MOORE RUBLE YUDELL

MOORE RUBLE YUDELL

THE FUTURE OF PLACE

未来空间

摩尔·乐伯·约德建筑事务所 编

贺丽 译

辽宁科学技术出版社

住宅空间

城市公共建筑

校园与社区建筑

总体规划与住宅

RESIDENTIAL

CIVIC

CAMPUS AND COMMUNITY

MASTERPLANNING AND HOUSING

建筑空间与空间建筑
迈克尔·J·克罗斯比

二十多年来，摩尔·乐伯·约德建筑事务所的设计师们一直秉承该事务所创办人查尔斯·摩尔精致、细腻的设计理念，并将这一优秀的设计精髓传承给年轻一代的建筑师。我个人认为，设计精英通过精诚合作、分享当代建筑理念和观点，保持鲜活、积极的设计状态是一个建筑成功设计的前提。成为一名建筑师，应该没有比这更吸引人的理由了吧？

本书中介绍了来自世界各地的多样化功能型建筑，并向读者证明一个细腻、周密的建筑价值体系能够使客户、用户或空间的要求得到满足。在摩尔·乐伯·约德建筑事务所看来，"空间"始终是设计的出发点：涉及对空间的了解、定义、衔接、打造和欣赏。建筑是人类幸福生活开始的地方。

摩尔·乐伯·约德建筑事务所通过对世界各地建筑的研究，熟谙不同文化背景下的建筑特色，汲取公众和个人的建筑智慧。他们深知将建筑与人类建筑价值理念的结合方式、正确表达这些价值观的路径，因此，对每一个项目的设计都做到仔细、缜密，从不武断，也从不仅仅为营造某种神秘效果而进行晦涩的空间布局。因建筑担负了为人类提供居住、生活、共享历史、分享个人回忆空间的重任，因此，在设计的过程中须将这些因素进行缜密研究，而这也成为设计中最强大的挑战之一。

摩尔·乐伯·约德建筑事务所的部分项目设计根据类型学进行划分。例如，图书馆建筑，强调空间的配置和形态、构成图书馆的基本材料以及所呈现的功能关系等。此外，设计师还对类型学的文化意义进行深入研究，涉及建筑周围环境所扮演的角色、城市规模以及一种类型建筑的诗意向度等。图书馆的诗意向度将为读者的生活产生何种影响？图书馆将会为读者的生活带来何种启发？如何令原建筑重新被赋予新的内涵，焕发活力？这些问题时刻萦绕在摩尔·乐伯·约德建筑事务所设计师的耳畔。本书为这些问题进行了完美诠释。

THE PLACE OF ARCHITECTURE, THE ARCHITECTURE OF PLACE
Michael J. Crosbie

The architects of Moore Ruble Yudell are reflective designers. In a practice that has spanned more than 30 years, the principals have expanded on the valuable lessons they learned from their teacher, Charles Moore, and have passed them on to younger generations of architects. This, to me, is how architecture should be practiced: a collaboration of talented people who continue to evolve a set of shared beliefs and values about architecture in response to contemporary life, keeping that vision alive for architects that will follow. What better reason is there to be an architect?

This book contains a range of recent projects of functional variety and from all over the world. It demonstrates that a carefully considered architectural value system can be adapted and suitable for virtually any client, use, or place. "Place" continues to be the bedrock of MRY's approach to architecture: the making of place, defining it, articulating in, inventing it, celebrating it. These architects see architecture as a place for human life to unfold.

MRY has studied architecture all over the world, attentive to the ways that human beings make themselves at home, in their culture, amid the collected wisdom of the civic and private worlds. MRY understands how architectural form connects with human worth—how architecture speaks to these values, articulates these values, and gives form to them. Because the architects understand how architecture helps us to make a place in the world, MRY's designs never appear arbitrary, or configured just for some arcane effect, or engage just with other architects. One senses in these buildings that architecture is always in service to larger ideas about living, about inhabiting, about making a place in the world to call your own—one connected to shared communal history and personal memory. It is, in short, one of the most demanding and challenging ways to design.

Part of MRY's place-making is aided with an understanding of typology's poetic power. This transforms typology from the way we usually understand it—the "type" of a library, for example, its configuration of spaces and forms, the materials that a library typically is composed of, the functional relationships that a library often displays. MRY also considers the cultural significance of typology—the role of the building in a neighborhood, or at the scale of the city—as well as the poetic weight of a type. What poetic dimension does the library bring to the reader's life? What fantasies does the library make possible in the reader's life? And, MRY asks, how can the type be reinvented to embody new meaning and give new life to the architectural assumptions about a type? The architecture here shows inventive responses to those questions.

书中介绍了四个建筑类型，我从每个类型中挑选出两个项目进行重点分析，希望能够体现出摩尔·乐伯·约德建筑事务所多年来的设计精髓。

住宅建筑是摩尔·乐伯·约德建筑事务所所有项目设计类型的试金石。哪里有房子，哪里就有建筑的存在。拉德尔家庭住宅（图1）是住宅设计的成功典范。从环境方面考虑，该建筑充分利用了所在地独特的地形条件，沿着小山的陡坡，向阳伸展开来。设计师约翰·乐伯和巴兹·约德对建筑中的凉亭在历史上扮演的角色（在遮篷下方勾勒出一方空间）进行了周密研究。实际上，拉德尔家庭住宅是一个对凉亭空间的研究成果。6个凉亭与自然环境和谐交融、错落有致，有效加强空间的通风、采光。室内外空间结合巧妙，没有尖锐的界限划分，"你中有我、我中有你"（其他项目中亦可见）。随着一天时间、温度、景致的变化，室内室外的定义及互动，一直在改变着。

位于美国加州的利弗莫尔家庭住宅（图2）的设计主题与拉德尔住宅类似。通过通风亭的精心设置，以及占地72,843,416平方米自然保护区的衬托，呈现出自然、和谐之美。泳池附近的杂色石雕在光影的变幻中呈现出万千姿态；镀锌屋顶在蓝天的映衬下分外抢眼；通风亭由结实的花旗松廊柱进行支撑；裸露的横梁天花板与硬朗的木纹地板遥相呼应。

fig. 1

From the well of this book's excellent projects, I have drawn eight that I believe capture the essence of such themes and their variations, pursued by MRY for many years. They neatly break down into two projects from each of the four typological realms that structure this book.

Residential Architecture has been a touchstone for MRY for all kinds of projects, residential or not. The house is the place where architecture starts. The Ruddell House (fig. 1) is rich in so many ways. Environmentally, it responds to its spectacular topical site. The house stretches out along the bluff of a hill, facing the sun. John Ruble and Buzz Yudell have reflected thoughtfully about the historical role of the pavilion in architecture— its power to define the place below a sheltering roof. Ruddell is a study in pavilion making. Six of them are tuned to the natural environment, catching prevailing breezes, sunlight, and views. There is also a game here of indoor and outdoor space (seen in many of their other projects) where one blends into the other, challenging us to find the line between the two. The game is never the same, as the time of day, the temperature, the views, and the inhabitants and their activities keep shifting the lines of what is outside and what is inside.

The Livermore House (fig. 2) in California contains some of the same themes as Ruddell, with a strong presence of materials. Throughout this arrangement of pavilions, which in turn are surrounded by an 18,000-acre nature reserve, one finds the celebration of natural materials. The rustic and variegated stonework near the pool is a play of light and shadow throughout the day; zinc roofs capture and reflect the hue of the blue sky; the pavilions are supported in some cases by stout columns of Douglas fir; exposed wood-beam ceilings are a counterpoint to the tight-grained wood floor below your feet.

fig. 2

美国加利福尼亚州贝克尔斯菲市法院大楼（图3），将我们的注意力从住宅设计转移到城市建筑，该项目阐释了二者之间的关系。入口附近的一个弧形混凝土墙彰显出小法院的公共建筑特色。室内设计与当地建筑风格保持一致。大堂的规模（作为一个室内外空间的中间地带）经由一个衔接流畅的木质天花板和木质与玻璃纹理的墙体完美界定出来，与美丽的湖景遥遥相望。

另一个公共建筑项目，美国驻圣多明各大使馆（图4）与多米尼加共和国的城市背景自然融为一体。与美国的其他前哨基地建筑不同，该建筑反映了所在城市的现代气息，并伴有一丝西班牙风采。在这里，摩尔·乐伯·约德建筑事务所的设计师探讨了雕塑的主题将其置于白色石灰岩幕墙之间。

一所大学的建筑是其公共特性的象征。美国弗吉尼亚大学由美国第3任总统托马斯·杰斐逊创办，声名显赫。在这个总统学府的旁边增设一个综合性建筑无疑是一项巨大的设计挑战。对于弗吉尼亚大学艺术与科学中心的设计，设计师并没有对杰斐逊"学术村"一味地效仿，而是巧妙打造了一个中央公共空间，与周围建筑自然衔接的同时，彰显自身特色。(图5)

摩尔·乐伯·约德建筑事务所为加利福尼亚州的伯克利大学分校校园中的斯普劳尔广场（图6）提供了一个崭新的总体规划方案，将大学和南端的社区衔接之后向北部的溪流和河岸生态系统进行延伸。在该项目的设计过程中，设计师注重与学生和教师员工之间的互动，听取他们的意见和建议，力图打造一个富有特色的个性化建筑。

fig. 3

fig. 4

The design of the U.S. Courthouse in Bakersfield, California (fig.3), shifts our focus from residential to civic architecture, but the connections between the two are explored in this project. This small courthouse has a civic presence, expressed in a monumental curved concrete wall near the entrance. The interior has a strong sense of domestic architecture, which seems entirely appropriate. The scale of the large lobby—an outdoor/indoor space—is carefully modulated with an articulated wood ceiling and a textured wall of wood and glass, which overlooks a lake.

Another civic project, the U.S. Embassy in Santo Domingo (fig. 4), speaks to the architectural context and sense of place of this Dominican Republic city. Rather than an outpost of U.S. architecture, the embassy reflects the presence of modern architecture in this city, albeit with a Spanish accent. Here, MRY explores a theme of sculpted volumes that slide past each other between screen walls of white limestone.

The architecture of a university is its public identity. The University of Virginia is known primarily through its architecture by Thomas Jefferson, and what could be more intimidating that adding a complex of buildings in close proximity to America's President-Architect? For a new College of Arts and Sciences Center, instead of recreating a miniature version of Jefferson's Great Lawn, MRY distilled UVA's DNA of pavilions on a green, punctuated by a circular central commons (fig. 5).

The identity of the University of California at Berkeley over the past 50 years has been that of an institution engaged with its surrounding community. MRY's re-designed master plan for Sproul Plaza on the Berkeley campus (fig. 6) forges a stronger connection between the university and the community to the south, and extends out to a creek and riparian ecosystem to the north. MRY maintains that its design sensitivity is a product of careful listening. For this project, workshops with students, faculty, and the community helped to define the project and its characteristics.

fig. 5

fig. 6

美国加州大学圣巴巴拉分校曼泽尼特村学生公寓（图7）的设计模式与斯普劳尔广场相似，不过在规模上有所差距。此外，也同样采用了可持续设计理念，向原有景观全方位延伸。建筑周围的开放空间角度不同，景致也各异。曼泽尼特村学生公寓的中央设置了一个开阔的中央广场，用来举办各种团体活动。

曼泽尼特村巧妙地运用不同的色彩将生活区和社区区分开来。在瑞典马尔默市的探戈住宅项目（图8）中，色彩扮演了一系列地标的角色。该住宅规划通过一个外墙与周围的城市环境进行完美衔接。内部庭院则作为生动的社区交流舞台。8个塔楼高度各异、色调迥异，犹如舞台上8个鲜活的人物角色。每个单元中的起居室呈堆叠状设计，用户则成为这个内外空间游戏的主角。在我看来，该项目可以被称之为住宅项目设计的成功典范。

随着中国经济的飞速发展和城市化进程的不断加快，中国的建筑已经全面进入高景气度时期，但有些建筑脱离了中国建筑尺度的传统。摩尔·乐伯·约德建筑事务所设计的天津新河总体规划（图9）展现了设计师对建筑尺度的独到理解以及室内外空间衔接的巧妙处理。该规划定义了两个活动中心：一个城市中心和一个商务中心，二者由一条蜿蜒的滨水散步长廊衔接在一起。附近的住宅区则沿着这条长廊向东西两侧延伸。这种滨水步行社区将可成为未来中国发展模式的典范。

今天，建筑的理念大多倾向于形式、古典主义、节能主义以及自由主义，似乎没有多余的空间去考虑空间的独特性、社区的协同性、材料运用的巧妙性、地域性以及建筑与周围环境的互融性。摩尔·乐伯·约德建筑事务所设计的作品告诉我们，建筑从外观上给人的感觉并不重要，重要的是能否真正解决用户的居住问题，能否为人们提供展开幸福生活的舞台。难道这种观点真的过时了吗？本书中的建筑给了我们答案。

fig. 7

fig. 8

At a different scale than Sproul, the Manzanita Residential Village at U.C. Santa Barbara (fig. 7) possesses a likewise visceral sense of place. Like Sproul, it is designed to be sustainable. It reaches out in all directions to the existing landscape. The open spaces around which the buildings meander are carefully designed to give the different quads their own unique identity. The central plaza at the heart of the village has the welcoming scale and sense of place of a small seaport village, where locals gather to celebrate community events.

Manzanita uses color to distinguish between living and community space. At Tango (fig. 8) in Malmö, Sweden, color is iconic as a series of vertical landmarks. This housing development has an outside wall that relates to the surrounding urban context. Its interior courtyard is a vibrant stage for community interaction. Eight towers in varying heights, each an intense color, step out like characters in a play. Containing stacked living rooms for each ring of units, the towers play the game of inside/outside space, and put the residents on stage as well. I can't think of a better place for a remake of "Rear Window".

The pace of development in China is break-neck, and the scale of much of this new building has been inhuman, disconnected from China's tradition of exquisitely scaled architecture. MRY's competition-winning master plan for the Tianjin Xin-He residential community (fig. 9) displays the firm's trademark sensitivity to scale and to indoor/outdoor connections. The plan defines two activity centers: a town center and a business center, connected by a meandering promenade along a river. Residential neighborhoods extend east and west from the promenade. Such walkable communities woven along a river could be models for future Chinese development.

Today the discipline of architecture seems all too fascinated with a mixture of formal blobism, recycled classicism, fascistic asceticism, and nihilistic sameness. There appears to be little room for the timeless human need for creating place, celebrating community, honoring materials, learning from the vernacular, building with the environment. The work of Moore Rubel Yudell shows us that great architecture needn't be monumental or self-conscious. Architecture is at its very best when it designed, first and foremost, as a theater for human existence. Have we already reached a point where such a notion is too passé?

The architecture herein says we have not.

9

THE FUTURE OF PLACE: CONTINUITY AND TRANSFORMATION

John Ruble and Buzz Yudell

Time and space appear to be shrinking under the influence of new technologies. Travel and electronic communication are transforming our lives—our relationships to one another and to place. The culture of architecture reflects this new globalization.

Aspects of this are energizing: cross-cultural understanding, communities of collaboration, extraordinary technologies, a vast array of cultural and environmental experiences.

Yet there are ominous trends in this period of transition. The globalization of architecture can default into the branding of place, the erasure of difference and the co-modification of the environment. How can we work creatively in a manner which embraces the energy of global transformation while celebrating the differences of place and the continuities of culture?

One effective approach is a region-based practice. Architects we greatly admire such as Kengo Kuma, Alvaro Siza, Glenn Murcutt, and Lake Flato have created powerful contemporary works that are inspired by continuities of place and culture.

Moore Ruble Yudell has taken a different path, pursuing an international practice based on a contemporary celebration of place, climate, context and regional culture. Even as we practice globally, our work is inseparable from its site, climate and context. While we explore contemporary ways of building and responding to evolving needs, we seek continuity with the specificity of culture and place. We are connecting to timeless lessons while creating places which nurture present communities and are flexible for future transformations.

The diversity of our practice presented in this volume are recent and current projects, each of which presents its own particular responses, all centered by a commitment to humanistic place making.

Respecting Heritage and Renewing Place

In certain contexts where a highly sensitive historic language of architecture and landscape has been nurtured, we have explored ways of building with great respect for these traditions, reinterpreting their principles with both traditional and contemporary expression.

At the University of Virginia, our South Lawn project revives the historic axis to distant mountains, which Jefferson had begun, only to have it later obstructed. The experience of the new building and landscape connects to the historic campus through classically inspired proportions and planning, yet surprises with an unfolding choreography of contemporary, light-filled places.

At Dartmouth College, we carefully studied the most successful patterns of historic buildings and landscape. Our new academic and residential buildings resonate with the proportions and cadences of the original campus. While the material palette connects to the historic fabric, subtle shifts in form and detail signal the newer rhythm of twenty-first century campus life.

14

未来空间：
延续与转型
约翰·乐伯与巴兹·约德

日新月异的科技发展正在逐渐使时间缩短，空间变小。旅游和电子通讯正在改变我们的生活、我们与他人或空间之间的关系。建筑文化将这种全球化新趋势彰显得淋漓尽致。

这种建筑文化主要表现为跨文化的认知、社区的合作、非凡的技术、广阔的文化与环境体验。

然而，在这个过渡时期也存在着一些不利影响：建筑全球化可能会导致区域独特性的缺失、环境的商品化等等。那么，我们如何才能开展创造性的工作方式，既能够符合能源全球化的发展趋势，又能够令空间具有独特性和文化的延续性？有效的措施之一是从项目所在地的实际出发。著名建筑设计师隈研吾、阿尔瓦罗·西扎、格伦·莫卡特以及莱克·弗拉托所打造的优秀建筑作品从地点和文化的实际出发，为当代建筑设计提供了成功典范。

摩尔·乐伯·约德建筑事务所独辟蹊径，力图打造一个从地点、气候、环境和区域文化出发的放之四海而皆准的设计理念，强调建筑与地点、气候和环境的完美结合。我们在开发新建筑设计方法、应对不断变化的需求的同时，探索地方与文化的特殊性和连续性，在为社区打造独一无二空间的同时，确保其能够灵活变幻、历久弥新。本书中所呈现的多样化设计作品，均以自身所在的独特地理环境为出发点，采用了人性化设计理念。

尊重历史遗产与空间的翻新
在那些高度敏感的历史性建筑和景观设计中，我们非常注重对传统的尊重，并将其奉行的原则用传统和现代的手法进行诠释。

在弗吉尼亚大学艺术与科学学院南罗恩学术中心的设计过程中，我们受所在地面积和规划以及现代、明亮的空间特色的启发，将新建筑和景观与历史校园有机衔接在一起。

在达特茅斯学院，我们对最成功的历史建筑和景观设计方式进行了仔细研究。新学术和住宅楼与原校园的比例和节奏相得益彰。材料的选用强调与历史结构的和谐统一，通过微妙的形态和细节设计赋予校园以崭新的二十一世纪新气象。

尊重传统与空间的改造

一些历史环境为传统的传承与空间的改造提供了机遇。在加州大学洛杉矶分校，世界艺术与文化大厅项目包括对历史建筑的翻新、空间及户外花园剧场馆等灵活空间的改造。互动的对比元素犹如一个节奏和主题相同的爵士乐章，各具表现力。整体空间通过当地艺术形态和新兴当代艺术探索的完美结合，有力彰显出学术研究方案的丰富性。

新空间 – 新典范

多样化的建筑文化背景以及丰富的建筑类型促使我们对设计手法进行不断探索，力求打造更新、更多的建筑典范。

瑞典的马尔默探戈住宅是环保项目设计的先锋。行人专用区的设计为一个衰败的工业用地注入了无限生机，并使该地的生态环境质量得以大大改善。该项目巧妙地将先进的环保技术和持续的低层、高密度、城市生活模式完美结合，作为设想中的城市实验室，在整个城市环境和设计中扮演了极为重要的角色。

此外，春森彼岸住宅总体规划面临着一个巨大的挑战，即如何在一个高密度聚居区打造一个人性化住宅。通常，这种人口高密度地区项目采用空间悬浮式结构，将没有特色的空间留在街面。我们的项目利用多层和高层建筑与地平面进行衔接。庭院、花园、小径和街道强调社区与环境的连接。新城市规划中还融入了历史古道和所在地的地质情况等元素。即使在一个人口密度更大的地点，对社区意识和空间独特性的塑造也是必不可少的。

在辛辛那提大学，我们与校园建筑师和同仁（包括Morphosis设计事务所、Gwathmey Siegel设计事务所、哈格里夫斯联合公司）进行合作，打造一个崭新的24/7学生生活中心。该校园刚刚建成了一系列标志性建筑（由著名设计师艾斯曼、盖里、格雷夫斯、裴·科布·弗莱德联合打造）。客户认为下一个挑战是如何打造出同样杰出的建筑，并使之互相协调统一，突出建筑与社区之间衔接的重要性。这一"协调性"设计过程包括建筑设计之前方案的拟定和整体规划的实施。经过周密的探讨和研究，我们最终创建了一个生动、活动的当代建筑群，被评为自弗吉尼亚

Respecting Tradition and Transforming Place

Some historic settings have provided the opportunity to be both respectful and transformative. At UCLA, the new home for World Arts and Cultures comprises components of historic restoration, adaptively renewed spaces and flexible contemporary places such as the new Kaufman Family Garden Theater. The contrasting elements interact like a jazz composition with shared rhythms and themes, but highly varied expressions. The ensemble reflects the richness of the academic program which embraces a range of art from vernacular to emerging contemporary exploration.

New Places—New Paradigms

Working across many cultures and building types has allowed us to explore evolving paradigms in place-making.

The Tango Housing in Malmö, Sweden is part of a pioneering environmental project. A pedestrian-oriented district was designed to restore vitality and environmental health to a degraded industrial site. The project employed both cutting-edge environmental technology and timeless patterns of low-rise, high-density, urban living. It was envisioned as an urban laboratory and has become a place of pilgrimage for its enlightened environmental and urban design.

On a much larger scale, new housing in the Chun Sen Bi An project in China takes on a daunting contemporary challenge: how to build humane housing at very high density. Typically, projects at this density have created repetitive monoliths which float in space, leaving anonymous and undefined spaces at the street level. Our project uses mid-rise and high-rise buildings to shape and connect the ground plane. Courtyards, gardens, paths and streets emphasize social and environmental connections. The historical pathways and geology of the site are recognized in the new urban planning. Even at great density, there is a strong sense of community and of specificity of place.

At the University of Cincinnati, we collaborated with campus architects and colleagues (Morphosis, Gwathmey Siegel, Hargreaves Associates) to create a new 24/7 center of student life. The campus had recently completed a series of iconic buildings by distinguished architects (Eiseman, Gehry, Graves, Pei Cobb Freed). The client felt that the next challenge was to build equally distinguished buildings but to plan them collaboratively so that the spaces between buildings and the places of community would be more important than the individual buildings. This collaborative process involved programming and masterplanning prior to building design. The result has been such a vibrant contemporary ensemble, that critics have considered it the most successful integrated piece of campus planning and design since Thomas Jefferson's Lawn at the University of Virginia.

New Places to Nurture Community

Each new project is a chance to shape places which in turn nurture community. At the Santa Monica Public Library, a quiet courtyard building is configured to welcome study and activity at many scales, from the single patron to large community gatherings. The building is shaped for environmental response, optimizing daylight and coastal breezes with a flow of interior and exterior space.

At a much larger scale, the new town center of Camana Bay creates a vibrant pedestrian-oriented mixed-use core, based on an extrapolation from the environmental wisdom of traditional building types. Computer modeling and contemporary materials raise the performance and comfort of buildings. Outside spaces are shaped for community and environmentally tempered by the architecture and landscape, allowing a broad range of 24/7 activity in a tropical climate.

New Places in Harmony with Nature

From the town center of Camana Bay to single-family houses, our architecture adapts to its environment and celebrates the specific qualities of its site. From tropical environments in the Caribbean and Hawaii to temperate sites in California and harsher climates of Scandinavia, we welcome the diversity of climate, landscape and culture. Understanding the specificity of places helps us to engage in a dynamic dialogue with the fundamental qualities of the context. This in turn creates new places which have meaningful and specific connections to nature.

In the Ruddell House in Kauai, the connection to precise views and sun angles informs the gently skewed geometry of the house's pavilions. In Malmö, Sweden, the apartments of the Tango Housing jostle like phototropic plants to gather the precious sunlight.

The diversity of our work is an expression of the diversity of place and culture, and of our on-going collaboration with clients and colleagues. We continue to approach each project as part of an evolving exploration, guided by humanistic principles.

Equally important, we understand that each work makes its own particular contribution to places that already exist—respecting, enriching, and sometimes transforming—but always recognizing the defining qualities of each context and setting. In that spirit, projects presented in *The Future of Place* are titled according to their location—a geographic perspective for architecture that is above all a celebration of place.

大学托马斯·杰斐逊"学术村"建立以来最成功的校园规划和设计作品。

社区新空间的建设

每一个新项目的设计将为空间塑造带来一个崭新的机遇，同时也为促进社区的合作提供新的平台。在圣莫尼卡公共图书馆项目中，一个静谧的庭院式建筑为学习、个人及社区活动提供一个良好的空间环境。该建筑的外观根据周围环境条件、室内外采光和通风效果进行设计。

此外，开曼湾新城市中心的总体规划打造了一个充满活力的行人专用多用途核心区，其设计灵感源自对传统建筑类型生态策略的参考。计算机模拟运用和现代材料的良好性能使建筑空间更加舒适、宜人。外部空间根据社区以及建筑和景观的环境背景而设计，确保与热带气候相协调。

打造与自然和谐的新空间

无论是开曼湾新城市中心总体规划项目，还是单体家庭住宅设计，我们的建筑在打造独特空间的同时，一直强调建筑与周围环境的自然融合。无论是热带气候的加勒比海和夏威夷，还是温和湿润的加利福尼亚州或是寒冷的斯堪的纳维亚半岛，我们一直注重气候、景观与文化之间的联系。了解地域的特殊性能够帮助我们与建筑环境的基本特性之间搭建桥梁。从而创造出的新空间能够与自然之间形成独特的联系。

在考艾岛拉德尔住宅中，周围自然景观以及采光角度巧妙地塑造了平缓的几何形状的亭阁外观；而瑞典马尔默探戈住宅公寓犹如一簇簇向阳植物，争先恐后地汲取太阳光。

作品的丰富性是地点和文化的多样化以及我们与客户和同仁不断合作的有力诠释。每个新项目的设计都是人性化理念引导下的一个崭新的设计尝试。与此同时，我们深知和谐处理新建筑与原建筑关系的重要性——坚持尊重、充实、转变的理念，并强调每个环境和背景的独特性，因此，《未来空间》中呈现的项目根据其所在地而命名——毕竟，地理角度在空间的设计中扮演了极其重要的角色。

住宅为
空间的创造者

房子是家的基本符
号，是人们栖身和获
得心灵安稳的一个不可替代的场所。对"梦想家
园"的追求亘古有之，许多人倾其所有，不惜举
债，为求一栖身之所，为之辛苦为之劳，而又甘
之如饴。近年来，流行杂志和图书中对独户住宅
的推崇更是将这种"追梦"热潮推到了至高点。

几千年来，房屋被各种社会组织以集中的方式进
行规划，旨在为团体提供生产、贸易和文化发展
的共享空间。这种配置是满足社会和环境要求的
有力展现。圆形、线型等基本的几何形状打造了
围墙、露台乃至街道与场区。建筑材料与技术的
运用与当地原材料和地形特征具有密切的关系。
房屋的外观应与其所在地的周围环境保持和谐、
统一。许多非洲的民居采用圆形结构，既确保环
境的安全，又能够在固定的范围内提供灵活发展
的空间，而建筑材料的选用则遵循就近原则，多
以泥土和枝条为主。建筑中，通常采用雕刻和切
割以及平面彩绘对室内进行装饰。

意大利南部阿布鲁佐地区的特鲁利房屋由多个平
缓的圆锥形单元构成。各单元之间衔接自然，位于
街面之上，形成一道美丽的街景(图1)。层次分明
的石灰石堆砌至一定的高度后再用片状的石灰石板
往上叠砌，逐步收窄封顶，形成了圆锥状的尖顶。

在这些古老的建筑形式中，建筑材料的运用旨在
作为一种身份的象征和情感的表达，至此，社会
情感的表达和家庭符号形成了和谐的统一体。

随着社会的发展，等级分化的日趋明显，在一些
国家，住宅的每个空间逐渐被细化，例如传统的
巴厘岛住宅，空间划分十分具体，涉及卧室、厨
房、储藏室、祠堂等。(图2)

这些住宅面向神圣的阿贡山沿街排列，自然衔
接，既保留了牢固的社会秩序，又体现了对传统
文化的尊崇。早期地中海文明影响下的别墅是财
富和权力的象征，而2000多年前罗马民居以庭院
为中心的设计风格一直延续至今。

THE HOUSE AS PLACEMAKER

The house is the elemental archetype of habitation. It manifests our primal needs for shelter and identity and is often the object of intense aspirations. It is not accidental that the phrase "dream house" has persisted for decades nor that popular magazines and books focus disproportionately on the single family house.

For millennia houses were aggregated in socially structured groups. These structures supported community, safety, shared production, trade and cultural development. The configurations were powerful diagrams of the social and environmental imperatives. Primary geometries of circle and line typically formed enclosures, terraces and eventually street and courts. The materials and tectonics of construction manifested a close connection to local materials and to the contours of the land. The shapes of the houses evolved in close harmony with the environmental needs of the region.

The circular enclosures of many African villages created security while also allowing for flexible growth within the protected boundary. The construction was of local materials—mud and wattle. Ornament and identity were provided by sculpting and incising patterns in relief and at times by bold graphic painting. The Trulli's of the Abruzzi region of southern Italy are houses formed by the aggregation of gently rounded conical units. Rooms are grouped into houses and houses linked to form streets (fig. 1). The plan and section of the house is the elegant result of the circumferential layering and tapering of flat stones, culminating at an ornamental roof vent.

In early house forms, the logic of material construction is married to an impulse to mark and ornament for identity and expression. There is harmony between the expression of the community and the marking of the family.

With prosperity came greater differentiation and hierarchy. In some cultures, the house became a set of uniquely expressed rooms, each of which met a specific need. In traditional Balinese villages, each room became a house unto itself: one for sleeping, one for cooking, one for storage, one for honoring ancestors (fig. 2).

A strong social order was maintained by aligning these house compounds along a street which oriented toward the mountaintop, the realm of the divine.

The villas of early Mediterranean civilizations developed as an expression of great affluence and power. The Roman villa organized around a series of courtyards is a powerful typology that persists after two thousand years.

住宅 RESIDENTIAL

fig. 1

fig. 2

如今，随着建筑产业的发展、施工工艺的进步、社会分工的细化，这些历史建筑，无论是乡村民居还是城市摩天大楼，其原始职能已逐渐转变为居住、工作、社交等。

可以说，住宅设计的发展与社会的进步密不可分，它由经济、政治等多种因素决定。

近30多年来，我们见证并参与了美国住宅的飞快转变。

二战结束以来，随着住宅信贷的膨胀和公路的扩展以及洲际高速的建立，美国住宅的建设开始逐步步向市郊延伸。人们也越来越向往拥有一个带有宽敞庭院的独立式住宅。有数据表明，美国平均每户住宅的面积已由上个世纪的130平方米逐渐上升至167平方米乃至今日的223平方米。

早期的房屋设计案例多以节约成本为前提，房屋格局设计遵循均衡、适度的原则。在20世纪70年代，我们还为设计师和年轻的学者提供57平方米的小户型设计。在那个时期，人们普遍认为167－223平方米的住宅面积最为合适，而279平方米的房间则稍显开阔些。事实上，小户型的房屋更能够激发创作灵感，设计理念也更为清晰。

现如今，我们设计的住宅面积已介于325平方米至929平方米之间。

对于一般收入的客户来说，寻找一个建筑师打造一个既经济又匠心独运的建筑并不是一件容易的事。

虽然，目前很少有机会参与小户型住房的设计，我们会将大部分精力投入到多层住宅的设计之中，并努力研究、开发各种环境下的建筑设计。

值得一提的是，住宅设计为我们打造成功建筑提供了很多参考，譬如如何协调建筑与环境及气候之间的关系；如何在有限的空间中构建各种规模的建筑物；如何处理光、影、色彩及建筑材料在使用上的契合度；以及如何应用节能技术来降低支付可持续性建筑成本等问题。

Grand houses evolved as places of residence, work and social and political intrigue, mirroring the ancient connection between living, working and socializing. This applied both to the country villa and the urban palazzo.

Even the briefest consideration of the evolution of the house demonstrates that it is charged with socio-economic and political implications and reflects the greater forces at work in a society.

In our own residential work of over thirty years we have witnessed and participated in the rapid transformation of the American house.

The post World War II expansion of housing financing and the proliferation of roads and interstate highways enable the spread and eventually sprawl of suburban housing. And as the dream of the single house with its ample yards proliferated the expectations for size of house rapidly expanded. In fact the average American house size has increased from 980 sf in 1950 to 1,500 sf in 1970, 2,080 sf in 1980 and 2,350 sf in 2004.

In our early practice, it was not unusual to design houses of modest means for clients with modest budgets. In the seventies we designed houses as small as 600 sf for artists and young academics. In that period, houses in the range of 1800 sf to 2,400 sf were considered comfortable and those over 3,000 sf were thought of as capacious. We often found that the smaller houses stimulated more invention and clearer concepts.

Our recent houses have ranged from about 3,500 sf to over 10,000. It is increasingly difficult for clients of modest means to design and build a house with an architect.

While we miss the challenges of the small urban house, we have been able to transfer that interest into the opportunities to design humane and imaginative homes in multi-unit housing . We continue to see the design of houses as a laboratory for exploring the many dimensions of habitation and placemaking.

Most importantly, our houses give us the chance to explore many of the issues that are fundamental to successful architecture: the connection of building to landscape and climate, the shaping and proportioning of spaces to accommodate varied scales of habitation, the choreography of space and the connections that nurture community, the use of passive techniques to create affordable sustainable buildings, the wonder of light and shadow, the integration of craft, materials and color.

总而言之，我们的设计主旨是开发和运用适当的设计元素，使建筑与周围环境自然融为一体，为客户提供最佳的居住环境。

这些设计经验和认知将在我们今后的多层住宅、城市综合体以及校园建筑的设计中发挥重要的作用。

另一方面，客户的想法和观点对我们的设计也起着重要的作用。有些客户来自三代同堂的大家庭，他们对设计元素的好恶和自身对居住环境所期待的设想对我们的设计有很大的帮助。这里所展示的五所住宅是我们当前最有代表性的作品。

这些大宅设计空间开阔，强调与周围建筑和景观的自然融合、注重光影的处理，为其乐融融的家庭打造温馨、惬意的居住空间。

光线与环境　此外，这些建筑也糅合了我们对自然的认知，借助光影变幻效果使房间与自然合二为一。利弗莫尔住宅便是这样一个充满诗情画意的建筑。约德/毕比住宅则巧妙地通过透明度的渐变效果以及自然的取景打造出完美的时间和空间感。

空间的舞蹈　通过对空间元素的动态设计强化了我们对个体与空间关系的认知。譬如，拉德尔住宅的通风亭设计，能够有效地加强室内通风效果，同时将远处景致成功引入到室内。柱梁颇有节奏地穿插于建筑之中，为空间增添了无限生机和活力。

利弗莫尔住宅中，精致的走廊为这个带有庭院的住宅打造了一个小型界道，令空间富于变化。界道的动态设计凸显了空间远景的变幻。

摩尔住宅，开阔、通透，各空间内衔接自然，连贯和谐，充分利用所在地的地貌特征。中规中矩的中心大厅与四周流线型空间的巧妙搭配，仿佛舞者曼妙的身姿，轻逸而充满旋律之美。

Our houses allow us to explore and exercise the fundamental elements which lead to creating buildings in harmony with their inhabitants and with their environments.

This experience and knowledge continuously inform our multi-unit residential design, our civic and campus work.

Another essential component of house design has been an intimate collaboration with our clients. Usually one family, but sometimes as many a three generations, are involved. We've been able to test ways of working which invite the participation, and dreams of our clients, while not abdicating our expertise in shaping place and exploring materials and technology.

The five houses presented here represent recent and current work. While most of these are large houses in spectacular settings, each has presented opportunities to explore the connection to place, to study the harmony of building and landscape, to reveal the wonder of light and shadow, to celebrate the life of the families within.

LIGHT AND LAND　Our houses are lenses which heighten our awareness of the natural world. Light and shadow are used dynamically as if painting space in time. The Livermore House explores the movement of light as a link between nature and the rooms we inhabit. The Yudell/Beebe house studies gradations of transparency and the framing of nature as a means of heightening the sense of time and place.

THE CHOREOGRAPHY OF PLACE　Our movement through space intensifies our awareness of the connection of body to place. At the Ruddell House a series of pavilions part and slide to welcome breezes and reveal distant landscapes. The columns of the house dance with a syncopated rhythm through space as markers of habitation.

In the Livermore House, a gallery forms a faceted street for the house, connecting alternating courtyards and carefully proportioned rooms. The movement of the street accentuates the shifting perspectives of spaces beyond.

The Moir House uses the great room as a central anchor of family life. From this all paths and rooms flow out and trace the contours of the land both uphill and down. As in a dancer's body, the center is still and the extremities are fluid.

打破空间界限：令室内外空间自然融合

在设计过程中，我们十分注重空间的层次感以及室内外空间的过渡。对于住宅来说，室内空间与外部环境的地位同等重要。马奎尔住宅的室内外空间风格保持一致。拉德尔住宅则是在一个共享的屋顶下打造了一系列独立的空间。

外观可持续空间

由设计大师查尔斯·摩尔及其MLTW设计事务所搭档和景观设计师拉里·哈普林共同设计的"海洋农场别墅"为我们的住宅设计提供了丰富的参考。

他们强调建筑与自然的和谐互融，同时通过可持续设计手法将建筑对生态自然景观的不利影响降到最低。

拉德尔住宅的外观设计在遵循设计理念的同时，十分注重与环境的互动。

该住宅通风效果良好，室外活动区光线适中，避免暴晒于骄阳之下。

约德/毕比住宅采用的一系列设计手法能够对未来的建筑设计提供有效参考。该项目遵循可持续的设计理念，注重空间的对流，确保室内冬暖夏凉。建筑采用环保可再生材料，并采用了最新低耗能设计手法。

从住宅设计中学到的

这些开阔的私人住宅设计，无论是外观、结构还是与自然环境的巧妙处理，将为我们今后在有限的空间和资金预算条件下打造城市公共建筑和校园建筑设计上提供大量参考及经验。

我们对城市公共建筑和校园建筑的设计得益于对住宅设计的研究和探讨。例如，对于弗雷斯诺法院大楼环境的塑造，令进入大楼的人们在第一时间体会到温馨、亲切之感。

无论是公共空间还是私人住宅，无论面积大小，我们都力图从客户的角度出发，将打造舒适、人性化的空间作为设计宗旨。

BREAKING BOUNDARIES: INSIDE OUT

All of our houses study the layering of space from defined rooms, through spaces which are transitional to the outside , and on to outdoor "rooms." Inside and out shape each other and are equal partners in habitation.

The Maguire House creates outdoor rooms as defined as those within. The Ruddell House literally breaks opens to become a series of individual rooms held together by a protective roof.

SHAPING SUSTAINABLE SPACE

All of our houses owe a debt to the early Sea Ranch explorations of Charles Moore and his MLTW partners and landscape architect Larry Halprin. There nature was studied and understood as a primary imperative in the discovery of form. Designing buildings in harmony with nature and understanding natural landscapes as ecosystems were prescient in their use of what is now called passive techniques for sustainable design. Understanding climate and place has continuously inspired our residential work. We see sustainable design as an evolving exploration, adding new tools while not losing timeless ways of building sustainably.

The Ruddell House pursues the extent to which shaping a house in plan and section can enhance its environmental responsiveness.

The house maximizes permeability to prevailing breezes, shades outdoor living and filters the strong daylight.

The Yudell/Beebe house takes a case study approach employing an array of strategies. It begins with passive design to shape the section and plan for maximum convection, shades in summer and captures winter sun for radiant heat storage. It then develops a spectrum of strategies based on renewable energy, sustainable materials and new technologies with the goal of approaching net-zero energy use.

LEARNING FROM HOUSES

These generous private houses hold lessons in shaping habitation and understanding the connection to nature. These lessons inform our work in multi-unit housing with many constraints on space and budget as well as our larger civic and campus work. Our affordable housing in California or Europe aspires to the same richness of experience we have brought these private house clients.

Our large Civic and Campus work benefits as well from understanding habitation in houses. It's been noted, for example, that our large Courthouse in Fresno provides a surprising sense of comfort and intimacy as one moves through the building.

Public or private, modest or grand, all buildings can provide humane places which celebrate our range of individual and communal life.

考艾岛

KAUAI

拉德尔住宅巧妙地利用了所在地独特的地形和气候条件。因住宅位于考爱岛北岸的西南端，因此该项目的设计理念是将优美的自然环境与建筑融为一体，打造浑然天成的视觉空间效果。造型别致的凉亭错落有致，通过拱形游廊、凉廊、庭院和走廊实现自然衔接，形成通透、开阔的视觉效果。室内外运用相似的动线设计巧妙地淡化了空间界限，再次强调了该地区独特的协同性生活方式。

开放式空间设计能够有效地增强室内通风，一个中央流通脊柱完美地将室内外空间衔接在一起。悬垂式结构能够对强烈的热带骄阳进行遮挡，并与当地的民居建筑特色保持和谐一致。通风塔上方设置的天窗能够时刻确保室内明媚、通透。每个部分的设计均以环境和项目主旨，即打造一个真正的、美妙的当代民居建筑为设计出发点。建筑通过现代设计手法为客户营造了一个舒适、惬意的家居环境。

The Ruddell House responds to unique regional and climatic challenges of the tropics. Situated on a south-west facing bluff on the north shore of Kauai, the design concept integrates environmental considerations into the aesthetic composition. The building mass is defined by a series of pavilions, interconnected by arcades, loggia, courtyards, and passageways, rendering the building threshold physically transparent. The interior/exterior boundary is dictated by common patterns of movement and habitation, allowing a synergistic lifestyle that is unique to the region.

Open spaces alternate with building masses to create a porous design that admits natural ventilation as well as weaving a fabric of interior and exterior spaces organized along a central circulation spine. Deep overhangs provide shelter from the harsh tropical sunlight and echo the vernacular architecture of the island. Despite the shading methods, the home maintains a well-lit interior environment through the use of clerestory windows open at the top of the pavilions to admit soft, indirect light into the heart of the home. Each design component is a multifaceted solution to environmental and programmatic goals: truly a contemporary aesthetic expression of vernacular architecture. The home facilitates the residents' active engagement with the environment through a modern design that is informed by the site, region and architectural heritage.

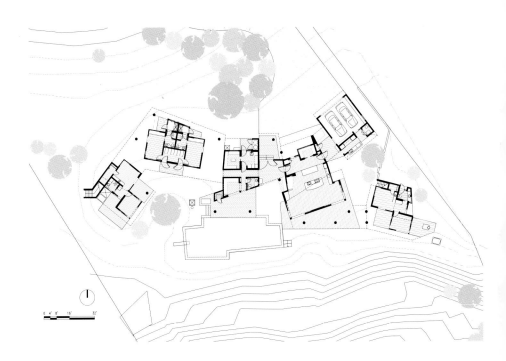

Pavilions part to frame views and catch trade winds.
通风塔有借景及让季节风流畅的功能。

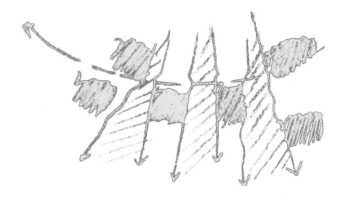

夏威夷，考艾岛
拉德尔家庭住宅

Kauai, Hawaii
RUDDELL FAMILY HOUSE

圣巴巴拉市

SANTA BARBARA

The architecture and the interior palette of the Maguire Beach House both reflect the oceanfront surroundings of the site. This existing beach house estate required a complete architectural re-configuration that included a revision to the first and second floor plans, a new beach façade, electrical, plumbing, HVAC and an entirely new interior finish palette.

The estate is composed of a tennis court, guest house and a main house facing the beach. The main house planning concept turned the former cluster of small, low-ceilinged rooms into a lofty plan that opens to the expansive beach view. Two decks with a new hot tub were added to the beach side of the house, and on the second floor, a spacious shower with floor-to-ceiling windows looks out onto the ocean. The second floor master bedroom suite enlarges the plan to reveal spaces that flow into one another: the dressing room communicates with bathroom, which flows into the sleeping area, the offices, and the decks.

Furnishings reflect the updated contemporary design and beachside setting: simple shapes with slip-covered upholstery keep the aesthetic clean and fresh. The architectural palette includes new wide-plank, bleached oak floors, concrete Caesarstone countertops, and stainless steel cabinets in the Baulthaup kitchen. Louis Poulsen Artichoke ceiling pendants recall seashells in the double-height main entry and contribute to the house's uniquely oceanfront aesthetic.

马奎尔海滨别墅的建筑结构和室内设计风格与其周围的海滨环境相得益彰。该项目旨在保留原建筑结构的基础上对一、二楼的布局进行改造，同时打造一个崭新的滨海外立面，完善室内电路、管道、暖通空调等设施，使室内环境重新焕发活力。

该住宅内设有一个网球场、客房和一个面朝大海的主室。主室的设计理念是转变之前低矮的天花板、狭小的格局，使之成为一个开阔、通透的海景空间。设计师巧妙地在住宅的滨海一侧增设了两个露台和一个热浴缸，并在二楼设置一个落地窗，能够将远处海景尽收眼底。二楼的主卧套房在原有的基础上进行了扩建，并加强了各空间的流通：更衣室与浴室相通，浴室又与卧室、办公室以及露台区相互贯通。

室内陈设具有浓厚的现代气息，并富于地方海滨特色：室内装潢线条简洁，营造洁净、清新之感。崭新的宽木板、漂白橡木地板搭配混凝土凯撒石台面以及厨房中的不锈钢橱柜为整个空间增添现代之感。令人联想起沙滩贝壳的路易斯·波尔森洋蓟状吊灯与双高入口的设计遥相呼应、妙趣横生，同时彰显独特的海滨风光。

An older beach house was opened horizontally and vertically to connect to the ocean and breezes.

该住宅的平面图和剖面图设计突出了可持续的设计理念。

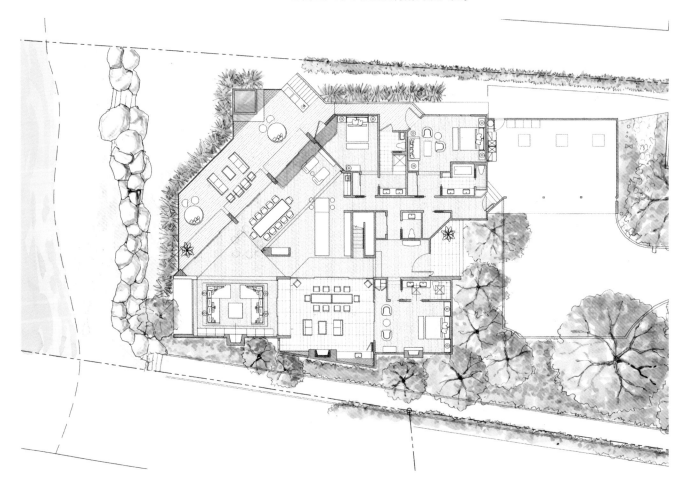

Santa Barbara, California
MAGUIRE HOUSE

加利福尼亚州, 圣巴巴拉市
马奎尔海滨别墅

卡梅尔市　CARMEL

The design concept of the Moir House in The Santa Lucia Preserve is informed by the landscape it inhabits. Indigenous California Oak trees serve as a frame surrounding the building as it opens to key focal elements —ridges, valleys and rock outcroppings—and allows their forms and palette to permeate the residence. Two primary design elements infuse the home with natural beauty: light monitors admit filtered northern light, while the H-shaped building layout forms a communication between two courtyards and draws a landscape path between the hilltop and stream.

The overarching woodland-inspired aesthetic is applied to the Client's request for a hacienda-style home. To achieve this, several central hacienda design elements were identified, distilled and merged with natural modernist style in a perfect synthesis to form the contemporary hacienda.

While open beamed ceilings and exterior overhangs recall the traditional Mexican ranch vernacular, the interior color, materials and furnishings reflect the surrounding environment. The qualities and textures of oak moss, rock outcroppings and wildflowers enter the home with a poetic arrangement of aged tree trunk slices that climb up the fireplace wall of the great room. Tanned leather recalls hacienda ranch days, while blending seamlessly with the earth-tone palette. The residence functions as a unified whole; traditional forms are imbued with organic qualities in a synthesis between structure and nature.

坐落于圣露西亚保护区的莫伊尔住宅，外观和结构设计均源自对其周围景观的参考。具有典型地方特色的加州橡树将建筑环抱其中，并与山脊、山谷和露岩等特有的环境元素融为一体。两个主要设计元素赋予建筑以自然之美：光线调节装置对来自北部的强光进行有效过滤；H形建筑布局将两个庭院进行巧妙衔接，完美地在山顶和溪流之间添加了景观小径，匠心独运。

森林美学理念在庄园式住宅设计中扮演了重要角色。因此，在设计过程中，往往先确定几个中央庄园设计元素，然后在探讨修改后使之与自然的现代主义风格完美融合，进而打造出独特的现代庄园空间。

显露的木梁天花和室外悬臂结构彰显了传统的墨西哥农场民居特色，其室内的色调、材料和家具均与周围环境相和谐一致。橡苔的质地和纹理，露岩和野花为空间增添了诗情画意。客厅中壁炉墙上方的老树干装饰将空间烘托得自然而惬意。鞣制皮革具有浓厚的农场庄园气息，并与泥土色调衔接自然，浑然一体。该住宅各部分空间衔接巧妙，具有较好的协同性。传统的建筑模式搭配有机材质充分实现了结构与自然的和谐统一。

The house is woven amongst great oak trees and terraces with natural topography.

该住宅处于加州橡树林之间并融入自然地形之中。

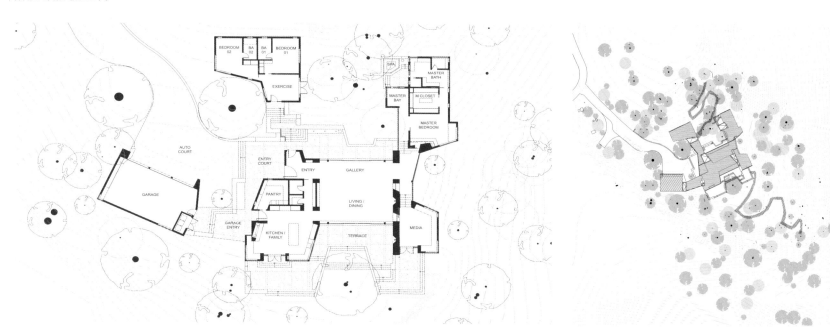

Carmel, California
MOIR FAMILY HOUSE

加利福尼亚州,卡梅尔市
莫伊尔住宅

卡梅尔市

CARMEL

坐落于加利福尼亚州蒙特雷生态保护区的利弗莫尔住宅对周围自然环境进行了周密思考，别致的造型与其所在地独特的地形条件密不可分。小丘、洼地和露岩为建筑模式及其临近的室外空间提供了重要设计源泉。

这幢建筑面积1,022平方米的住宅中包括主室和客室两大部分，二者沿曲线型车道分隔开来，同时一个重建的河岸走廊与车道相交后形成空间的入口。月牙形主室的设计保留了小丘的地形特点，能够将南端的加利福尼亚海岸山脉和北部的山脊景致尽收眼底。月牙形室内外空间，因外观、面积、特征和朝向不同而各具特色，令人目不暇接。整体镀锌屋顶能够避免南向的露台和庭院遭受北风的侵袭，同时将来自北部的光线成功引入室内。光线透过光线调节装置倾洒到室内，飘窗和楼梯有效增强了色彩及自然光线的相互作用。

The Livermore House is sensitively integrated with an ecological preserve in Monterey, California, and is shaped by the uniquely varied topography. Knolls, swales and rock outcrops provide critical inspiration for the architectural forms and their adjacent exterior spaces.

Access to both the 11,000 sf main residence and guest cottage is along a curvilinear driveway; tucked into the natural topography, a restored riparian corridor intersects the driveway to frame the entry to the site. The crescent shape of the main residence preserves the knoll, while optimizing views both south to the distant California coastal range and north to adjacent ridge lines. The house is articulated as a weaving crescent of interior and exterior spaces, each varying in form, size, character, and orientation. A sweeping zinc roof protects the south facing leeward terraces and courtyards from the predominant northerly winds, while maximizing opportunities for north light. Light floods the home through monitors, habitable bay windows and stairways that frame the interaction of color and natural light.

Rooms and courts are linked to a gallery which traces the shape of the land.

随着地形设计的廊道将室内空间及庭院串连起来。

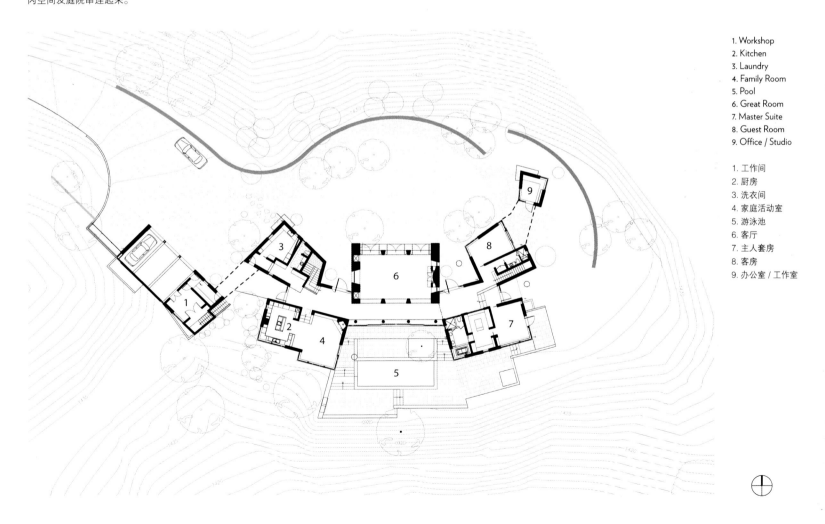

1. Workshop
2. Kitchen
3. Laundry
4. Family Room
5. Pool
6. Great Room
7. Master Suite
8. Guest Room
9. Office / Studio

1. 工作间
2. 厨房
3. 洗衣间
4. 家庭活动室
5. 游泳池
6. 客厅
7. 主人套房
8. 客房
9. 办公室 / 工作室

加利福尼亚州,卡梅尔市

利弗莫尔家庭住宅

Carmel, California

LIVERMORE FAMILY HOUSE

Acting both as designers and clients enabled us to treat the project as a case study in which creating a place of harmony and wonder could be totally aligned with ambitious environmental goals including working toward a net-zero energy house.

The environmental strategies for the house reflect a tiered approach:

Passive design: The house is shaped in section and plan to optimize convection, natural cooling, daylight, shading, and winter heat gain. The "section" of the house is extruded throughout so that every room participates in this passive design.

The two-story space at the core of the house is not only environmentally critical but functions as a kind of piazza which links all the living spaces. All rooms benefit from the careful washing of daylight and the framing of the landscape. At night the same shaping allows indirect lighting to create its own nuanced environment.

In plan, the house develops as a "yin-yang" diagram with interior and exterior complementing and overlapping along a flexible boundary. This creates long diagonal views and movements on a tight urban lot. A gallery-like space links all the rooms and creates a transitional zone between inside and out.

Renewables: Photovoltaic panels are designed to provide over 100% of the electric energy. Solar water panels are designed to provide radiant heat, domestic hot water and pool heating.

Landscape: The landscape focuses on drought-tolerant native materials, a roof garden of native grasses, and onsite water retention.

Materials and technology: Throughout the house, materials were selected for minimal environmental impact. An array of low-energy-consuming products such as LED lighting significantly reduces the energy loads.

Monitoring: Systems are designed so that monitoring and adjustments can take places over years of inhabiting the house. This is critical so that we can use the house as a laboratory for our clients and ourselves.

While designing sustainably, we found that we could further elevate our concerns for the choreography of space, the magic of light and shadow and the harmony between building and landscape. The house is evolving with a richness and subtlety of experience, a range of transitions between inside and out and an ever-changing awareness of the magic of the natural elements.

设计师和客户的双重身份使我们将该项目作为个案研究，力图打造一个和谐、奇妙的住宅空间，并与周围环境完美融合在一起，该项目为我们提供了一个实现零能源消耗设计目标的契机。

该空间设计的环境战略具体可分为如下几个步骤：

被动设计：该住宅的平面图和剖面图设计突出了可持续的设计理念，强调空间的自然通风、采光效果，注重空间的遮阳、冬季的取暖以及室内外空间界限的灵活性。同时，突出住宅的"剖面"，确保每个房间参与到这个被动设计之中。

位于住宅核心的一个两层空间在装点外观的同时，扮演走廊的角色，将所有生活空间连接到一起。确保所有房间沐浴在明媚的阳光中，同时将秀美的景观尽收眼底。夜色降临之时，间接照明灯具将空间烘托得分外迷人。

对于空间的平面布局，我们设计了一个"阴－阳"关系图，即强调内外空间的相互补充，并沿一个不定边界进行重叠。这种布局能够在一个拥挤的城市空间中打造一个狭长的对角线景观。一个走廊状的空间将所有房间有机衔接在一起，并巧妙打造了室内外空间的过渡地带。

可再生能源：光伏板能够提供100%的电能。太阳能板的设计提供辐射热、生活热水和游泳池加热。

景观：景观的设计以本土耐旱材料为主要原料，屋顶花园种植的原生草皮起到贮水的作用。

材料与技术：整个住宅材料的选用力图将对环境的影响降到最低。低能源消耗产品，如LED照明设备能够有效降低能源的负荷。

监测系统：监测系统的设计能够对空间进行监测和调整，使之历久弥新。这是设计的关键，这样我们可以将它作为我们和客户的实验室。

在可持续设计中，我们发现空间的布局、光影效果的处理以及建筑与景观的关系的调节还存在一定的上升空间。整个空间中，丰富而微妙的感官体验、内外空间的自然过渡以及自然元素间的神奇变幻，将为未来住宅空间的设计提供完美的示范作用。

The house is shaped in plan and section to optimize its sustainable design.

该住宅的平面图和剖面图设计突出了可持续的设计理念。

Santa Monica, California

YUDELL/BEEBE HOUSE (in progress)

加利福尼亚州,圣莫尼卡市

约德/毕比 住宅 (建设中)

圣莫尼卡市
SANTA MONICA

PASSIVE DESIGN STRATEGIES

building orientation & shape
day lighting
natural ventilation & stack effect
shading
thermal mass

ACTIVE DESIGN STRATEGIES

EnergyStar appliances
energy efficient & dimmable lighting
high-efficiency gas boiler
hydronic radiant heating & cooling
no air-conditioning
variable-speed pool pump

RENEWABLE ENERGY

photovoltaic panels
solar hot water supplies:
    domestic hot water
    radiant heating
    seasonal pool heating

MATERIALS & METHODS

100% engineered lumber
100% FSC-certified plywood
80% of pre-existing house was donated
    and recycled
durable materials
formaldehyde-free millwork
FSC-certified wood veneer
low-waste framing & millwork practices
no or Low-VOC paints, adhesives, finishes,
    and sealants
recycled/recyclable materials
    (steel, glass, aluminum)
renewable resources (bamboo, young trees)

LANDSCAPE & WATER

drought-tolerant planting
drip irrigation
permeable paving
zero run-off (storm water collection)

被动设计战略

建筑方位与外观
采光
自然通风与烟囱效应
遮阳
热式质量流量计

主动设计战略

节能产品认证设备
节能与调光系统
高效燃气锅炉
循环辐射供暖与制冷系统
无空调装置
变速泳池水泵

可再生能源

光伏板
太阳能热水供应：
生活热水
辐射采暖
季节性的泳池加热

材料与方法

100% 复合木料
100% FSC认证胶合板
80% 原建筑材料的再利用
耐用材料
不含甲醛的木制品
FSC认证木单板
低损耗框架及预制木制材料
无或低 VOC 涂料，粘合剂，
    抛光剂，密封剂
回收/可循环再造物料
    （钢铁、玻璃、铝）
可再生资源（竹子、小树）

景观与水土保持

耐旱植物的种植
滴灌
透水路面
零径流（收集雨水）

1. Summer
2. Winter
3. Sun shading
4. Pool
5. Hydronic floor heating system
6. Solar hot water panels
7. Photovoltaic panels
8. Indirect daylight
9. Natural ventilation
10. Electricity to house and grid
11. Water storage and pump

1. 夏季
2. 冬季
3. 遮阳系统
4. 游泳池
5. 循环地板加热系统
6. 太阳能热水板
7. 光伏板
8. 间接光源
9. 自然通风
10. 电力供应
11. 蓄水与泵水

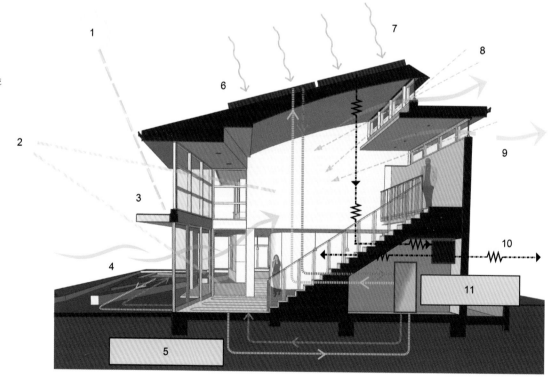

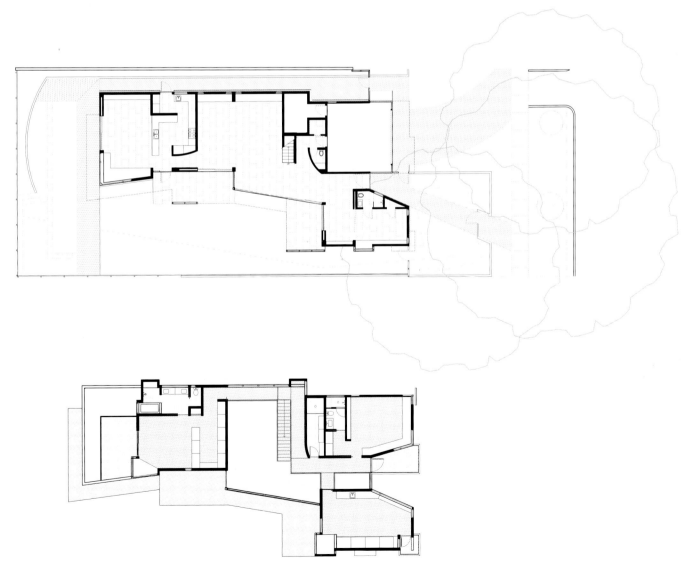

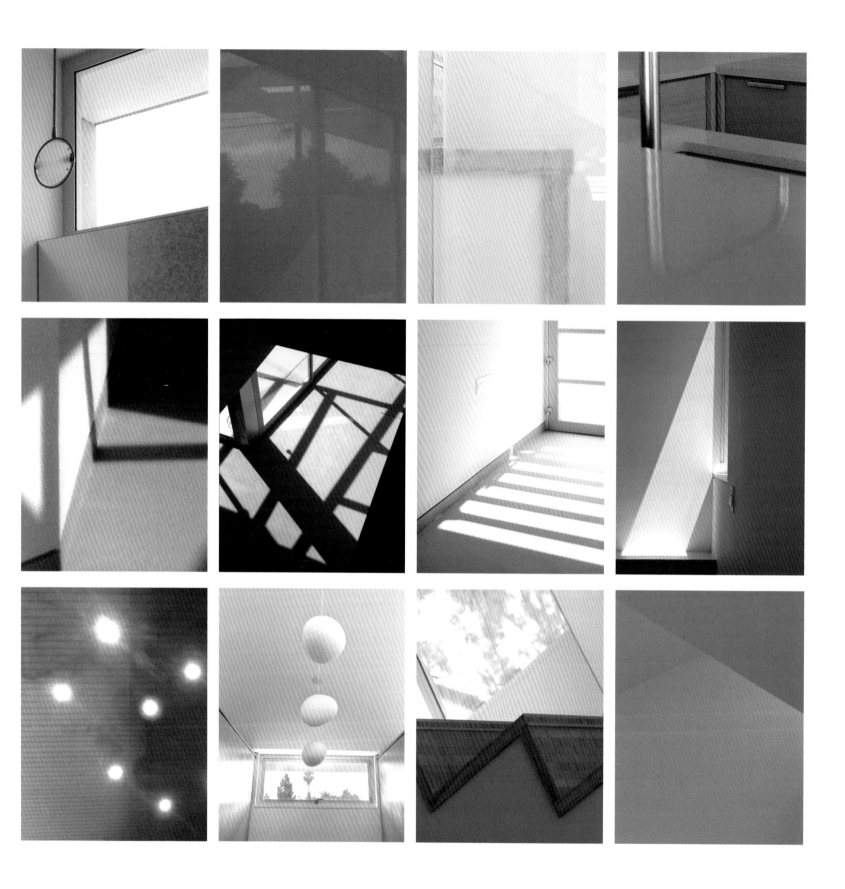

YUDELL/BEEBE HOUSE 约德/毕比 住宅

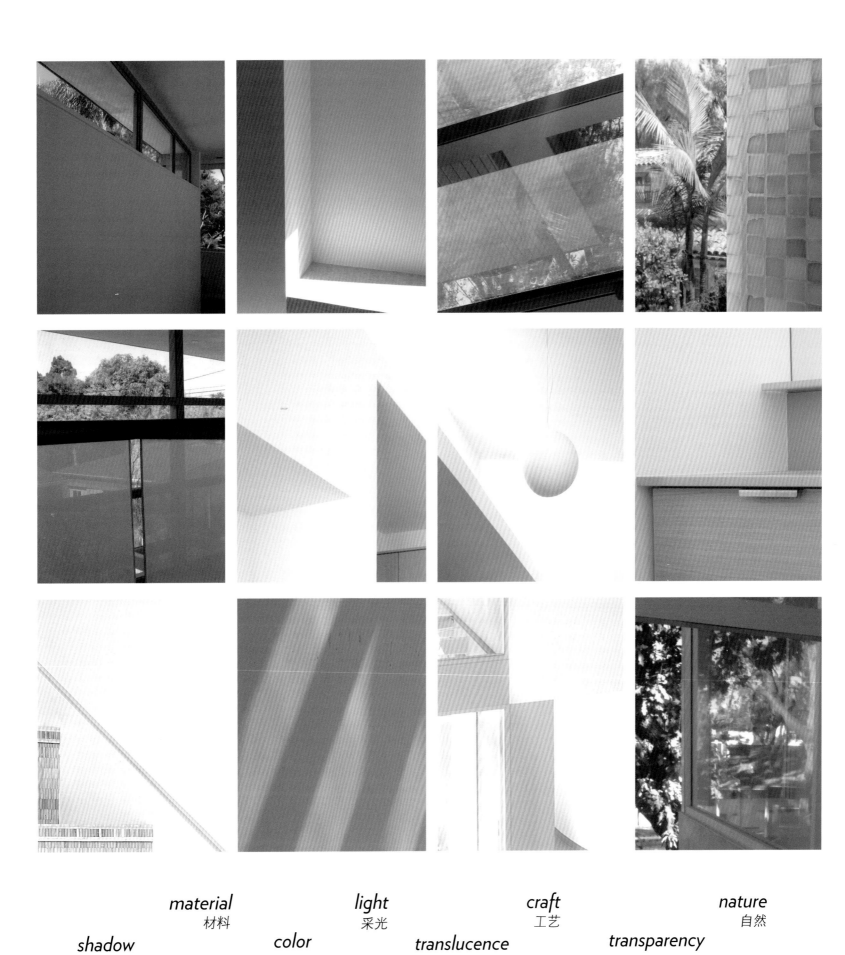

material
材料

light
采光

craft
工艺

nature
自然

shadow
遮阳

color
色彩

translucence
半透明

transparency
通透

城市公共建筑和机构建筑设计

城市公共建筑将我们与对公共生活和社会联系得更加紧密。在纷繁复杂的都市世界中，我们依然可以找到城市建筑一个经典的代表——寺庙会所，每个会所由于宗教仪式、政治或文化的不同功能，从而确认不同的社会体制。在布局和设计主旨方面，城市公共建筑为民主价值观的展现提供了足够的机会和支持。

选址和意义

城市公共建筑通常位于城市的历史中心，其醒目的核心位置彰显了独特的社会地位。对城市中心的当代城市设施进行重建或翻新意味着将为整个城市注入新鲜活力，使之焕然一新。位于美国的弗雷斯诺罗伯特·科伊尔法院大楼即是这样一个经典案例。尽管高速公路拉近了郊区与市区的距离，法院最终还是决定选址在已有的市民公园附近，以带动整个弗雷斯诺地区的复兴。

同样，位于快速发展的城市中心地带的新圣莫尼卡公共图书馆为城市街头面貌打造了一道亮丽的风景。静谧的庭院花园为市民提供了一块远离尘嚣的净土，市民于此既可以充分享受个人空间带来的自由，也可以与他人进行互动交流。此外，花园中还设置了咖啡馆，与随处可见的街角咖啡店相比，此处更显高雅、幽静。

因此，城市公共建筑的空间设计与结构设计同等重要。法院广场在法院大楼的设计中扮演了重要角色，同时，广场或者公园也是整体建设中不可忽视的部分。对于我们设计的纪念性建筑项目在文化中的地位来说，援引伟大的地理学家巴顿杰克逊提出的设计理论，即强调其建筑在城市公共景观中"显眼"的重要性。随着现代城市公共建筑尺度的增大，其周围的商业和住宅建筑扩张的更快,为图书馆或法院这类城市公共建筑设计提供街道退缩或开放式公共空间，使其独特性分外明显。

CIVIC AND INSTITUTIONAL WORKS

Civic architecture connects us to the most fundamental agreements we have about public life and society. Embedded in the complexity of our sprawling metropolitan world we can still find echoes of the classical representation of civitas: a gathering of temples—each housing its particular institution devoted to religious observances, government, or culture—that in its form and function identifies a society in terms of placement and in terms of unique, specific purpose, civic architecture offers extraordinary opportunities for the expression—and the support—of democratic values.

PLACE AND MEANING

Our understanding of the city as giving form to social order is heightened by the placement of civic buildings at its heart—often in the historic center of town. Replacing or re-building contemporary civic facilities in the heart of downtown makes an important statement of commitment to the vitality and relevance of urban centers. A classic example is the Robert E. Coyle US Courthouse in Fresno. Early studies considered suburban sites that were "freeway close" to town. Yet the decision by the courts to find a site adjacent to the existing civic campus led to new development and a revitalization of Fresno's ailing core.

Similarly, the location of the new Santa Monica Public Library in the middle of a fast developing downtown residential district has given the library its special meaning as "the living room of the city". Its tranquil courtyard garden provides an oasis of calm and a place of community. While the garden also includes a café, the presence of the library provides an alternative to more commercial gathering places—a quieter place of destination in contrast to the ubiquitous street corner coffee shops.

Thus civic architecture is as much about place making as about buildings. The courthouse gives meaning and importance to the courthouse square, but it also needs the square—or the park—as a setting. In describing the place of monuments in our cultural landscape, geographer J.B. Jackson attributed great importance to "visibility"—relative visual prominence of the civic marker in relation to its context. Even as the scale of modern civic buildings has increased, the scale of surrounding commercial and residential buildings has grown more, and the hierarchic uniqueness of the library or courthouse is best expressed by notable setback from the street, or by presiding over a patch of open space.

城市公共建筑 CIVIC

Our proposal for a new US Courthouse in Bakersfield takes maximum advantage of the adjacent public park—an attractive, watery green space in a dry, dusty western town. The building and the park are inseparable—stitched together by a long glassy gallery so that each is bounded by the other. The Fresno courthouse makes a similar connection between public garden and lobby—a continuous work of art titled "Once upon a time in Fresno..." by landscape architect Pamela Burton and San Francisco artists Anna Valentina Murch and Doug Hollis. The garden and lobby fulfill the first priority of Judge Coyle, for whom the courthouse is named, that the building give something of importance to the city— "a magnificent public place".

FUNCTION AND PURPOSE That civic buildings are a reflection of their function may seem self-evident, but functions evolve with time. Behind or within the shifting complexity of function is the deeper and relatively unchanging understanding of purpose. For civic programs, this idea of purpose is embodied in the concept of the building as a type. Thus a library is both a building and an institution. Contemporary re-namings like "educational resource center" or "justice center" attempt to broaden the content of the program, but also tend to imply the building as an invisible support system for a set of activities.

Yet the buildings and their latent meaning as forms will not go away. Every architect of a courthouse eventually confronts the question— "how is this design like or not like the popular image of a courthouse?" Our civic architecture will always represent something—and that something is ultimately "the purpose of the institution"—whether we want to address the issue or not. How to translate these timeless meanings into contemporary form is among architecture's most satisfying challenges.

位于贝克斯菲尔德地区的美国新法院坐落于一个绿意盎然的公共公园旁，该公园作为干燥的西部城市中心的一块绿洲，为此地打造了一道清新的绿色景观，而法院大楼的扩建充分抓住了这一地形优势，利用一个狭长的玻璃走廊实现了与公园的有机衔接。同时，该建筑还在公共花园和大堂之间建立了相似的公共衔接区域，其中陈列了一系列艺术作品，涉及景观设计师帕梅拉·伯顿和旧金山艺术家安娜·瓦伦蒂娜默奇和多戈·霍利斯设计主题为"曾经的弗雷斯诺"的作品等。花园和大堂按照著名法官科伊尔的提议而设计，该法官因长期致力于法律事业而闻名，而建筑也以该法官名字命名，这座新法院的落成为城市打造了又一个意义深远的公共空间。

功能和目的 城市公共建筑反映出的功能性似乎不言自明，然而其功能也随着时间的推移而逐渐发生变化。复杂的功能性转变的背后是相对不变的设计宗旨。对于公共项目而言，设计理念体现设计的目的。因此，图书馆既是一个建筑，同时也是一个机构。随着社会的发展，传统的建筑机构开始衍生出新的名称，诸如"教育资源中心"或者"司法中心"，这些新生词汇似乎延伸了项目的内涵，但是同时也暗示了该建筑背后的一系列无形支持体系。

当然，建筑物及其潜在的内涵并不会消失。该法院大楼的建筑师最终面临的问题是如何打造一个独特的法院大楼形象，不落俗套的同时不辜负绝大部分公众的期待。对于城市公共建筑来说，具有丰富的象征意义是设计的亮点所在，如何将这些永恒的意义转化成充满现代气息的建筑模式是设计中面临的最大的挑战。

城市公共建筑设计目的的当代定义

2008年，在设计美国驻柏林使馆的过程中，我们经常会被问道："使馆的安全性考虑是否会影响到设计？"对一个临街的建筑进行改变，建筑物退缩设计的确会影响建筑的城市特征，不过这样的提问，这样的假设听起来是有点荒谬的。在一个现代城市公共建筑的设计过程中，这个问题的答案就存在于问题之中，即设计体现设计计划和目的。

1995年，在新使馆的设计大赛中，美国国务院针对这个项目提出了四个要求也可以说是目标，即公众形象、功能性、可持续性和灵活性。这四个要求并重，缺一不可。尽管这设计竞赛看起来似乎偏重于更注重建筑物的公众形象，我们却将这四个要求看成是四个相互依存的统一体。事实上，美国国务院的提议是对21世纪的城市公共建筑和机构提出了一个总体要求。

在使馆的建设过程中，我们将整个建筑结构看成是一个统一的整体，无论是室内还是室外空间，均能够彰显功能性和代表性。办公环境的优越本身就是一种公众形象的塑造。可持续发展的设计理念和空间的灵活性结合在一起能够实现建筑的历久弥新。

新使馆的建立也可以看作是城市复兴计划的一部分，该城市复兴计划的重点是完成对勃兰登堡门这一欧洲最负盛名的古迹的改造。对于这一重要的城市计划，首要条件是加强对这一建筑类型的了解，在这种情况下，我们打造了一个典型的柏林庭院式建筑，使之承担多种功能。庭院模式能够为一个安全的中心花园提供充足的光线，同时满足了城市对绿色空间的要求。

城市公共建筑因丰富的功能性而布局上较为细化，划分为公众入口大厅、活动场所、聚集场所以及办公空间等。弗雷斯诺法院大楼、圣莫尼卡图书馆以及柏林使馆均设置了精致的入口，并通过运用玻璃材料打造了通透的楼顶玻璃封闭空间，犹如城市中的灯塔，十分醒目。

CONTEMPORARY DEFINITIONS OF CIVIC PURPOSE

At the 2008 dedication of our new US Embassy in Berlin members of the press repeatedly asked "Did the embassy's requirements (for security) interfere with your design?" While the need for a revised setback along the major street front did certainly impact the urban character of the block, in a more general sense the journalists' assumption was dubious at best. In designing a modern civic building the answer does indeed lie within the question—design embodies both program and purpose.

In the 1995 design competition for the new embassy the State Department set forth four requirements or goals for the project, with the emphasis that they were all equally important: public image, functionality, sustainability, and flexibility. While the dynamics of a design competition would seem to favor public image—dominated by visual presentation—we chose to see all four aspects as interdependent. Indeed, the State Department's listing of its priorities sounds a lot like Vitruvius (commodity, firmness, delight) and provides the ultimate user's definition of what a civic or institutional building is in the 21st century.

Our proposal for the Embassy takes the building fabric as a whole, inside and out, to be simultaneously functional and representational. The quality of the workplace is itself an aspect of public image. The interrelated concerns of sustainability and flexibility add up to making the building long-lasting—which to be successful requires a deep exploration of functional relationships.

The new embassy also has a part to play as part of the reconstruction of the city—in particular of Pariser Platz as a frame for the Brandenburg Gate—one of Europe's most recognized monuments. Our starting point for this critical urban design issue was to understand the building as a type—in this case a classic Berlin courtyard block—which became the parti for organizing the embassy's many complex functions. While urbanistically relevant, the courtyard format also provides abundant daylight around a secure central garden, which in turn helped meet the city's requirement for green space replacement.

Civic buildings provide a rich repertoire of functions to express: public arrival, event spaces such as courtrooms, gathering places, and the presence of public officials. The courthouse in Fresno, the library in Santa Monica, and the embassy in Berlin all use and activate public places with dramatic entrances, and animate their rooftops with glass-enclosed rooms that act as civic lanterns to celebrate the presence of the institution in the city.

INSTITUTING SUSTAINABILITY

Increasingly civic projects have taken on the responsibility to lead the way to a greener future. While it preceded the LEED requirements of the General Service Administration's current projects, the Robert E. Coyle US Courthouse has proven to be distinguished in terms of building performance, flexible public use, and urban conservation. The Santa Monica Public Library holds a LEED Gold certification, and demonstrates an integrated design approach with multi-functional features like its rain-collecting inverted roof, which also functions as a light-scoop for the reading room.

For our clients at the State Department, the challenge of a worldwide spectrum of climate types, often in remote locations, combined with the system-wide requirement for uniform interior air conditioning has made climate-responsive design an imperative. Our proposal for a new embassy in Santo Domingo seeks to address energy performance and regional relevance with a carefully conceived building envelope. Deep overhangs, floating canopies, and projecting walls shade window openings and walkways, sheltering the public throughout a series of indoor and outdoor waiting areas. This influence of climate leads to an evidently tropical modernism, linking the architecture of the embassy to the context of Latin America's vibrant contemporary design culture.

实行可持续发展理念

越来越多的城市公共建筑倾向于打造一个完美的绿色空间。目前设计的总务管理局项目达到了LEED认证标准，罗伯特科伊尔弗雷斯诺法院大楼则堪称是造型独特、公共空间应用灵活、功能性优良的绿色建筑。圣莫尼卡公共图书馆获得了LEED金级认证，采用了多功能的综合设计方法，诸如倒置式屋顶既能够储存雨水，又确保阅览室光线充足。

对于客户美国国务院来说，打造统一的室内空调系统是设计的关键所在。而圣多明各新使馆的设计主旨则是解决建筑的节能以及与周围环境的衔接问题。悬臂、浮檐篷、投影墙、遮阳窗和行人通道等细节设计，巧妙地打造了一个集公共空间与室内外休息区于一体的公共建筑。受热带气候的影响，该建筑的设计风格奔放、充满活力，与拉丁美洲独特的现代设计文化相得益彰。

fig. 1

城市公共建筑的地域性

由于机构建筑类型具有相对独立的功能性，因此区域化带给设计的影响深远而明显。在弗雷斯诺科伊尔法院大楼的设计过程中，清楚地阐述问题显得尤为重要。"21世纪的法院形象是怎样的？"这个问题并不是我们的设计团队所思考的，而我们真正考虑的是："21世纪加利福尼亚的法院形象是怎样的?或者更进一步说，21世纪加利福尼亚中央谷地的法院形象是怎样的?"该建筑的设计灵感源自风景秀丽的山麓，崎岖的山脉以及大片的农业模式。气势雄伟的外观设计既彰显了法律的威严又实现了与当地环境的和谐统一，同时暗示法院作为社会的一部分，其行使的职能不容小觑。（图1）

对于贝克斯菲尔德法院大楼来说，该建筑与弗雷斯诺科伊尔法院大楼相比规模较小，不过设计背景类似。有这样一个问题，即"法院在一个西部地区小城镇中扮演什么角色？"县级法院建筑模式对加利福尼亚州的其他小城镇也同样适用。所不同的是，其他县级法院位于当地的核心地带，而我们设计的这个小法院则位列一侧。在设计过程中，我们打造了华丽的整体屋顶和一个玻璃结构的封闭走廊。该走廊呈西向设计，一个以木材和金属为原料的全高柱廊为其进行遮阳，并巧妙地将环境和城建标准融为一体。此外，该走廊将作为多功能性空间，这同时也是该项目的亮点所在，并满足了城市公共建筑对型式、风格以及公共生活空间塑造的要求。

CIVIC REGIONALISM

Because institutional building types have such a clear DNA in terms of their programs, regional influences on design can be especially meaningful and legible. When designing the Coyle Courthouse in Fresno, it was important to state the problem clearly. Instead of asking "What is a 21st century Courthouse?" our team considered the question "What is a 21st century Courthouse in California?" and more to the point, in the Central Valley. Inspiration was all around in the form of beautiful foothills, rugged mountain ranges, and sweeping agricultural patterns. The building that resulted represents the Federal Government without looking like a visitor from Washington—an important message of local relevance and a reminder that the courts are part of the community (fig. 1).

For the much smaller program of the courthouse in Bakersfield—a very similar context to Fresno—the question was "What does a courthouse mean to a small western town?" The familiar form of the county courthouse has great significance for small towns in California, as elsewhere. While their typical position is at the center of a block, our project stood off to one side. The county courthouse gained civic stature by being mounted atop a steep set of steps—taboo in our time of universal access. Our design for the courthouse reinterprets civic gesture with a dramatic sweep of roof and a glass-enclosed gallery. The gallery faces west—the harshest orientation in a hot climate—and so is shaded by a grand colonnade of full-height wood and metal fins, combining environmental performance and civic statement in one. The gallery would provide the community with the kind of multi-use venue that has been a great success in Fresno, and points to the most relevant kind of regionalism: supporting the pattern, style, and place of public life.

圣莫尼卡市

SANTA MONICA

作为一个崭新的公共空间，新公共图书馆彰显了圣莫尼卡独特的地方特色，为公众营造了极具加州南部沿海风格的舒适空间。为加强公众意识，并鼓励民众参与到公共环境之中，该建筑的各部分设计元素均采用适中的比例，并且全方位开放，空间通透，视野开阔。

通过一系列的会议讨论，该图书馆最终决定将大型遮光玻璃、姹紫嫣红的小型花园与可持续设计理念相结合，这与独特的圣莫尼卡气候相得益彰，该设计获得了LEED金牌认证。整个空间的中心是一个大型封闭式庭院，内设一个小咖啡馆，衔接巧妙，毫无突兀之感。北部场区和中央花园与一个可容纳200人的礼堂和多功能室相结合，作为公共场地之用。此外，一个小型博物馆和灵活空间可为展览和非正式会议提供场所。矗立于飞速发展的住宅和商业楼群之中，该建筑以其独特的城市绿洲身份装点着城市的天际线，并扮演了"城市客厅"的角色。

The new Public Library reflects the character of Santa Monica as a place and as a community, supporting a well-informed public in the comfort of the benign coastal climate of southern California. Seeking to enhance community awareness and encourage public use, the design presents a building of approachable scale and civic proportions, opening in all directions to access, daylight, and views into and out of the building.

Designed through a series of community meetings, the library responds to Santa Monica's breezy-but-enlightened culture by incorporating large, sun-shaded windows, colorful pocket gardens, and a broad spectrum of sustainability features—ultimately winning the project LEED Gold certification. At the center of the whole is a large enclosed garden court containing a small cafe with wireless connectivity. The north court and central garden/café combine with a 200-seat auditorium and multi-purpose rooms to offer a dynamic venue for public use. In addition, a small museum and flexible spaces can alternately accommodate exhibitions and informal presentations. The building serves as an urban oasis at the center of fast-paced residential and commercial redevelopment, earning its title as the "Living Room of the City".

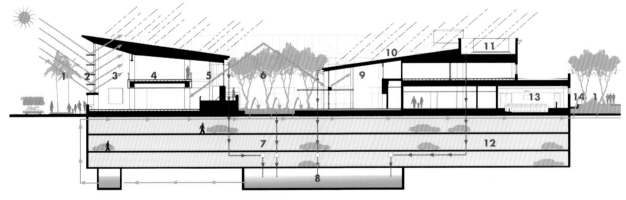

Roof slopes inflect to the courtyard to gather day-light and rain water.

屋顶向中庭倾斜,达到采光及收集雨水的功能。

1. Native planting 2. Sunshades and glazing 3. Reading room / library stacks 4. Raised flooring for HVAC and electrical 5. Main staircase 6. Central courtyard 7. Rainwater filter 8. 200,000 gallon rainwater cistern 9. Cafe 10. Sloped impluvium roof 11. HVAC equipment 12. Below-ground parking 13. Auditorium 14. Rainwater for irrigation

1. 原生植物种植区 2. 遮光系统与反射 3. 阅览室 / 图书馆书库 4. 空调与配电室 5. 主楼梯 6. 中央庭院 7. 雨水处理系统 8. 200,000加仑雨水蓄水池 9. 自助餐厅 10. 方形蓄水池倾斜屋顶 11. 暖通空调设备 12. 地下停车场 13. 礼堂 14. 雨水灌溉系统

Santa Monica, California

加利福尼亚州,圣莫尼卡市

SANTA MONICA PUBLIC LIBRARY

圣莫尼卡市

SANTA MONICA

圣莫尼卡市民停车场结构设计巧妙，在市中心附近的建筑群中，其地位不可或缺。该结构已远远超越了传统的停车库模式，其扮演的公众生活态枢纽角色不容小觑。

该停车场占地27,871平方米，不但能够提供882个有效车位(地上六层，地下两层)，同时也为各种设施的设置提供了足够空间。位于五楼的公共会议室是公众中心的一个主导空间，身居于此，可将壮美的太平洋海景和城市景观以及广场上的咖啡馆和穿梭的人流尽收眼底。

该项目作为首个获得美国停车结构LEED®认证的建筑，要归功于以下几个元素：屋顶上的太阳能板；东、西两侧立面设计为建筑提供能源所需；而檐篷及太阳能光伏板等元素则能够为空间进行有效的温度调节。建筑采用了大量的可再生材料，诸如粉煤灰、可循环再造钢筋框架等。

停车区结构同样也是公众中心的一个视觉标志。斑驳陆离的墙面上嵌有棱纹状水泥板，使停放的车辆在光线的作用下，实现光影交汇的艺术效果。由槽形彩色玻璃制成的一系列隔间，打破了沉闷的空间布局，多角度设置能够时刻确保空间内部明亮、通透。夜色来临之时，剔透的玻璃和熠熠生辉的窗帘交相辉映，令空间分外迷人。

The striking design of the Santa Monica Civic Parking Structure establishes a strong presence within a cluster of civic buildings near downtown Santa Monica. The structure was conceived as much more than a traditional parking garage—rather, a functionally dynamic hub of civic life. The 300,000 sf parking structure effectively provides not only 882 parking spaces (accommodated in six levels above grade and two below grade) but also a wide variety of amenities to the community. Serving as an easily identifiable marker for the entire civic center, the building affords spectacular views of the Pacific Ocean and the city from the upper levels, while a cafe on the main plaza terrace animates the pedestrian traffic flow.

Many factors contribute to the building's status as one of the first LEED® certified parking structures in the United States. Photovoltaic panels on the roof provide for all of the building's energy needs, while canopies and photovoltaic panels facilitate self-shading. Materials with a high recycled content were used, including fly-ash replacement for cement, and recycled-content reinforcing steel and framing.

The Parking Structure is a visually iconic presence in the Civic Center. Ribbed concrete panels are set in a rhythmic, variegated pattern on all facades, capturing and enhancing the rich play of shadows while screening the presence of parked cars. A series of bays made of channeled colored glass breaks down the scale of the structure and are set at varying angles to bring a light, luminous and ever-changing quality to the building. The character of the structure changes yet again in the evening, when the glass is illuminated and appears to glow as a shimmering curtain.

加利福尼亚州, 圣莫尼卡市
圣莫尼卡公共停车建筑

Santa Monica, California
CIVIC CENTER PARKING STRUCTURE

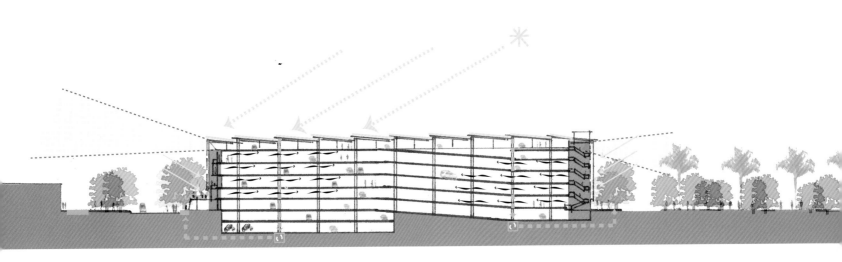

Photovoltaic canopies shade
vehicles and collect power.

太阳能板不但能收集能
源并提供为汽车遮荫的
功能。

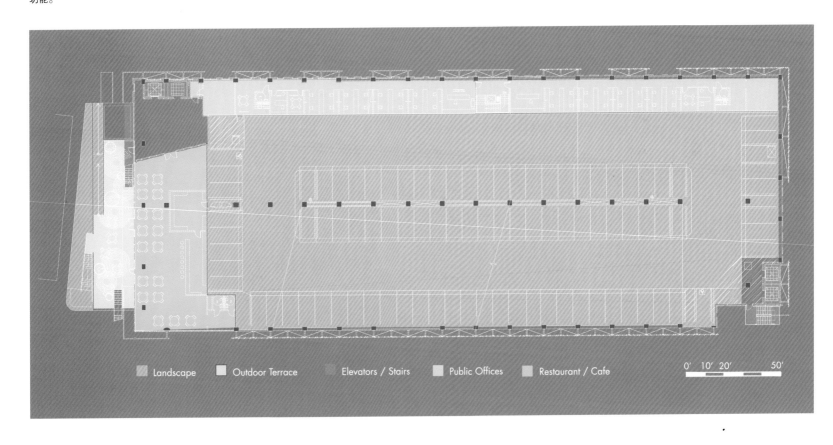

■ Landscape　■ Outdoor Terrace　Elevators / Stairs　■ Public Offices　■ Restaurant / Cafe

0' 10' 20'　　　50'

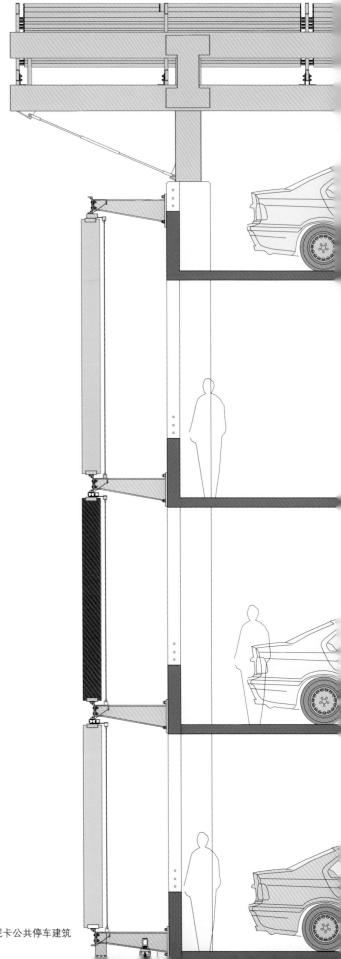

CIVIC CENTER PARKING STRUCTURE 圣莫尼卡公共停车建筑

弗雷斯诺市

FRESNO

The United States Courthouse in Fresno adds a new landmark to the downtown and enhances the cultural environment of the city as a whole. A major public garden, large multi-use lobby, cafe, library, and other amenities make the courthouse an integral part of urban and community life. The context of the greater Central Valley and the nearby Sierra Nevada Mountains are reflected in the bold sculpting of the mass of the building and the use of a unique system of textured precast concrete panels.

The mass is folded into an L of two intersecting volumes, with solid shoulders and sloping tops, capped by a grand loggia at the apex.

The L-shape of the building frames a large public garden—a collaboration between the artists and landscape architect—as a tableau to be seen from the lobby. The garden, entitled "Once Upon a Time in Fresno..." creates a whole environment that celebrates the natural history of the San Joaquin Valley—the region that the courthouse was built to serve.

A defining aspect of the courthouse is its unique skin of sculptural precast concrete. The variation of concrete surface patterns across the elevations of the courthouse are intended to suggest the rugged nature of the landscape in the region, particularly the majestic faces of the Sierra Nevada Mountains rising to the east. Crucial technical requirements are also fulfilled: the panels meet the building's blast-resistance criteria, provide acoustical insulation, and ensure the durability of the building's envelope. Moreover, on such a large building, the faceted nature of the 1,260 individual concrete panels mediates the scale of the massive wall surfaces and heightens the sculptural effect of the entire building form.

美国弗雷斯诺法院大楼为该地成功塑造了一个新型地标，提高了整个城市的文化环境。公共花园、大型多功能大厅、咖啡厅、图书馆和其他设施将法院与城市和社区生活紧密联系在一起。大胆的建筑造型搭配独特的预制混凝土板纹理与中央山谷和内华达山脉的自然景致遥相呼应，美不胜收。

两个体量交叉合拢后形成"L"形外观，两侧呈立体结构，倾斜的顶端上设置了一个开阔的凉廊。

L形的建筑框架巧妙打造了一个大型公共花园，其中优美的艺术作品和景观设计从入口大厅即可窥见一二。这个名为"曾经的弗雷斯诺"的公共花园彰显了法院所在地圣华金河谷优美的自然景观。

该建筑外部采用的雕刻预制混凝土表层，匠心独运、不拘一格，是整个设计的焦点所在。千变万化的混凝土图案象征着该地区崎岖的自然景观，与东侧雄伟的内华达山脉遥相呼应。此外，牢固的嵌板符合建筑防爆标准，具有良好的隔音效果，耐久性能一流。同时，1,260个小型混凝土嵌板能够对墙面的比例进行有效调节，并为整个建筑外观增强雕塑效果。

The Courthouse garden opens toward the civic axis of city hall.

法院的花园面向市政中心的主轴开放。

加利福尼亚州,弗雷斯诺市

弗雷斯诺罗伯特·科伊尔法院大楼

Fresno, California

ROBERT E. COYLE UNITED STATES COURTHOUSE

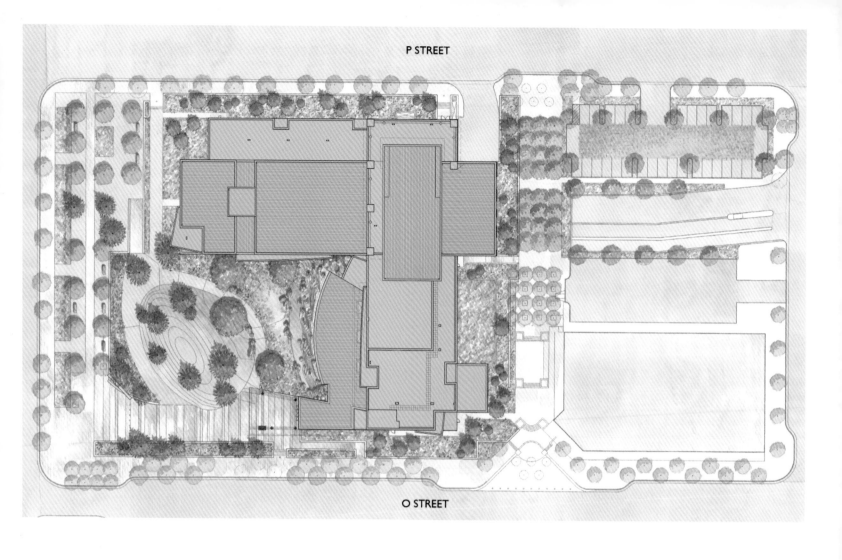

P STREET

弗雷斯诺罗伯特·科伊尔法院大楼

O STREET

FRESNO COURTHOUSE 弗雷斯诺罗伯特·科伊尔法院大楼

贝克斯菲尔德市

BAKERSFIELD

The new United States Courthouse will be a focal landmark of a redeveloped district of Bakersfield, but a landmark with appropriate scale. The fundamental design approach is to respond to the local environment and context. Planning for the courthouse takes maximum advantage of daylight, frames views of the nearby park and canal, and introduces daylight into the courtrooms via north-facing clerestory windows. A light court in the center of the building allows daylight to penetrate into spaces that would otherwise be cut off from the external environment.

The entry plaza of the courthouse is framed by a monumental curved wall of finely-textured concrete, over which a grand roof canopy sweeps up at an angle for a dynamic, contemporary expression of civic dignity. The courthouse is organized as a linear sequence of arrival and movement, using a glassy gallery that parallels the canal. The west-facing Lobby Gallery is characterized by a series of full-height fins that mediate potential solar heat gain and recall the order of a classical colonnade. In the context of a beautiful park, the courthouse will be the center of a new neighborhood and be an icon of the next phase in the life of the city.

The design concept for the new U.S. Courthouse in Bakersfield approaches the project in broad terms as a demonstration of new means and methods. Just as the finished building may be seen as a test case for new design approaches, Design-Build with Design Excellence as a procurement approach has equally important lessons for our current and future economy. Thus the new U.S. Courthouse in Bakersfield is more than a small, one-room courthouse—indeed, its modest scale invites it to be a laboratory for big ideas.

新美国法院的建立将成为复兴中的贝克斯菲尔德地区一个崭新的地标性建筑。该建筑的设计理念是巧妙利用所在地的自然环境，并使之与建筑实现自然融合。法院大楼充分利用自然光线，并与周围公园和运河景观进行有机衔接，通过设置一个北向的长廊将自然光线成功引入到审判室之中。位于建筑中央的天井时刻确保室内光线充足，视野开阔，同时淡化室内外界限。

法院入口广场上，一个巨大的弧形混凝土墙体上方经由一个开阔的屋顶檐篷覆盖，极具动态之美，同时彰显庄严、肃穆之感。空间内采用线性结构布局，一个玻璃画廊与外部运河呈平行状设置。西向的大堂画廊中的一系列散热翅片能够有效调节室温并与经典的柱廊排列遥相呼应。在绿意盎然的公园衬托之下，该法院大楼将成为城市生活中又一处亮点。

该法院大楼的设计理念是运用全新的设计手段和设计手法。就如同每一个建筑的竣工都是一次对设计手段新的尝试。设计建造经验与卓越的设计理念并重，是目前以及未来经济体系下，一个重要的学习经验。因此，贝克斯菲尔德菲市法院大楼不仅仅是一个小型一室法院建筑，其适度的规模更是一次伟大设计概念的大胆尝试。

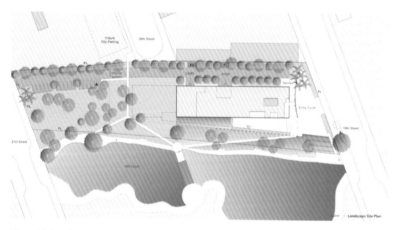

Natural light adds dignity, drama, and orientation to the courtrooms.

自然采光增添了法院的尊严、戏剧感及方向性。

加利福尼亚州,贝克斯菲尔德市

美国贝克斯菲尔德市法院大楼

Bakersfield, California

UNITED STATES COURTHOUSE

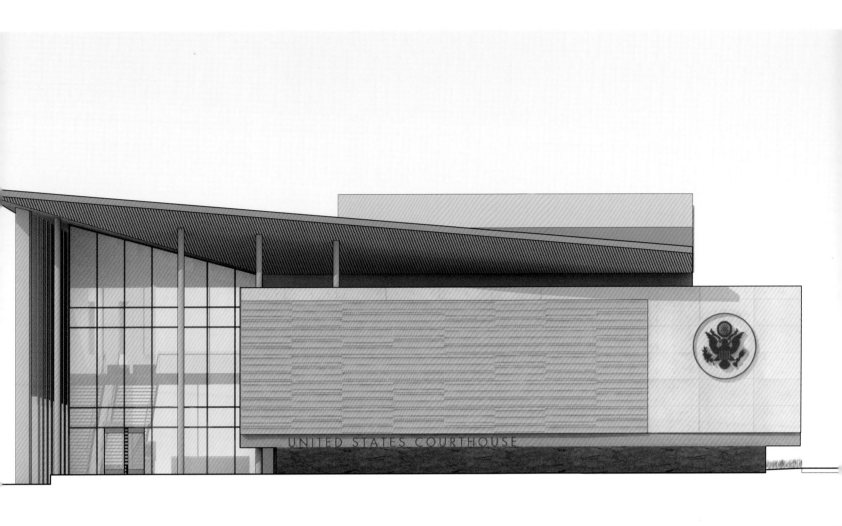

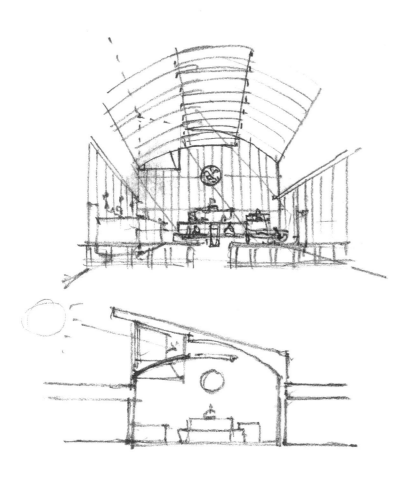

BAKERSFIELD COURTHOUSE 贝克斯菲尔德市法院大楼

柏林

BERLIN

美国驻柏林大使馆巧妙地将历史、城市背景与未来发展构想融为一体。该建筑与其附近的勃兰登堡门位于德意志联邦德国的政治中心地带，扮演城市地标的角色。入口设计精致而高雅，符合安全标准。巴黎广场上的主要大厅犹如一个开放的庭院，将自然光线透过立面直接引入室内。办公大楼内优雅、开阔的大厅为午宴和高层接待会提供了充足的空间，大楼因毗邻新政府中心和德国国会大厦而备受瞩目。

使馆顶端采用了绿化屋顶设计，与绿意盎然的庭院景观遥相呼应，从上端俯视，仿佛是建筑的第五立面。独特的美洲景观材料为使馆空间注入了无限生机，同时与蒂尔加滕公园自然融为一体。夜幕降临之时，柔和的灯光将室内照亮。大厅上方的红铜和玻璃灯笼式天窗与国会大厦的穹顶以及勃兰登堡门的战车雕塑遥遥相望，共同描绘着城市的天际线。从灯笼式天窗望去，战车雕塑仿佛刚刚从使馆屋顶的花坛园中驶过。

The competition-winning design for the U.S. Embassy in Berlin is both synergistic to its sensitive historic, urban context and clear in its development of a new identity for the Embassy. The building serves simultaneously as background and partner for the nearby Brandenburg Gate, occupying a focal position at the symbolic and political center of the reunified Germany. Gracious entry sequences in the interior carefully meet security criteria, while the main lobby on Pariser Platz has the feel of an open courtyard, allowing direct and reflected sunlight to break through the facade. The Chancery's elegant State Room is a compelling venue for luncheons and other high-level receptions, owing to the proximity of the new government center and the spectacular view of the Reichstag.

The Embassy features green rooftops and landscaped courtyards, treating the bird's eye view of the building as a "fifth elevation". Landscape materials inspired by the American continent give the Embassy a green narrative, and link the site to the grand context of the Tiergarten. Using only soft interior lighting at night, the copper and glass lantern of the rooftop State Room Pavilion joins both the Reichstag's dome and the Quadriga sculpture on the Brandenburg Gate as part of the civic district's collection of skyline landmarks. The view from the Lantern has been carefully composed to show the Quadriga as it seems to ride across the Embassy's rooftop parterre garden of native American grasses.

Berlin, Germany

UNITED STATES EMBASSY, BERLIN

德国，柏林

美国驻柏林大使馆

105

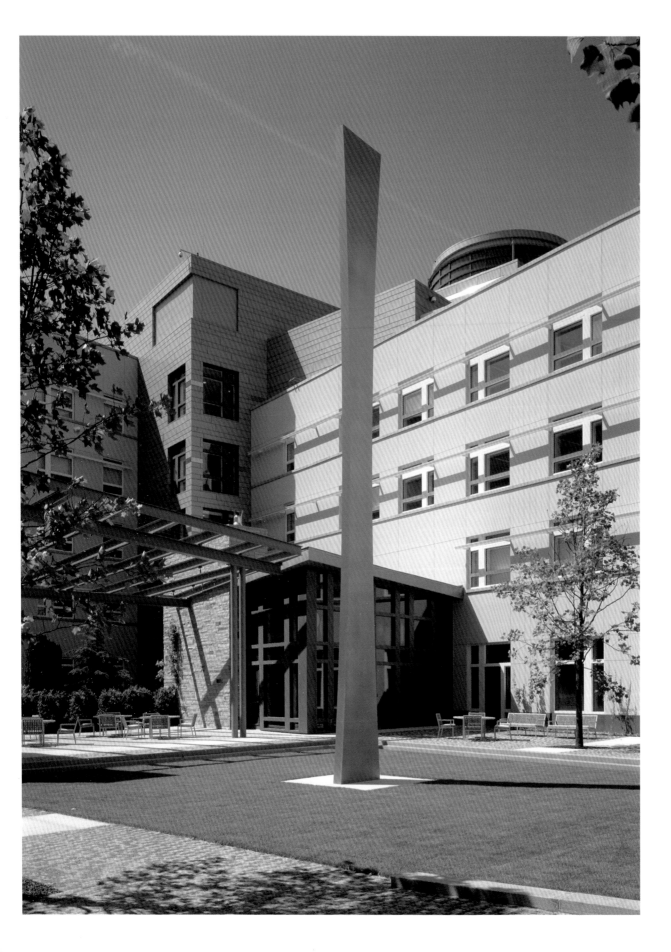

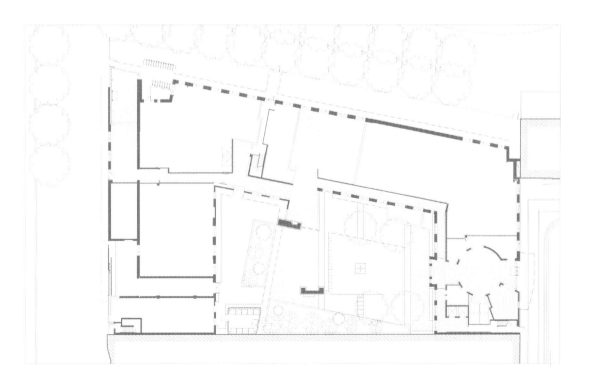

圣多明各

SANTO DOMINGO

This new embassy for the Dominican Republic serves an island nation with close cultural ties to the United States—evidenced by a consulate large enough to feel like a border crossing. In response to its warm tropical climate, the new Chancery has been designed to allow abundant natural light into the interior spaces while providing deep canopies to shade exterior terraces, plazas and walks. At the heart of the Chancery a dynamic full-height atrium brings light into the center of the workplace, where the main lobby, dining, and meeting spaces for visitors and employees are gathered.

The 6.5-hectare site is organized into distinct zones related to use: Public and Consular functions at the front, Diplomatic and Embassy Community uses in the center, and Support and Service at the back, separated by garden walls and landscape. Giving order to the whole is a sculptural system of parallel walls of various heights, clad in limestone, creating layers of interior and exterior space all across the site. Landscape designed by Pamela Burton complements this geometric pattern with a continuous flow of sinuous curves, accented by rows of native palms and ornamental plantings. Inspired by the Brazilian landscape architect Roberto Burle-Marx, the free-form movement of broad lawns and planting is continued in exterior paving patterns, and inside by the soaring vaults of the atrium.

Given its island context, the new embassy is virtually self-sustaining in terms of energy and basic utilities. Through such initiatives as photovoltaic power generation and intensive storm water management the project has been designed to attain LEED Silver certification.

多米尼加共和国新使馆犹如一个边境通道，彰显了小岛国与美国之间密切的文化联系。新办公大楼采光系统良好，能够时刻确保室内光线充足，同时别致的檐篷能够为户外露台、广场和步行区提供有效遮荫。在办公大楼的中央，一个充满活力的全高中庭将光线成功引入到办公空间的中央，为设置于此的大堂、餐饮中心以及访客和员工的聚会区营造舒适、通透的环境氛围。

该建筑占地6.5万平方米，各区间划分清晰：公共区和领事区位于前端，外交区和使馆区位于空间的中央，服务区则位于空间的后身，经由园林和景观墙与前端的空间分隔开来。不同高度的石灰石雕塑墙呈平行式设计，实现空间的有序衔接，并加强了室内外空间的联系。由设计师帕梅拉·伯顿设计的景观主要由原生棕榈树和观赏植物构成，蜿蜒曲折的形态与几何型雕塑墙交相辉映，妙趣横生。受巴西景观设计师罗伯特·布雷·马克思的启发，室外铺路模式和中庭的穹顶延续了室内绿地和植物设计的自由形态，彰显随意、动态之美。

鉴于该建筑优良的基础设备和能源自给功能，诸如太阳能光伏发电和雨水处理等设施的运用，该项目获得了LEED的银级认证。

Santo Domingo, Dominican Republic

UNITED STATES EMBASSY, SANTO DOMINGO

多米尼加共和国，圣多明各

美国驻圣多明各大使馆

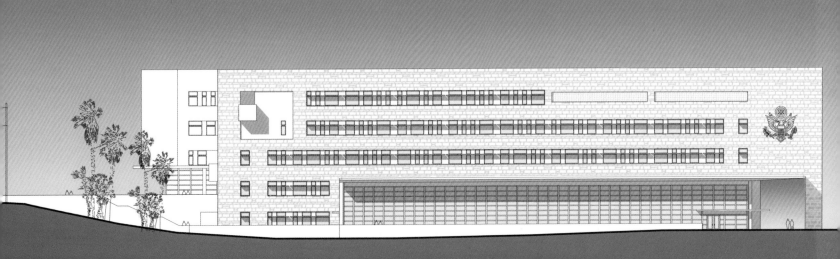

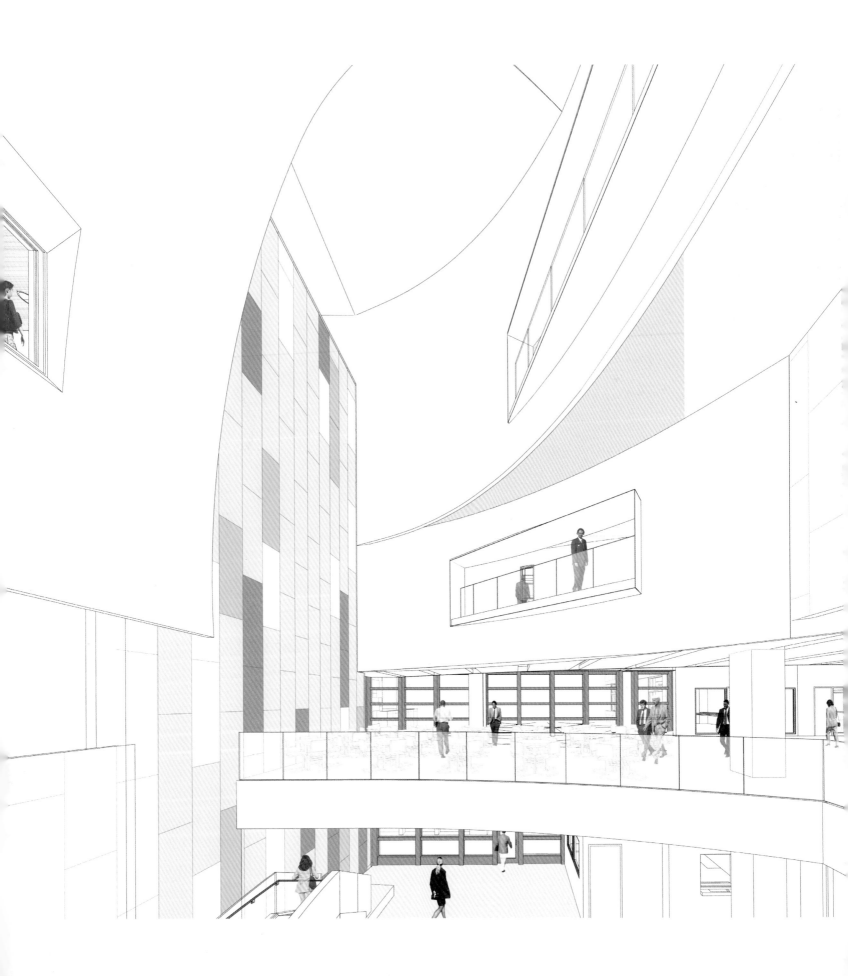

台北市

TAIPEI

美国在台协会建筑因空间功能性强、所在地区地形复杂，对设计手法和应用技术要求很高。总体规划和设计需要满足一个大型、复杂的建筑功能要求，同时与地形及周围环境自然融为一体，而无突兀之感。开阔的入口能够同时满足车辆和行人的需要，并严格遵循建筑安全标准。建筑共包括办公大楼（占地面积为18,800平方米）和设施服务大楼（占地面积为2,950平方米）两个部分。建筑十分注重细节设计，走廊、回廊等空间设计彰显出浓厚的台湾文化。在台湾，人们对建筑的风水说法十分讲究，因此，在该建筑中，风水同样扮演了重要角色。这座雄伟的综合性建筑与周围其他台湾建筑融合得恰到好处。

The American Institute of Taiwan is technically complex, consisting of multiple buildings on a topographically challenging site. The master planning and design had to meet the functional requirements of a large, complex program, while effectively negotiating the site topography and related landscape design specifications. Site access for a large number of vehicles and pedestrians, as well as the concomitant security considerations posed challenges, particularly in a project of this scope. It includes a new Chancery Office Building of approximately 18,800 GSM and support facilities of approximately 2,950 GSM. The design extends beyond masterplanning, to details such as interior expressions; the concepts of passage, privacy and procession in Taiwanese culture are explored and echo throughout the building. These ideas combined with Feng Shui practices play an integral part of the interior design development. The American Institute is a complex building with a strong presence that is carefully integrated into the landscape of Taiwan.

Taipei, Taiwan

AMERICAN INSTITUTE IN TAIWAN

台湾，台北市

美国在台协会

An etched glass wall chart
of Chinese characters
animates the lobby.

刻上中国汉字的玻璃墙表
使大厅具有生气。

校园与社区建筑

CAMPUS AND COMMUNITY: PLANNING AND ARCHITECTURE

美国校园是至高文化理念和文化成就的独特体现，彰显一定价值取向的人文精神。植根于启蒙运动的人文原则和之后的民主平等信条，这些教学机构以为学生营造开放、自由、积极的学习环境为主旨。

美国的校园十分注重培养学生的创新意识和团队精神。学生可以畅所欲言，尽情展示自我。

他们鼓励校园文化的多元性和开放性，来自不同国家、不同文化的学生通过互相交流和学习能够增进对世界的了解。

新的挑战和趋势　校园空间的建设需要同时满足集体和个人以及团队的学习和研究的需要。

美国校园的形式多种多样，无论是田园般的杰斐逊"学术村"，还是极具城市化建筑特色的麻省理工学院，如今都面临着新的挑战。

1990年至2007年经济繁荣期过后，政府拨款，私人慈善和捐赠基金因经济的萧条而大大缩水，无论是社区学院还是重点大学几乎都遭遇新经济时代带来的冲击。

打造校园品质生活

然而，学校为了保持顽强的竞争力，即需要营造优秀的教学环境和学习环境。在过去20年来，学校一直致力于宿舍、餐厅、学生中心和体育设施的改建，以提高学生的生活品质。

科技的发展与时间和空间的缩小

科技和全球化可以看作是一种现象的两个方面：世界范围逐渐缩小，发展节奏也越来越快。学生是这个新世界的化身，他们淡化了时间和空间的界限。在辛辛那提大学的一次学生研讨会上，他们这样说道："忘记大学里学到的一切。我们时刻与世界进行沟通。"

这种沟通的结果是远程教育和全球协作的出现以及多学科研究的飞速发展。几年前，麻省理工学院的建筑工作室与一个欧洲学校进行了全天候视

The American Campus is a unique embodiment of the highest aspirations and achievements of the culture. Rooted in the humanistic principles of the enlightenment and expanded by the democratic commitment to equality of opportunity, these institutions have been central to the development of a society of great innovation, mobility and expectations.

Our campuses have created places which encourage inquiry, nurture community and protect freedom of expression. They create a safe zone for almost limitless exploration of ideas from the arcane to the provocative. They support a community in which people of diverse backgrounds come together for an intensely communal experience where they learn about themselves and others, realizing a better understanding of the complexities and opportunities of the greater world.

EMERGING CHALLENGES AND TRENDS The places made on the Campus scale nurture community and support individual and group study and research. While our campuses have diverse physical forms, from Jefferson's idyllic "academical village" to the urban compounds of MIT, they share emerging challenges.

After the boom years of the 1990's to 2007, virtually all campuses from modest community colleges to powerhouse prestige schools are challenged by a new economic era. Government funding, private philanthropy and endowments are all under pressure.

Building the Quality of Student Life

Yet, campuses need to provide attractive, nurturing environments to remain competitive. During the last twenty years schools have been intent on improving the quality of student life through improved dormitories, dining, student centers and athletic facilities. This has, in turn, raised expectations.

Technology and the Shrinking of Space and Time

Technology and globalization can be seen as two sides of one phenomenon: the world is becoming smaller and faster.

Students arrive at campuses as the avatars of this new world. They ignore the boundaries of time and space. At a student workshop at the University of Cincinnati in Ohio, they told us "Forget about everything you experienced in college. We live twenty four-seven and communicate globally."

Corollaries of this include the rise of *distance learning, collaboration on a global scale* and the increase of *multi-disciplinary research*. At MIT several years ago an architecture studio maintained a twenty-four hour video link to a studio at a European school. Both studios worked on similar design projects and students could interact with their transatlantic peers at any time and in any social configuration: individual or groups, structured or informal.

An equally powerful trend is the *creation of partnerships or academic branches internationally*. This has been evolving for years, but the pace is accelerating and the reach expanding. While high profile initiatives such as NYU's new campus in Abu Dhabi get press, local institutions feel the need for similar initiatives.

Many campuses see *increasing professionalization of the curriculum*. As economic malaise continues, schools increase their appeals to students who are concerned about employment prospects. This often parallels a diminishing funding and role of the arts and humanities. The *expansion of "for profit" education* also troubles many due to its potential to optimize for the company rather than the student.

Such trends challenge the core humanistic values of higher education and the core strengths of a liberal education which is meant to teach critical thinking and ignite a lifelong love of learning—strengths which have been at the core of the artistic and scientific vitality of our society.

STRATEGIES FOR MAINTAINING VITALITY AND LEADERSHIP

Faced with the challenges of the economy, technology, globalization, professionalization and privatization, how can our colleges and universities remain competitive and vibrant?

We have tested a number of strategies in our planning and architecture.

Synergies and Partnerships

In an age of tighter budgets but expanding horizons we and our clients look for synergies and partnerships which yield benefits to all participants. *Cross or multi-disciplinary education and research* is one of the more important evolving developments.

At UCLA, the Department of World Arts and Culture supports the study and practice of dance, music, and material culture in both popular and classical forms and brings extraordinary talent from around the world to collaborate, study and teach. We helped to develop a new home for WAC in the historic 1929 Women's Gym. Since the program is protean and innovative it was necessary to develop an array of teaching and performance spaces with great flexibility and a range of technology to accommodate both the avant-garde and the traditional. The resulting physical hybrid of restored historic, adapted re-use and new, creates a dynamic synergy which both reflects the program goals and inspires new explorations (fig. 1).

频链接。两个工作室的设计项目相似，学生们可以通过视频随时与大洋彼岸的学生、有组织的团体或非正式团体进行互动。

此外，与之并驾齐驱的另一股趋势是国际学术伙伴关系和分支的相继建立。几年来，随着全球化进程的加快，该趋势发展迅猛。享誉全球的纽约大学计划在迪拜创建分校，而其他的美国院校也拟定了设立分校的计划。

许多大学越来越注重课程的专业化。由于经济的持续萎靡，学校出于对学生就业前景的考虑，逐渐减少了对艺术和人文科学的投入。这种重工作而轻教学的"牟利教育"为以人文价值观为教育核心、注重培养严谨思维和学习精神的高等教育带来了巨大挑战。

保持活力，维系领导地位的战略方法　　在经济、科技、全球化、专业化和私有化的挑战面前，我们的高等教育如何才能保持竞争力和活力？

我们在建筑设计的过程中，尝试了诸多方法。

互动和伙伴关系
在预算紧缩时期，扩大视野、加强协作，将令所有的参与者受益。

交叉或跨学科的教育和研究是重要的演变发展之一。

在加州大学洛杉矶分校，世界艺术和文化专业同时也注重对流行与古典形式下的舞蹈、音乐、物质文化的学习与研究，号召世界各地有关精英进行沟通与协作。这一次，我们应邀为其打造一个女子健身中心。该项目的设计理念是构建一个灵活、开阔的教学与表演空间，令前卫与传统风格并存。在创建新空间的同时对原有空间进行充分利用，最终令该校园得以焕然一新。（图1）

目前，我们正在为美国加州大学圣巴巴拉分校生物技术研究专业提供建筑设计。该建筑方案反映了学科之间的科研界限正在逐渐的淡化。纳米技术和生物科技领域将通过相互交流和空间共享以推动科技的进步。该项目旨在通过构建一个精致的层次化社会空间、研究实验室、教室和办公室加强社区间的互动与相互支持。高度可持续发展设计理念从长远的利益角度出发，将对环境的负面影响降到最低，同时令建筑历久弥新。

美国加州大学伯克利分校则采用了更为积极的方式，倡导与哈斯商学院及博尔特法律学校建立共享空间。

该建筑的设计大大促进了协同作用的发展，从实际和文化角度与已有的哈斯商学院及博尔特法律学校实现了有效衔接。

建筑巧妙地加强了两个学校间的南北互动，通过学术与社会空间的共享真正实现了学术的交流与互动。一个东西向的通道将校园进行自然衔接，并与多功能广场和户外圆形剧场融为一体。

科技

技术的发展，为社会意识和空间意识带来了机遇和挑战。

麻省理工学院一直是教学应用新技术开发的领导者。由物理系开发的一个原型教室（旨在利用科技提高学习能动性）能够为实时协作、教学和测试提供广泛支持。多角度设计可以帮助教师对每个小组进行观察。每个小组可进行电子化合作，

At the University of California Santa Barbara we are designing a building for state of the art Biotechnology research. The building program reflects the evolving nature of scientific research where boundaries between disciplines have been rapidly falling. Here diverse areas of research will cross-fertilize and share space. The building is designed to enhance interaction and support community by the careful shaping of a hierarchy of social spaces, research laboratories, classrooms and offices. Highly sustainable design optimizes passive design and future flexibility, a key element of the building's long-term viability.

A more radical initiative at the University of California Berkeley involved design of a building to be shared by the Haas School of Business and the Boalt School of Law. The design for the building develops the synergies of connections. The building physically and culturally links the existing Law and Business School Buildings. It maximizes north-south movement between the schools and intersects that movement with shared academic and social spaces. An east-west pathway links to the campus and connects to the multi-use forum and outdoor amphitheater.

Technology

As technology evolves it presents both the opportunities for advancement and challenges to our sense of community and place.

MIT has been a leader in exploring the pedagogic applications of new technology. The physics department developed a prototype classroom call the TEAL (Technology Enhanced Active Learning). This supports a broad range of real time collaboration, teaching and testing. It works at many scales so that the faculty can monitor the work of over 100 students at tables of nine. Teams at each table can collaborate electronically, and the work of an individual, a group or the aggregation of the whole class can be digitally tallied, projected, and critiqued.

fig. 1

fig. 2

Working with faculty staff and students on new facilities for MIT's Sloan School of Management we explored the form, type and technology of classrooms. The designs that evolved accommodated a range of teaching spaces from a version of the TEAL classroom to a technologically updated version of the classic tiered case-study room, to highly flexible flat floored seminar rooms. Dimensions, structure and systems were developed so that rooms could be changed over many years. Opinions about the relation between form and pedagogy varied greatly. Case-study advocates wanted classrooms designed within the millimeter to optimize view angles and face-to-face interaction. The faculty dealing with more behavioral aspects of management wanted flexibility of spatial arrangement for student interaction in well daylit flat-floored space. Technology was, for them supportive, but not primary to their teaching.

Strategic Use of Time and Resources

Not only are costs a greater concern but we are in an era of greater awareness of the preciousness of all resources. Among these are our use of land, our treatment of existing buildings and our stewardship of natural resources. Early planning provides the best opportunity to positively deploy limited resources.

Our study for a revitalized student center at the Lower Sproul Plaza of UC Berkeley is another bellwether of a strategic approach to resources. The Plaza and its four surrounding buildings were built in the early 1960's with the idea of creating a lively urban Plaza. While this functioned well initially, it became a harsh and uninviting landscape and the surrounding buildings have not accommodated evolving student needs (fig. 2).

The plan, developed in close collaboration with students and staff, is based on the strategic insertion of new pieces, and the phased revitalization of existing buildings. The program optimizes cultural diversity, sustainability and phased transformation. The students recently voted by a two to one margin to pay additional fees to help finance the project, a surprise to many in these times.

In Dublin our master plan for the new Grangegorman Urban Quarter will create a campus for Dublin Institute of Technology (DIT), Health Service Executive (HSE) and the local community. The project builds strategically in the historic setting of St. Brendan's Psychiatric Hospital. Our plan involves the careful re-use and expansion of historic buildings, complemented by harmonious contemporary structures. The old and new inform one another, connecting to the past and aspiring to the future. Equally important is the careful connection to the surrounding urban fabric. Linkages to transit, pedestrian connections and the chance to help revitalize the neighborhood commercially and culturally were critical to gaining the support of the surrounding community (fig. 3).

个人、集体或整个班级的作品将被采用数字式记录、预测和点评。

我们与麻省理工学院全体师生合作为斯隆管理学院教室的外观、类型及应用技术进行设计。

设计旨在创建一系列教学空间，涉及原型教室、新一代阶梯教室、高度灵活的平板地板研讨室。空间尺寸、结构和系统经全面改进后可应对时间的考验。对于空间形式和教学二者之间的关系众说纷纭。

案例研究人士认为教室应设计成圆形，以优化视角从而实现大家面对面的互动。教师则更注重课堂上的管理，希望打造一个灵活的空间布局，在一个光线充足的平板地板空间中更能够加强学生间的互动。在他们看来，科技是一种后期支持，并不在教学中扮演重要角色。

时间和能源的战略性应用

对于当前设计来说，除了资金预算问题，同时还要考虑能源的合理利用。这其中包括对土地的有效利用、对现有建筑的合理改建以及对天然资源的管理。之前的规划项目为能源的战略性应用提供了良机。

位于劳尔·斯普劳尔广场上的加州大学伯克利分校学生中心的设计方案即以能源利用为设计的出发点。该广场及其周边建筑均建于20世纪60年代，以打造生动的城市广场为理念。该设计起初运作良好，然而，终因缺乏与景观的协调性和不能满足学生的需求而最终受到非议。（图2）

该项目的设计，旨在通过与全体师生的密切配合，在原有建筑的基础上扩建一个崭新的空间，并对原建筑进行修缮，使之重新焕发活力。该项目丰富了文化的多样性、强调能源的可持续性和阶段性的转变。近期，学生们通过投票表决决定将支付一些额外费用，以资助该项目，这一举措无疑是一个意外的惊喜。

而我们为都柏林理工学院提供的新Grangegorman校园设计则采用了环境战略，即以历史建筑为设计背景。该建筑的前身是一个

fig. 3

拥有多年历史的废弃疗养院。该规划的主旨是在巧妙利用原建筑的基础上进行扩建，并使扩建的现代建筑与原建筑自然融为一体。新老建筑的巧妙融合既体现了对历史的尊重，又彰显出对未来的无限憧憬。此外，该规划的另一个重点是实现建筑与周围景观的自然衔接。一系列过渡地带及行人通道的设置有效地推动了周边商业和文化的发展，从而赢得了周边社区的高度评价。（图3）

可持续规划与设计

我们的诸多校园设计作品表明，可持续设计理念与技术应用同等重要。

达特茅斯学院因广泛运用传统和时尚的设计手法打造的一系列可持续性空间而活力四射。北部校园核心扩建计划在可持续空间设计理念的基础上，加强了与学生的积极互动。该建筑要求具有相当强大的耐久性，至少可持续使用100年。因此，在传统的结构基础上，欧洲先进机械设备的运用使空间更为舒适，尽可能的降低了成本。

该建筑试用不久，学生们自发对其能源的利用进行监测，他们还发明了一个有趣的北极熊能源监测软件，当能源消耗量低时，北极熊即会露出笑脸，反之，北极熊则会沮丧。设计精巧，十分耐人寻味。

该系统的应用目前已经普及到全国所有的校园之中。可持续设计与购买那些实质利用的设备相比要实用得多。

最近的校园设计经验使我们相信，当代挑战可以激发更多新策略的产生，通过采用可持续设计理念，更能够打造一个优良的育人环境。

Sustainable Planning and Design

Our work on many campuses has emphasized that sustainable design is as much a cultural process as a technical application.

Dartmouth College is committed to a vigorous campus wide application of sustainable living with both innovative and traditional methods. In our plan for the expansion of the campus north of its core, we built on this culture with active participation of students in the planning. The college budgeted for 100-year structures with robust building envelopes and durable materials. This approach to traditional quality was complemented by a willingness to employ cutting edge European mechanical systems as long as comfort and cost were optimized.

Soon after the housing was occupied, the students took the initiative to monitor energy use and developed graphically playful software called GreenLite—a polar bear on an ice-floe smiles when energy use is low and frowns as it rises.

This initiative has now inspired students across the country. Living sustainably is far more effective than buying technology which is not well used.

Our recent experiences give us confidence that contemporary challenges can inspire new strategies for revitalizing our campuses in ways that are affordable and implementable, while shaping places to nurture community.

圣巴巴拉市

SANTA BARBARA

生物工程大楼是一个多学科服务设施建筑，旨在为工程和生命科学发展的交叉学科提供完美空间。化学实验室空间与由设备和程序支持的传统仪器室均匀地分布在整个建筑之中。这些功能区与建筑研究总部行政套房衔接自然，相得益彰。

加州大学圣巴巴拉分校科学院坐落于两个主要流通路线的交叉点上，是科学学院与公共学院的中心地带，因此，该区既是一个交通枢纽，同时也可称之为"碰撞空间"。经过长时间的讨论，最终决定方案是拟建三个科研楼层和一个大型植物园以及神经血管外科套房，该套房位于地下室，为生物工程大楼及其周围的科研团体提供研究空间。

这一强调整体性而不增加额外成本的设计手法为最终获得LEED认证资格创造了有利条件。建筑十分注重空间的采光与通风，地热、冷梁技术的利用彰显了重要的环保理念。

The Bioengineering Building is conceived as a multi-disciplinary facility that serves the growing intersection between engineering and the life sciences. Dry, computational laboratory space is balanced with traditional wet laboratories that are served by an extensive array of equipment and procedure support space. These functions are complemented by administrative suites for defined research groups headquartered within the building.

Envisioned as a hub, or "collision-space", for the scientific community at UCSB, the site chosen anchors the intersection of two primary campus circulation routes and is centrally placed within the science and engineering district. Initiated through an extensive programming phase, the design embraces its important site while providing three research floors and a large vivarium and neurovascular surgical suite placed discretely within the basement that will serve research both within the Bioengineering Building as well as the surrounding research community.

The project has been undertaken within an integrated design approach leading to a current LEED target status that nears Platinum without incurring added cost. Extensive use of natural ventilation, daylighting, geothermal and active chilled beam technologies all support an ambitious goal towards environmental responsibility.

加利福尼亚州，圣巴巴拉市

加州大学圣巴巴拉分校
生物工程大楼

University of California, Santa Barbara

UC SANTA BARBARA
BIOENGINEERING BUILDING

1. Fresh air introduction thru office windows-moves to atrium thru acoustical baffle
2. Natural ventilation induced as hot air rises in atrium – roof shaped to facilitate air movement
3. High-reflectance roofing to mitigate heat island effect
4. Canopy framework provides for a variety of shading systems – PV panels, tensile fabric, trellis
5. Screen wall provides thermal mass and structural shear
6. Useable terrace and green roof
7. Displacement ventilation

1.办公空间的窗户能够完美地将新鲜的空气带到室内,并穿过声障板流通到中庭之中
2.良好的自然通风效果能够有效地带走中庭的热空气,独特的屋顶设计为加强空气流通提供了条件
3.高反射率屋顶,能够有效缓解热岛效应
4.檐篷框架提供了多样化的遮阳系统,包括光伏电池板、可拉伸构造、网格结构
5.分隔墙扮演保温和稳固的角色
6.可利用阳台和绿化屋顶
7.置换通风

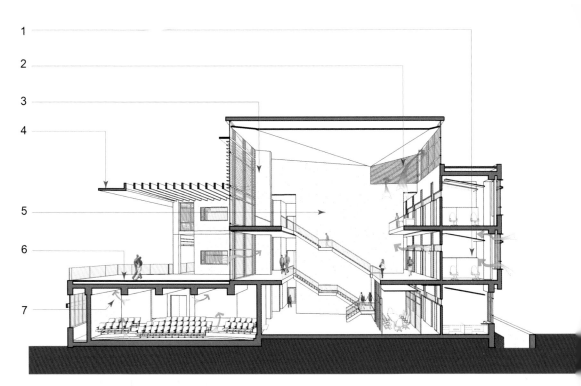

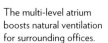

The multi-level atrium boosts natural ventilation for surrounding offices.

多层的入口大厅,加强了周围办公室的自然对流通风。

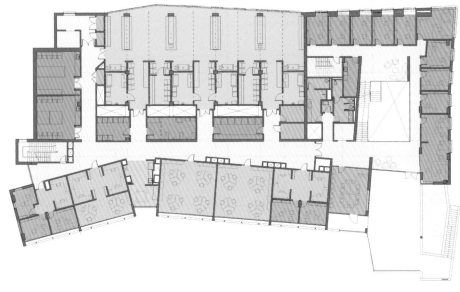

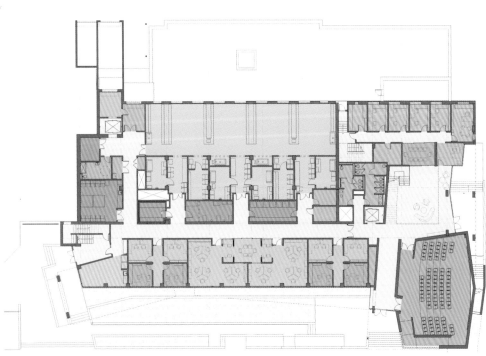

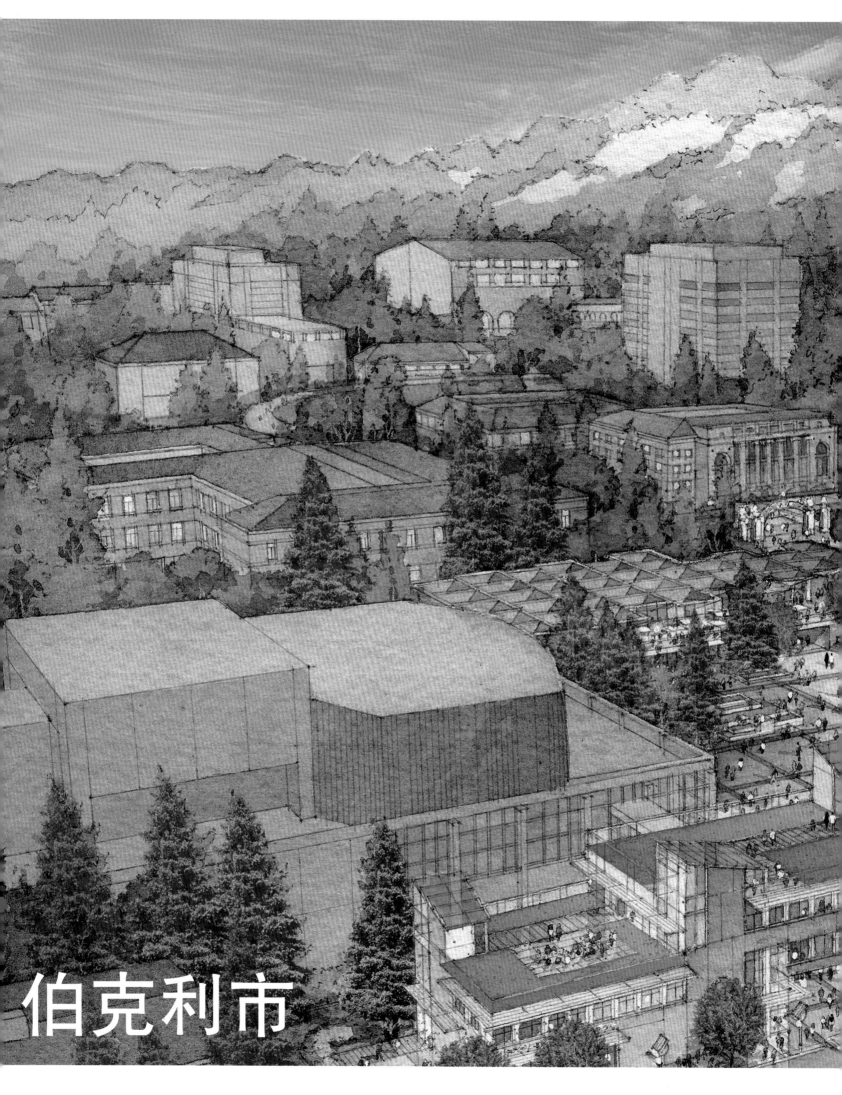

伯克利市

BERKELEY

The strategic master plan for the adaptive reuse, new construction, and revitalization of the Southwest Campus District will affect a transformation of the new multi-building Student Community Center (SCC) and neighborhood. The SCC is a student-based initiative that calls for recasting the existing mid-century buildings in the district into a revitalized state-of-the-art facility rooted in sustainable practices. The master plan balances physical and programming needs, celebrates the diverse community of students, faculty and staff, and creates a Living Room for student life and learning. Modern flexible spaces will accommodate the evolving needs of future generations of students for student services, retail, food service, meeting areas, and space for student organizations and student government.

The SCC site at the edge of campus makes it a gateway between campus and community. A transit center on Bancroft Way—a thriving neighborhood retail street—will reinforce 24/7 activity. The north site boundary is defined by Strawberry Creek, a verdant riparian ecosystem. Our master plan intensifies visual connections to the city, creek, and campus landmarks, while encouraging pedestrian movement and outdoor gathering.

西南校区的规划项目旨在通过空间的再利用、扩建以及修缮打造一个崭新的多功能学生社区中心和周边环境。学生社区中心以学生为出发点，对一个建于中世纪的古建筑进行改造，通过采用最先进的环保设施使建筑重新焕发活力，展现昔日风采。该总体规划强调外观与规划要求的平衡性，彰显丰富多样化的师生团队，同时为学生生活和学习提供了一个"客厅"空间。现代灵活的空间可为学生提供零售、餐饮、聚会、学生自治等多种服务，满足学生未来不断变化和增长的需要。

位于校园边缘地带的学生社区中心将校园与社区之间有效衔接在一起。建筑的北端是一个青翠繁茂的草莓河生态系统。我们的总体规划旨在强调城市、河流、校园标志性建筑之间的有序衔接，为行人的户外运动及聚会提供完美空间。

University of California, Berkeley

UC BERKELEY SPROUL PLAZA STUDENT COMMUNITY CENTER

加利福尼亚州，伯克利市

加州大学伯克利分校
斯普劳尔广场学生社区中心

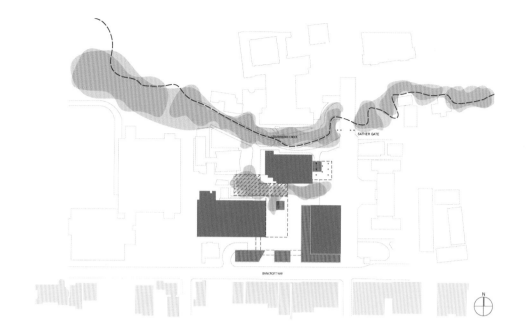

The intersection of city
and campus becomes the
focus of active new uses
and energy.

城市和校园的交汇处成为
新的活动及活力集聚点。

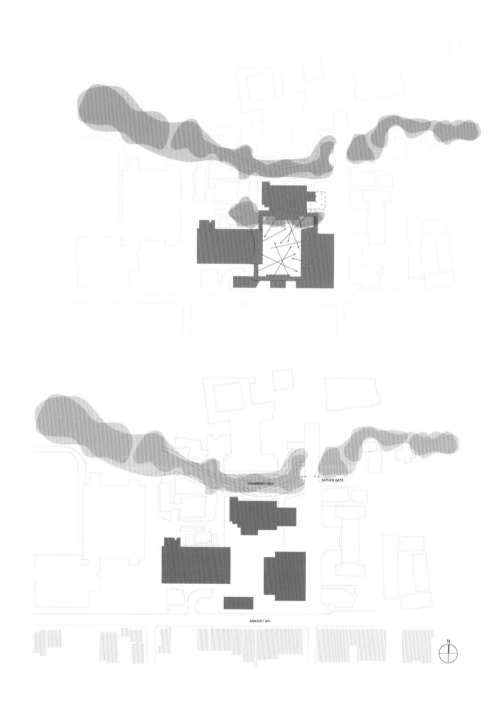

UC BERKELEY SPROUL PLAZA STUDENT COMMUNITY CENTER 加州大学伯克利分校斯普劳尔广场学生社区中心

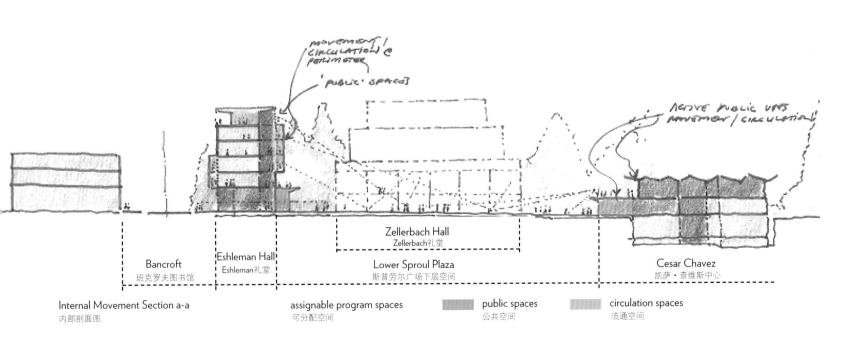

MOVEMENT/
CIRCULATION @
PERIMETER

'PUBLIC' SPACES

ACTIVE PUBLIC USES
MOVEMENT / CIRCULATION

Zellerbach Hall
Zellerbach礼堂

Bancroft
班克罗夫图书馆

Eshleman Hall
Eshleman礼堂

Lower Sproul Plaza
斯普劳尔广场下层空间

Cesar Chavez
凯萨·查维斯中心

Internal Movement Section a-a
内部剖面图

assignable program spaces
可分配空间

public spaces
公共空间

circulation spaces
流通空间

UC BERKELEY SPROUL PLAZA STUDENT COMMUNITY CENTER 加州大学伯克利分校斯普劳尔广场学生社区中心

伯克利市

BERKELEY

哈斯商学院和博尔特法律学校之间的法律与商业衔接建筑占地17,977平方米，该建筑从形态和学术领域为二者的沟通搭建了桥梁。该设计在两个学校的两端分别创建了一系列共享会议室和社交空间，两端设计风格各具特色，同与其"接壤"的院校特色相得益彰。每一端皆为师生提供一个集教室、办公室、自由空间（囊括了研究中心和会议室）于一体的综合性空间。

共享建筑的核心是一个三层的广场，可作为正式和非正式的交流空间之用。该空间向外延伸，与一个露台花园完美衔接，该花园同时也可作为一个公共活动空间。在广场附近设置的咖啡厅、汇报厅、研讨室和小组学习区有效加强了空间的灵活性。

该建筑巧妙地将设备系统与结构相结合，将对能源的消耗降到最低。两端建筑的定向设计有效减少了热量的吸收，并加强了室内通风。外部遮阳系统与室内遮阳导光板的充分结合在确保室内光线充足的同时，对室内温度进行适度调节。屋顶平台上种植的原生植被起到了保湿和净化空气的作用。

The new 193,500 sf Law and Business Connection physically and academically bridges the programs of the Haas School of Business and the Boalt School of Law. Developed as two academic wings with a series of shared conference and social spaces, each academic wing has an identity and close association with its respective professional school. Each wing supports faculty and graduate student research with a combination of classrooms, faculty offices, and flexible shared space for research centers and conference rooms.

The shared central core of the building is focused around a three-story forum that can be configured for both formal and informal interaction. The space extends to a terraced garden which also allows for a broad range of activities and presentations. A cafe, lecture hall, seminar rooms, and group study areas are arrayed in close adjacency to the forum to further support its flexible use.

The building is designed to be environmentally sustainable by carefully integrating mechanical and structural systems to reduce energy consumption. The orientation of the wings minimizes heat gain while optimizing prevailing breezes and regional views. Exterior shading combined with interior "light shelves" cut heat gain while increasing interior daylighting. Roof terraces planted with native vegetation increase water retention and air quality.

加州大学伯克利分校,伯克利市
法律与商业衔接建筑

University of California, Berkeley
UC BERKELEY LAW BUSINESS CONNECTION

辛辛那提市

JOSEPH A. STEGER STUDENT LIFE CENTER

CINCINNATI

辛辛那提大学弦月形的学生生活中心巧妙地将学术空间、零售中心以及社会空间融为一体，为学生提供了一个多元化的服务空间。教室、学生组织、计算机实验室、餐饮、零售、信息和资源等空间的综合利用为学生营造了一个充满活力的学习和生活坏境，也因此，该项目获得了LEED质量认证。

这些空间通过一系列室内步行广场、餐饮和休息区自然衔接在一起。同时，通道、入口和门廊实现了视觉上的衔接。建筑的水平和垂直运动为非正式的互动和社交活动提供了充足空间，"社会阶梯"的应用将画廊、步行广场和中庭有机衔接在了一起。这些元素促进了广泛的互动，多功能空间全天24小时都充满活力。学生生活中心毗邻学生会和娱乐中心，为校园中心带来了多样性的活动。

The crescent-shaped Student Life Center at the University of Cincinnati carefully connects academic, retail, and social spaces to best serve a diverse community of students. The varied mix of uses includes classrooms, student organizations, computer labs, dining, retail, and information and resource areas, within a socially dynamic and supportive environment and LEED Certified building.

These aspirations are developed at the campus scale through connections for pedestrian movement, such as covered arcades for walking, dining and relaxing. Visual linkages are reinforced by pathways, portals, and porches. At the scale of the individual building, horizontal and vertical movement is designed to encourage informal interaction and socializing, using "social stairs", naturally lighted galleries, arcades and an atrium. These elements encourage a broad array of interactions, from casual to programmed, while the varied mix of uses creates a lively 24 hour energy. Closely relating the Student Life Center to the nearby student union and recreation centers engenders a magnet for activity in the heart of the campus.

辛辛那提大学

约瑟夫A.斯泰格
学生生活中心

University of Cincinnati

JOSEPH A. STEGER
STUDENT LIFE CENTER

151

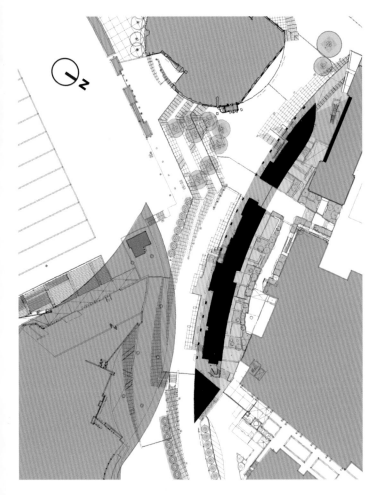

The long thin building
animates a new Main Street
and weaves connections
to its neighbors.

长条状的建筑带动了新的
主要街道,以波浪形状与邻
近环境衔接。

UNIVERSITY OF CINCINNATI JOSEPH A. STEGER STUDENT LIFE CENTER 辛辛那提大学约瑟夫A.斯泰格学生生活中心

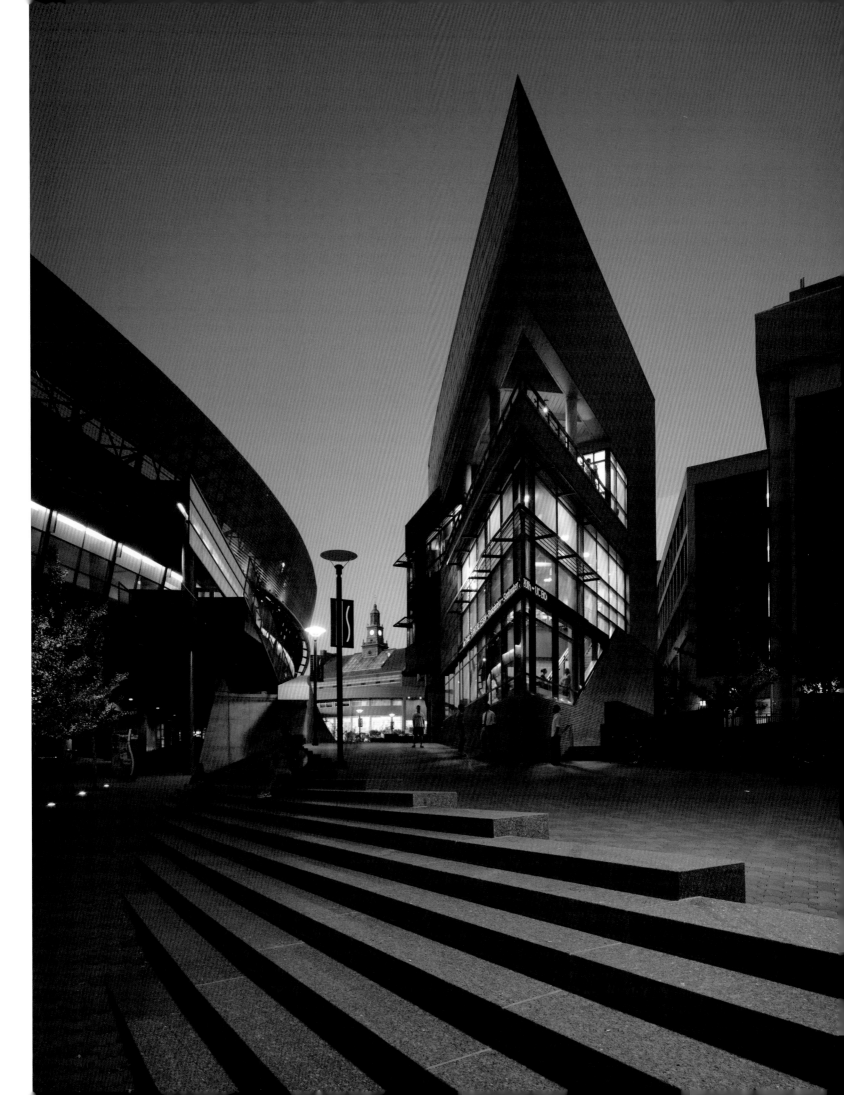

夏洛茨维市尔

CHARLOTTESVILLE

南罗恩学术中心的人居密度几乎是托马斯杰斐逊原有"学术村"的10倍，占地10,000平方米，与周围建筑和景观自然衔接，是艺术和科学学院的一个新学术空间。从视觉角度上看，该空间相对独立，通过一个开阔的园景露台巧妙地将原罗恩学术中心的轴心与杰斐逊公园大道衔接在一起。其设计的灵感源自对托马斯杰斐逊"学术村"的参考。

衔接是该项目的主题，旨在将新罗恩中心与其附近的新卡贝尔大厅（建于1950年）通过一个楼梯和走廊自然衔接在一起。该项目将圆形的远景阳台作为一个枢纽，构建了一个新东西向轴线，将学院与其附近的福斯特家族历史建筑融为一体，并向附近的医疗中心进行延伸。由谢里尔·巴顿和沃尔特·胡德提供的景观设计完美地将水文、历史、地形和行人的活动融为一体，浑然天成。

At almost 10 times the density of Thomas Jefferson's original "Academical Village", the South Lawn is a new neighborhood, planned with the utmost concern for the harmony of buildings and landscape, and providing over 10,000 square meters of new academic program for the College of Arts and Sciences. While visually separated, and some 20 meters of elevation downhill from the Central Grounds, the project effectively extends the axis of the original Lawn across Jefferson Park Avenue with a broad landscaped terrace. Inspiration was drawn from the classical composition, character, and scale of Jefferson's great design without resorting to imitation.

Connectivity is the ultimate theme of the project, beginning with the new lawn itself, linked to the adjacent 1950 New Cabell Hall with a grand stair and porch. With its circular "Vista Point Terrace" as a hinge, the project sets up a new east-west axis, linking the College to the adjacent Foster Family historical site and gesturing to future development that will extend in the direction of the nearby medical center. Landscape design by Cheryl Barton and Walter Hood is a sweeping reintegration of site hydrology, history, topography, and pedestrian movement.

弗吉尼亚大学
艺术与科学学院
南罗恩学术中心

University of Virginia
COLLEGE OF ARTS
& SCIENCES SOUTH LAWN

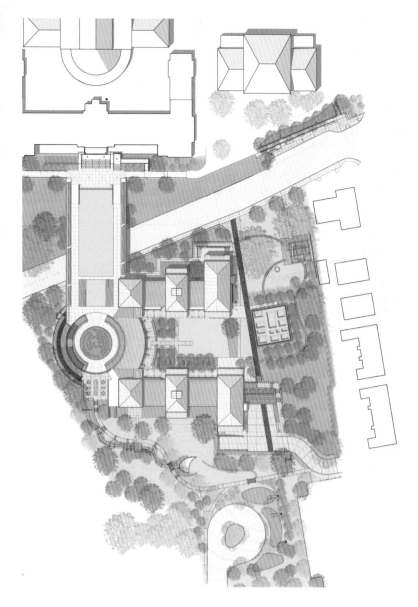

Starting at the lawn terrace, the central Commons gathers pedestrian traffic from multiple levels and directions and redistributes movement vertically and horizontally throughout the College. The 4-story wings of the new building frame a 20-meter-wide courtyard with a matrix of offices, classrooms, meeting rooms, and "flow spaces", fulfilling the University's philosophy of integrating students and faculty. Appropriate scale is achieved by articulating the plan into a series of interconnected houses that step back with open terraces at the fourth floor.

As one of the University's earliest planned LEED projects, the South Lawn began with the requirement for basic certification, but is now tracking for LEED Gold.

从罗恩露台开始，中央共享区将来自各个楼层的人们进行了有序分流。整个学院空间纵横交错。新大楼的一侧建筑共四层，一个20米宽的庭院周围设置了办公室、教室、会议室以及流动空间，彰显大学倡导的学生和教师和谐互动的理念。四楼一系列相通空间墙体后缩与开放式阳台一同确保了建筑体量的适中。

作为最早获得LEED认证的校园项目之一，南罗恩中心的设计满足了LEED认证的基本要求，目前正为最终获得LEED金级认证而努力。

UNIVERSITY OF VIRGINIA COLLEGE OF ARTS & SCIENCES SOUTH LAWN 弗吉尼亚大学艺术与科学学院南罗恩学术中心

达拉谟市

DURHAM

法国家庭科学中心通过对新设施的改进和对其附近的生物科学和人工气候室进行选择性的装修，巧妙地将杜克大学的重点专业从形态和知识结构角度自然衔接在一起。通过广泛的总体规划和详细部署，最终，这个四层新设施中心设置了最先进的研究实验室和化学、生物和物理配套空间以及本科教学实验室、互动空间、会议室、报告厅、院系办公室和一个开阔的温室研究中心。该空间设计灵活，构思巧妙，使跨学科的实验室实现了完美衔接。

实验室、实验室配套设施以及教师办公室围绕通透的多层中庭进行集中布局，便于加强空间中水平和垂直方向的流通。非正式会议区和正式会议区贯穿整个中庭，便于跨学科的科学文化调查。名为"法式烘焙坊"的咖啡店位于入口和中庭的交叉点上，为人们提供了优美的休息空间。

在科学中心总体规划的构想中，科学梯田打造了一个全新的校园园区，作为新设施中心及其旁边的物理和生物大楼的入口，并通过草坪和露天剧场的设置，从视觉角度和空间角度实现了与校园核心的巧妙衔接。

大学和设计团队通过一系列环保材料和系统的运用实现了可持续的设计目标。良好的室内采光设备、能源管理与回收系统、材料选取的就地原则以及本土植物对环境的美化作用为该项目获得LEED银级认证提供了有力保证。

The French Family Science Center provides, through the development of new facilities and selected renovations within the adjacent Biological Sciences and Phytotron buildings, a way of linking both physically and intellectually the primary science disciplines at Duke University. Initiated through extensive master planning and detailed programming phases, the four-story facility provides state-of-the-art research laboratories and support spaces for Chemistry, Biology and Physics, as well as undergraduate teaching laboratories, interaction spaces, conference rooms, a lecture hall, faculty and departmental offices and an extensive set of research greenhouses. The design incorporates truly flexible research spaces that allow for seamless conversions of laboratory types across disciplines.

Laboratories, lab support facilities and faculty offices are organized in grouped clusters along and within the sky-lit, multi-story atrium that provides the building's primary horizontal and vertical circulation. Generously placed throughout the Atrium are casual and formal meeting areas that serve a culture of interdisciplinary scientific investigation. The coffee shop—The French Roast—anchors the busy crossroads of entry and Atrium.

Integrally conceived in the development of the Science Center, Science Terrace creates a new campus quad that provides the primary entry space for the new facility as well as entrances into the adjoining Physics and Biology Buildings. Science Terrace creates a visual and physical connection to the heart of the campus while providing a lawn and amphitheater for a variety of campus activities.

The University and design team met their ambitious goals for environmental responsibility through the use of daylighting, energy management and recovery, locally obtained materials, and sensitive landscaping using native plant materials resulting in an LEED Silver certification.

杜克大学
法国家庭科学中心

Duke University
FRENCH FAMILY SCIENCE CENTER

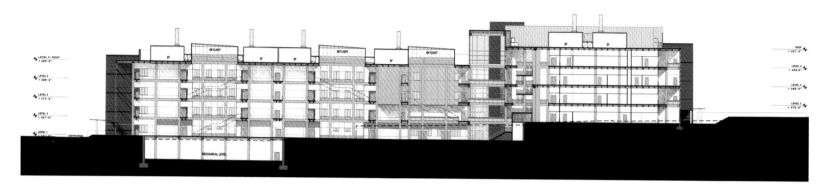

The interior street climbs
through the site, linking
buildings and sciences.

室内街道贯通基地，
串联了建筑与科学。

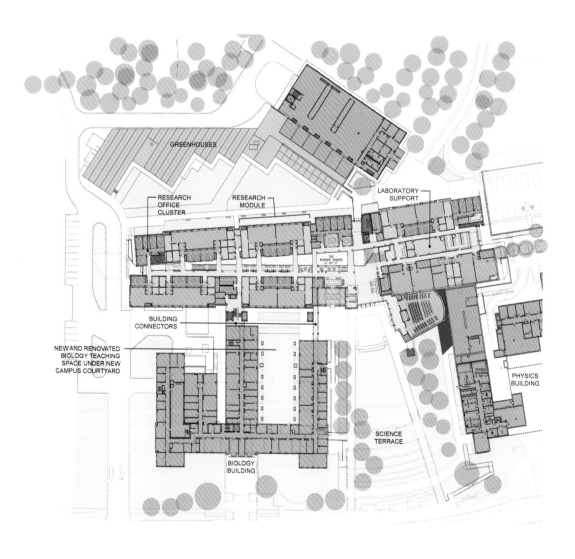

DUKE UNIVERSITY FRENCH FAMILY SCIENCE CENTER 杜克大学法国家庭科学中心

汉诺威市

HANOVER

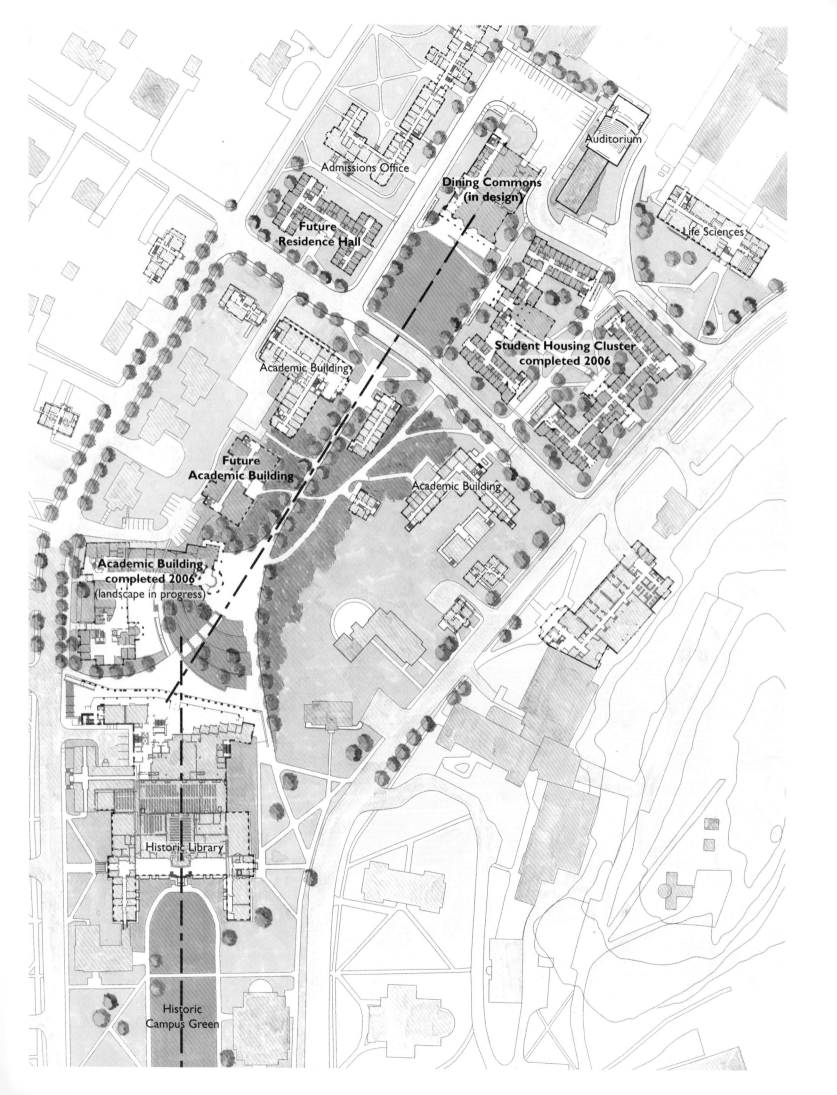

Admissions Office

Auditorium

**Dining Commons
(in design)**

**Future
Residence Hall**

Life Sciences

Academic Building

**Student Housing Cluster
completed 2006**

**Future
Academic Building**

Academic Building

**Academic Building
completed 2006**
(landscape in progress)

Historic Library

Historic
Campus Green

达特茅斯学院规划项目占地28,328平方米，与其北侧的共享商业区和大学城一同打造了一个崭新的校园空间。该规划涉及数学与人文系的新校舍、学生宿舍、新餐饮中心以及科学中心和其他校园停车场的建设，以满足未来发展的需要。

新建筑物与达特茅斯校园其他建筑和谐互融，在尊重建筑悠久历史的同时运用现代材料，形成了一个充满活力的校园，其意义远远超过了各部分空间的总和。

该建筑的设计严格遵循了可持续设计的新标准，最大限度地灵活利用建筑系统，以应对建筑在未来100年的发展。可持续措施包括辐射热供暖和制冷设施的运用；废热回收、低VOC涂料和黏合剂的应用；雨水再利用系统以及再生材料的运用。室内空气质量传感器能够有效减少二氧化碳的排放，设备规模适中以降低对能源的消耗。

麦克劳克林学生公寓获得了金级认证，共包括一个三层宿舍、一个四层宿舍（共设置了343个床位）、一个中央公共区、一个干部公寓以及学习和生活空间。该项目的设计促进了学生之间的互动，并为自由学习和聚会营造了良好氛围。该公寓的多功能入口与街面和中央庭院交相辉映，并有效加强了校园间的衔接。

凯梅尼·霍尔与霍尔德曼中心将分散在校园各处的数学系和三个人文专业进行了集中布局，并获得了LEED银级认证。该建筑将校园的核心部分与达特茅斯标志性建筑以及校园北部的新建筑完美衔接起来。顶层的壁龛将自然光线成功引入室内走廊，时刻确保教师和职员办公室通透、明亮。毗邻教室和会议室的公共空间为人们在活动或研讨会结束后提供良好的互动和交流空间。

The master plan for this seven-acre site at Dartmouth College reconfigures the area directly north of the shared town and college Green into a major new campus space. The program includes a new home for the Math and Humanities departments, Student Housing, and a major new dining center, as well as allowing for future programmatic needs, such as expansion of the Science Center and additional campus parking.

The new buildings weave connections with the rest of the Dartmouth campus, and are designed to be sympathetic with their historic context while representing contemporary needs and materials, to create a dynamic campus that will be more than the sum of its parts.

The buildings adhere to new standards for sustainability by maximizing the long-term flexibility of building systems to provide a 100-year building life. Sustainable measures include radiant floor heating and cooling, carefully sized equipment to limit energy consumption, heat recovery from return air and water, low VOC paints and adhesives, indoor air quality sensors to minimize CO_2, stormwater retention systems, and the use of rapidly renewable and recycled materials.

The McLaughlin Cluster Student Housing, awarded Gold certification, consists of two 3- and 4-story residence halls with 343 total beds, a central social Commons, a director's apartment, study and living spaces. The project design fosters social interaction among the students by providing many opportunities for casual study and gathering. Multiple entries to the Cluster animate the street and central courtyard, and serve as connections across campus.

The LEED® Silver certified Kemeny Hall & Haldeman Center is the new, consolidated home for the Math Department and three Humanities departments that were previously dispersed throughout the campus. The building provides a connection between the central portion of the campus and the iconic Dartmouth Green as well as the newer buildings on the north portion of campus. Upper floor alcoves allow natural daylight to enter the corridors, making them attractive, sunny extensions of the faculty and staff offices. Public space adjacent to classrooms and conference rooms encourages people to "spill out and spread out" so that the exchange of ideas can continue long after an event or seminar has concluded.

达特茅斯学院

北校区新区规划：麦克劳克林学生公寓，凯梅尼·霍尔与霍尔德曼中心

Dartmouth College

NORTH CAMPUS DISTRICT PLAN: MCLAUGHLIN HOUSING, KEMENEY HALL & HALDEMAN CENTERS

New buildings extend
campus core to the north,
framing new paths and
courtyards.

新建筑物将校园的核心
北移,并营造了新的行道
及庭院。

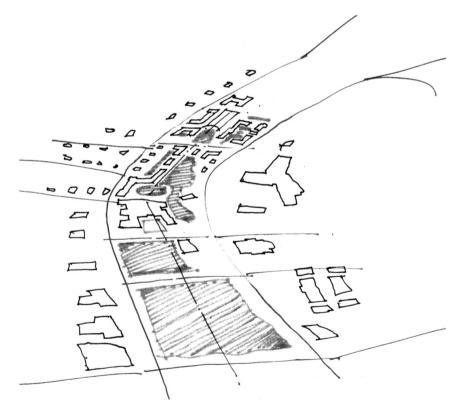

1. Intake / Exhaust through rooftop "chimneys" minimizing airborne contaminants
2. Ventilation air independent of heating and cooling to ensure indoor air quality
3. Low-flow toilets and shower fixtures
4. Wood harvested from Dartmouth College's forest used for dorm furniture
5. Radiant floor heating and cooling in all rooms from exposed concrete slab(s)
6. Heat from warm shower water drains exchanged and transferred to hot water supply
7. Supply
8. Exhaust
9. Enthalpy Wheel / Heat Exchange: (1). In the Winter, warm exhaust air passes it's heat on to pre-heat incoming air supply. (2). During the Summer, cool exhaust air absorbs heat from warm incoming air, thus pre-cooling it.
10. Robust Exterior Envelope: Brick, air space, poly-iso spray-on insulation, CMU with metal stud back-up
11. CO_2 sensors used in assembly spaces with VAV air system
12. Radiant floor heating and cooling beneath bamboo flooring
13. Double and triple-glazed windows allow natural light while limiting heat loss and gain. Artificial lighting loads are less than 1 W/ft
14. 50% of power required obtained from renewable energy such as wind and solar electric

1. 进气/排气，通过屋顶"烟囱"最大限度地减少对空气的污染
2. 独立的加热与制冷通风设备，以确保室内空气质量
3. 低流量卫生间和淋浴装置
4. 宿舍的家具木料全部来自达特茅斯学院附近的森林
5. 所有房间中裸露的混凝土板为地板辐射采暖和制冷提供了条件
6. 来自热水淋浴排水沟的热量经过能量交换转变为热水补给系统
7. 补给
8. 排气装置
9. 焓/热交换：(1)在冬季，温热的排气将其热量传递给进入到室内的外部空气。(2)在夏季，凉爽的排气将进入室内的温热空气进行吸收并预冷

10. 强大的外围防护结构：砖、空心处、聚异丁烯绝缘涂层、备用金属螺栓管道管理部件
11. 在VAV空调系统装配空间使用二氧化碳传感器
12. 竹木地板下方的辐射采暖与制冷
13. 双层和三层玻璃窗能够确保光线自然进入室内，并对强光进行有效过滤。人工照明负载量不高于1瓦特/英尺
14. 50%的电力来自对可再生能源的利用，包括风能、太阳能等

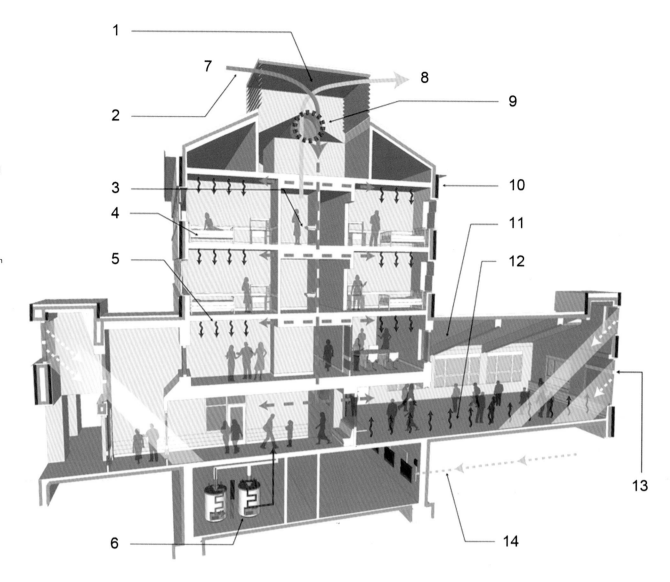

DARTMOUTH COLLEGE NORTH CAMPUS DISTRICT PLAN 达特茅斯学院北校区新区规划

香港 HONG KONG

这个高密度的学术综合建筑入口位于丘陵之上，学生从附近的火车站下车之后可直接进入到校园之中。该项目的总体规划，拟建一个电梯入口和普通入口以及一个25米长的坡道，其设计灵感源自香港兰桂坊区规划的启发。开阔的阶梯与一个内设大型汇报厅和国际学生中心的六层建筑相通。

该建筑巧妙利用了当地复杂的地形特征，强调与环境的自然融合。采用了人工绿化屋顶、节能机械系统、室内与室外水资源保护措施，光滑的玻璃窗口以及良好的定位能够对自然光线进行有效调节，并确保室内环境清新，通透明亮。灌浇混凝土、瓷砖、铝合金框架等建筑元素的利用为建筑的持久、耐用提供了优越条件。

针对高人口密度校园的布局，2ITB设计公司提出了几个设计方案。其构建的国际学生中心作为设计的重点为通勤学生构建了一个集咖啡馆和活动空间于一体的新校园环境。该建筑与一个通往学生中心的玻璃亭台以及一个景观台相通。这两个分别为10层和14层的建筑实现了教室、工作室、教师办公室的共享，应用较为灵活，可随着时间的推移而适度调整。在规划中，建筑呈倾斜状设计，与其附近的学生宿舍楼相对，华美的露天楼梯犹如垂直悬挂的灯笼，为空间注入了无限活力。开阔的楼梯同时也在整个新项目中扮演了中轴线的角色，如同一个全天候的活动"街道"。

This high-density academic complex takes a gateway position on CUHK's hilly campus, greeting students as they arrive from the nearby train station. As a demonstration of our proposed Master Plan concept, 2ITB provides escalator-powered access—and universal access as well—up and down some 25 meters of hillside, in a scheme inspired by Hong Kong's Lan Kwai Fong district. The Grand Stairway also connects six stories of podium containing large lecture halls and an International Student Center.

The complex addresses environmental responsibility goals through the use of planted roofs, energy efficient mechanical systems, interior and exterior water conservation measures, and glazed openings shaped and shaded by their orientation to the sun and views. Long-term maintenance of the structure was carefully considered through the use of poured concrete, porcelain tiles, and aluminum framing on the building's exterior.

Responding to the opportunities of campus place-making at higher density, 2ITB shows several strategies. Its "workhorse" program of general use facilities is enlivened by the International Student Center, providing a campus home for commuting students, with cafe, and activity spaces. The building mass is articulated into multiple forms—a glassy pavilion entry for the student center, and a landscaped podium that engages the surrounding green hillsides. With a combination of classrooms, studios, and faculty offices, the 10-and 14-story towers may be flexibly programmed over time. In plan the towers are splayed to maintain views from neighboring residence halls, and their open stairways serve as colorful, vertical lanterns. The Grand Stairway itself provides a dramatic central axis up through the site, a diagonal "street" of 24/7 activity and a new campus prototype.

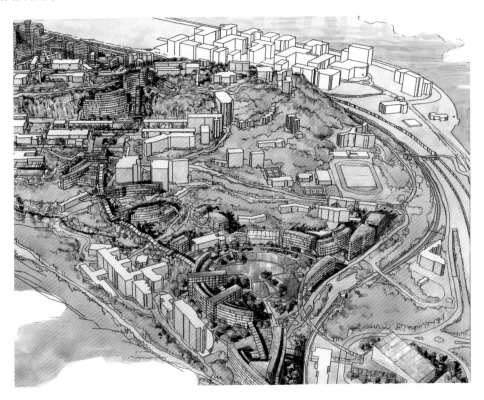

Chinese University of Hong Kong, China

TWO INTEGRATED TEACHING BUILDING

中国香港中文大学

两个综合教学楼

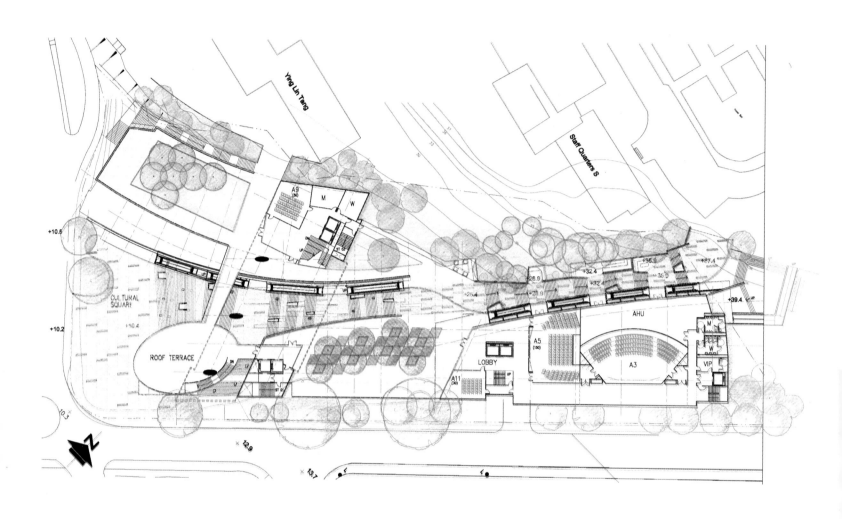

Ying Lin Tang

Staff Quarters S

+10.5

CULTURAL
SQUARE

+10.2

+10.4

ROOF TERRACE

A9
(30)

M

W

ST Q

A11
(30)

LOBBY

ST Q

A5
(150)

AHU

A3

M

W

VIP

+26.9

+26.4

+28.9

+32.4

+32

+35.9

+36.9

+37.4

+39.4

10.3

12.9

13.7

N

圣彼得堡市

ST. PETERSBURG

A Business Library will be integrated as a fundamental part of the new campus of St. Petersburg University. The campus plan adds new buildings to a restored 19th century palace located at the Mikhailskaya Dacha (Summer House) outside of the city. Within a strict limit of 53,800 GSF, this state-of-the-art library emphasizes efficiency and flexibility, while counterpointing a contemporary image at the entrance to the GSOM's historic site. The program combines digital media and a printed materials collection with a variety of team-oriented student work spaces, all contained in a simple modular format that assures adaptable space.

The site is sculpted to bring daylight into a lower ground floor, allowing three levels of program to fit within a strict height limit of 33 feet. Under a green roof, a minimally gradated envelope of white fritted glass is surrounded by a rotated rugged screen of reclaimed Russian railroad timbers. The raw wood speaks to the forested site and filters daylight while protecting the lower floor windows from winter snowdrifts. By night, the Library serves as a lantern to illuminate the main path between dormitories and classrooms, becoming a warm focal point of campus.

商学院图书馆是圣彼得堡大学新校区的一个基本组成部分。该校园的规划旨在于市郊避暑别墅附近的19世纪宫殿旁打造几个全新建筑。这个占地4,998平方米的图书馆强调功效性与灵活性的巧妙结合，在具有浓厚历史气息的环境中打造一个充满现代感的入口。该项目将数字媒体和纸质印刷品收藏室充分结合，为学生提供了一个优良的团队合作空间。

该项目注重建筑低层的采光，三层高的建筑不高于10米。绿化屋顶下，一个白色多孔玻璃表层由一个旋转的俄罗斯铁路再生木屏覆盖。原生木材与周围浓郁茂盛的自然环境交相呼应，并对光线进行有效调节，确保低层的窗口免受冬季风雪的侵袭。夜幕降临之时，图书馆仿佛一盏明灯，照亮了学生宿舍和教室之间的主要通道，成为校园一处惬意的景观。

St. Petersburg, Russia

ST. PETERSBURG STATE UNIVERSITY GRADUATE SCHOOL OF MANAGEMENT LIBRARY

俄罗斯，圣彼得堡市

圣彼得堡国立大学 研究生管理学院图书馆

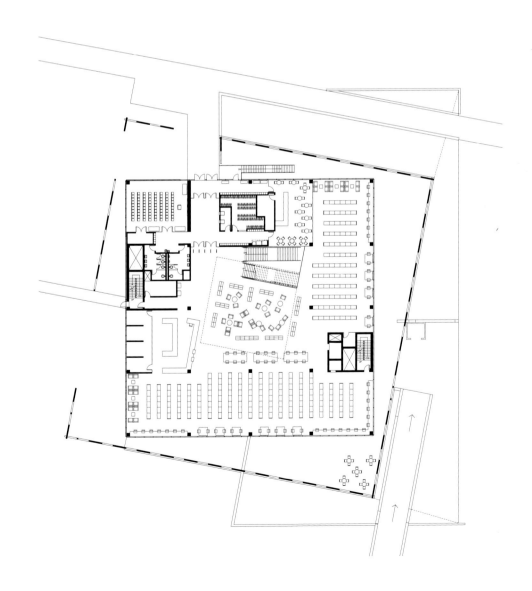

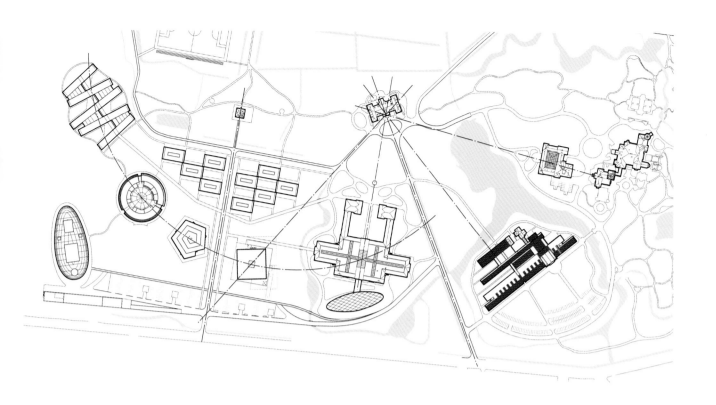

ST. PETERSBURG STATE UNIVERSITY LIBRARY 圣彼得堡国立大学图书馆

圣克鲁斯市

SANTA CRUZ

物理科学大楼占地13,006平方米，作为科学山的北入口，内设了研究和教学实验室、配套空间、微机室、会议室、教师和研究生办公室以及综合性教室和报告厅。设计强调布局的清晰、合理，以一个四层的中庭为核心，该核心同时也作为横向和纵向的枢纽。化学与环境毒理学实验室设在图书馆的一侧，而位于建筑末端的配套空间，能够对设施进行灵活配置，并与主流通道相通。此外，位于配套空间中的研究生办事处，能够将流通区域的景致尽收眼底。穿过中庭和图书馆，可直接到达室外园区。

该项目建筑在原停车场的位置上，尽量减少对附近红木树林的破坏，融合了多种节能和可持续设计手法。项目中采用了诸多自然通风策略：北向的封闭空调实验室能够降低热量的获取；南向的办公室内设有可移动玻璃窗，巧妙利用地形和风向特征，确保室内夜间通风；利用中庭作为温度调节器加强上下空间的通风，提高室内空气质量，减少能源消耗。

Marking the north entry to the campus's Science Hill, the 140,000 sf Physical Sciences Building houses research and teaching laboratories, support spaces, computer rooms, conference rooms, faculty and graduate student offices, as well as, general assignment classrooms and lecture halls. The design emphasizes clarity of organization centered on a four-story atrium called the Spine, which acts as a horizontal and vertical hub. Laboratory wings for Chemistry and Environmental Toxicology allow for flexible reconfiguration by placing support spaces at ends of blocks and within a flex-use band bordering main circulation routes. This support zone also houses graduate student offices that have views to circulation areas, the Spine, and through the laboratories to the forested exterior beyond.

Developed on an existing parking lot to minimize the destruction of the adjoining redwood forest, the building incorporates a wide variety of energy saving and environmentally sustainable approaches. The project includes various natural ventilation strategies including facing the sealed, air-conditioned laboratories north to reduce heat gain, locating offices with operable windows on the south to take advantage of the site's prevailing wind patterns, providing nighttime air flush, using the Spine as a thermal chimney to actively pull fresh air through occupied areas and vent stale air at the top of the space, and exposing thermal mass to temper daily temperature swings all contribute to enhanced indoor air quality and reduced energy consumption.

加利福尼亚州，圣克鲁斯市

美国加州大学
圣克鲁斯分校
物理科学大楼

University of California, Santa Cruz

UC SANTA CRUZ
PHYSICAL SCIENCES
BUILDING

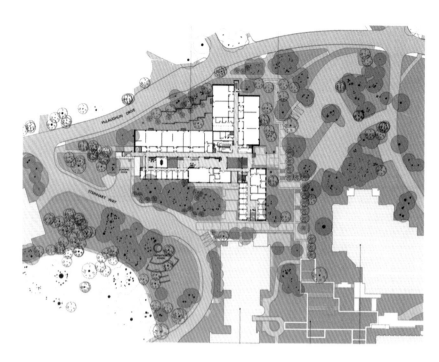

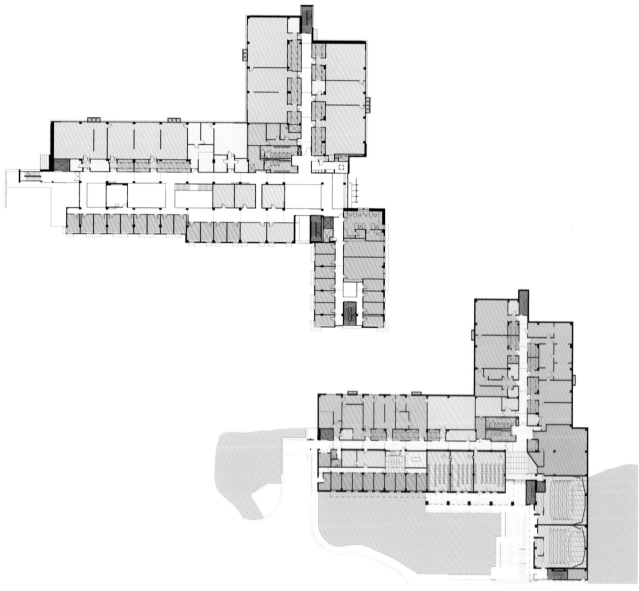

UC SANTA CRUZ PHYSICAL SCIENCES BULDING 美国加州大学圣克鲁斯分校物理科学大楼

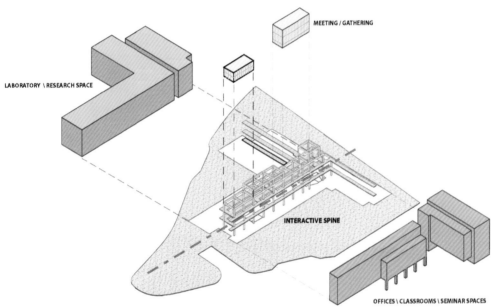

LABORATORY \ RESEARCH SPACE

MEETING / GATHERING

INTERACTIVE SPINE

OFFICES \ CLASSROOMS \ SEMINAR SPACES

The atrium "Spine" draws
pedestrians through the
surrounding redwood trees.

脊状入口大厅引导行人
穿越红树林进入建筑。

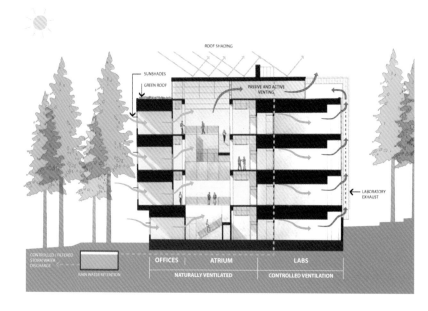

台州市　TAIZHOU

中国台州时代医疗公司总部——科学园项目，强调可持续设计理念与环保和新信息技术的巧妙融合。该设计成为致力于生物医学和制药等行业的国家级高新技术园区未来生活与工作规划项目的优秀典范。该建筑的竣工将成为台州市一个崭新的地标性建筑，通过独特的外观和结构彰显其独特的医疗和科学形态。

我们的设计理念是打造一高、一低的两个建筑，通过一个室内天桥和环绕四周的水池使二者相结合。较低的建筑中设有酒店式公寓和一个训练中心，而较高的建筑中则设有台州时代医疗公司总部办公空间。为优化公共入口和改善空间环境，建筑还增设了附加公共空间，该空间中包括位于楼上和顶层的餐厅、观景台以及医药和科学主题展览画廊。夜色中，建筑外部的显示屏将整个建筑照亮的同时，为整个城市的夜色增添了无限活力。

建筑通过在屋顶和墙体中安装光电太阳能板自行发电，微型涡轮机的设置将对能源的消耗降到最低。太阳能板既能够将自然光线引入到室内，同时为建筑外部的显示器提供能源供给。绿化屋顶、绿色墙体、可种植阳台、温室为办公空间和住宅区营造了一个"空中花园"，将对空调的利用率降到最低。优良的蓄水系统和灰水再利用设施能够对种植区进行有效灌溉，一楼的水体和倒影池同时也扮演了滞留池的角色。

The Science Park Towers headquarters for Time-Medical Inc. in Taizhou, China incorporates state-of-the-art sustainable, environmentally friendly and information-technology features to make it an outstanding precedent for future live/work developments in the "Medical City"— China's newly-formed national hi-tech park dedicated to biomedical and pharmaceutical industries. The structure is envisioned to become a landmark symbol of Taizhou, evoking medical and science-related forms through an architectural statement that captures the energy of this unique place.

Our design concept is based on a powerful, sculptural configuration of two towers—one higher and one lower—linked by a verdant "conservatory bridge" and surrounded by reflecting pools. The lower tower accommodate hotel-style apartments and a Training Center, while the higher tower provides office space for the headquarters of Time-Medical Corporation. In order to optimize public access and promote the project as a health and sciences-oriented visitor destination, additional public spaces have been incorporated including iconic restaurants on the upper floors and roofs, observatories to provide views of the city, and exhibition galleries with medicine and science-related themes. At night, the exterior surfaces of the towers are illuminated as "media facades" to become glowing lanterns for the city.

The towers reduce energy usage by generating their own electricity through building-integrated Photovoltaic solar panels on the roofs and walls, and a micro-turbine. The solar panels double as partial shading elements that permit light passage to the interiors, as well as feeding the "media facade" skin of the buildings. Grass roofs, green cladding on walls, planted terraces and greenhouses create a vertical movement of "sky garden" offices and residential units while minimizing the need for heating and air conditioning. Rainwater is collected, and gray water recycled to irrigate planted areas, while water features and reflecting pools on the ground floor double as retention ponds.

中国，台州
时代医疗公司总部大楼

Taizhou, China
TIME-MEDICAL INC. TOWERS

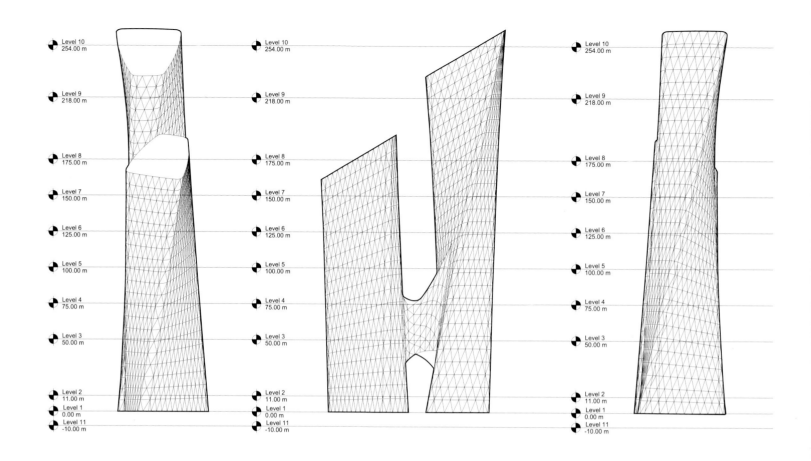

Level 10
254.00 m

Level 9
218.00 m

Level 8
175.00 m

Level 7
150.00 m

Level 6
125.00 m

Level 5
100.00 m

Level 4
75.00 m

Level 3
50.00 m

Level 2
11.00 m

Level 1
0.00 m

Level 11
-10.00 m

Level 10
254.00 m

Level 9
218.00 m

Level 8
175.00 m

Level 7
150.00 m

Level 6
125.00 m

Level 5
100.00 m

Level 4
75.00 m

Level 3
50.00 m

Level 2
11.00 m

Level 1
0.00 m

Level 11
-10.00 m

Level 10
254.00 m

Level 9
218.00 m

Level 8
175.00 m

Level 7
150.00 m

Level 6
125.00 m

Level 5
100.00 m

Level 4
75.00 m

Level 3
50.00 m

Level 2
11.00 m

Level 1
0.00 m

Level 11
-10.00 m

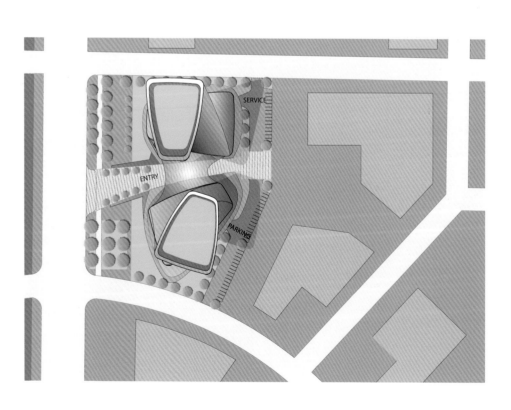

SERVICE

ENTRY

PARKING

A multi-level bridge raises
shared facilities up into the
towers.

多层连接桥梁将建筑的
共享设施空间提升至塔
楼之间。

剑桥市

CAMBRIDGE

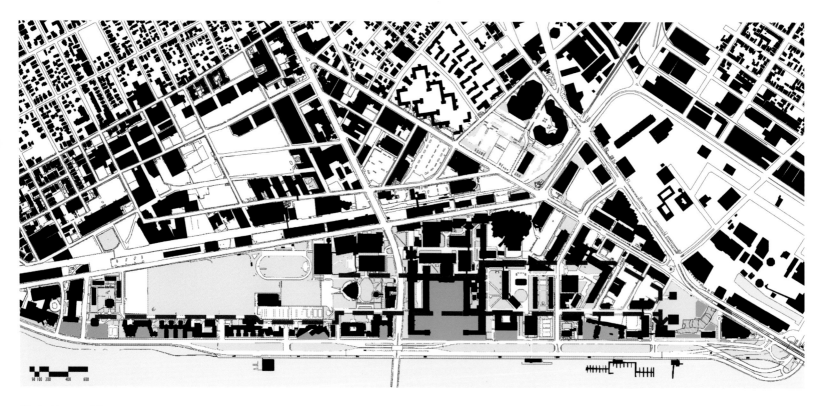

The building carefully
connects historic buildings
facing the river and frames
a new entry court toward
the city.

透过精心安排，新建筑
连接了面向河岸的历史
性建物，并成为城市一
个新的入口庭院。

美国麻省理工学院斯隆管理学院是校园的一个基本组成部分。新建筑与总体规划加强了与麻省理工学院和剑桥地区的连接，构建了一个集社交、学术和象征性于一体的新东部校区，促进全体教师的合作与交流。环境优美的建筑内，灵活的空间布局为未来发展提供了先决条件。这个总占地面积为216,000平方米的项目包括斯隆学院办公室、斯隆教室、行政教育区、餐饮、小组研究区、相关的社交空间以及地下停车库等空间。

这一高性能的建筑能够实现能源利用的最优化并且营造一个健康的室内环境。可持续设计元素涉及建筑外墙保温和窗口系统、遮阳设备和太阳能光伏板等等。三楼的屋顶平台绿草茵茵，既美化了建筑，同时也起到了节能和降低雨水径流峰值的作用。

建立和加强衔接是该项目的首要目标之一。这些衔接不仅仅指的是城市和校园之间的连接，同时也寓意教师和学生之间更大的互动。位于一楼的画廊通透、明亮，是斯隆校园的一个社交核心区域，该画廊由餐饮区、学生休息室、商务中心等区域环绕，同时将室内与景观的连接纽带——河畔园区拥抱其中。斯隆学院作为麻省理工学院校园的一个重要组成部分，与整体自然融合的同时，因独特的建筑风格而相对独立。

The Sloan School of Management at the Massachusetts Institute of Technology is an integral part of the campus on many levels. The new building and masterplan strengthens connections to the MIT Campus and Cambridge region, creates a social, academic and symbolic "Heart" within the East Campus and consolidates faculty to promote intellectual collaboration. This is achieved within an environmentally optimized building that allows for flexible programmatic implementation in the future. The 215,000 GSF project includes MIT Sloan faculty offices, classrooms, executive education, dining, group study, related social spaces and below-grade parking.

The building is high-performance, providing superior energy efficiency and creating a healthy environment by design. Sustainable elements include an effectively insulating building exterior and window system, sun shading devices and is ready to accept photovoltaic panels. The third floor flat roof is designed as a "green" sedum roof that is attractive, low-maintenance and reduces peak rainwater runoff.

Creating and strengthening connections at multiple scales is one of the project's primary goals. The design establishes these connections, which range from urban and campus-wide connections to fostering greater interaction between faculty and students on an individual level. The daylight-filled Gallery on the ground floor provides a social heart to the MIT Sloan campus. Encompassed by the dining facility, student lounges, business center and breakout spaces, the Gallery embraces the river court, which connects the interior to the landscape. The MIT Sloan School of Management is a vital part of the connective tissue of the MIT campus as a whole, while simultaneously existing as an independent entity, unique in character.

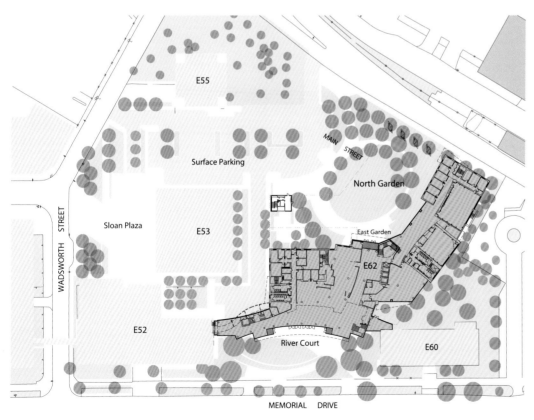

The new building connects to key campus and city pathways.

新建筑衔接了校园及城市的主要步道.

Massachusetts Institute of Technology

MIT SLOAN SCHOOL OF MANAGEMENT

麻省理工学院
斯隆管理学院

MIT SLOAN SCHOOL OF MANAGEMENT 麻省理工学院斯隆管理学院

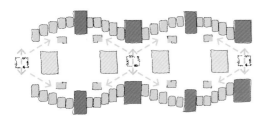

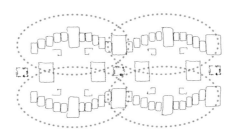

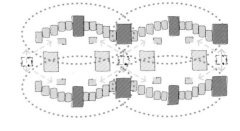

The "DNA" of faculty office clusters balances intimacy within groups and connections across disciplines.

建筑群以"DNA"的形状配置安排，平衡了私密性及跨学科交流的需求。

圣何塞市

SAN JOSE

霍勒斯·曼恩小学占地6,596平方米，位于历史名城圣何塞市中心，能够容纳从幼儿园到小学五年级的学生。校园中设有教室、行政大楼、附有媒体中心的图书馆以及实验室和作为特殊之用的灵活空间等。为促进学校社区间的广泛互动，该方案同时也增设了公共服务设施，诸如用于举办讲座、演出和其他社团聚会的多用途报告厅。

新建筑结合了当地城市的规划背景，三层建筑中设置的庭院、草坪游乐区、露台、聚会空间加强了学校与大型社区间的视觉衔接。建筑的特殊结构便于室内采光，并加强室内通风，为全体师生营造了一个舒适、静谧的工作和学习环境。

Horace Mann Elementary School accommodates students from kindergarten to fifth grade on its 71,000 sf site near historic downtown San Jose. The campus houses classrooms, an administration wing, a library with an expanded media center, and unassigned or "lab" classrooms to be outfitted for special uses. In an effort to foster community involvement in the school, the program was augmented to include public-serving amenities such as a multi-purpose hall for lectures, plays, and other community gatherings.

The new buildings respond to the urban context, stepping from one to three stories in height, while the various courtyards, turf play areas, terraces, and gathering spaces provide a visual link between the school and the larger community. The organization of the buildings is designed to maximize natural light access and ventilation for all occupants, contributing to a high-quality learning and work environment.

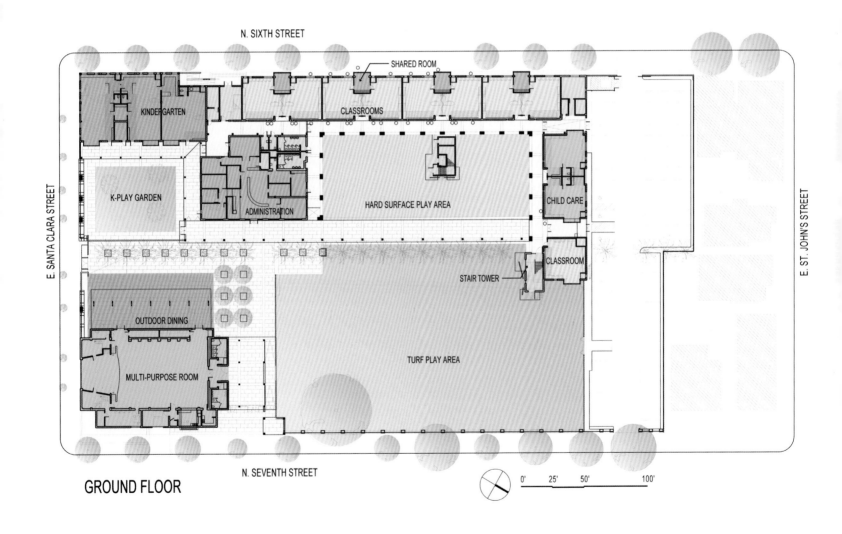

N. SIXTH STREET

SHARED ROOM

KINDERGARTEN

CLASSROOMS

E. SANTA CLARA STREET

K-PLAY GARDEN

ADMINISTRATION

HARD SURFACE PLAY AREA

CHILD CARE

E. ST. JOHN'S STREET

STAIR TOWER

CLASSROOM

OUTDOOR DINING

TURF PLAY AREA

MULTI-PURPOSE ROOM

N. SEVENTH STREET

GROUND FLOOR

0' 25' 50' 100'

San Jose, California

加利福尼亚州，圣何塞市
霍勒斯·曼恩小学

HORACE MANN ELEMENTARY SCHOOL

HORACE MANN ELEMENTARY SCHOOL 美国加州圣何塞市霍勒斯·曼恩小学

Glorya Kaufman Hall is the new home for the Department of World Arts and Cultures. The building is an adaptive re-use of a 1932 Italian Romanesque building originally designed as the women's gym and badly damaged in the 1992 Northridge earthquake. This historic building, part of the original core campus, has been transformed into a state-of-the-art performance venue, including a new 300-seat reconfigurable theater, an outdoor garden theater pavilion, five dance rehearsal studios, multi-media laboratories, offices, and classrooms.

The flexibility of major performance and practice spaces in this 94,500 sf building has led to an extraordinary range of collaborations by faculty, visiting artists and students. Informal circulation spaces lead to impromptu creative uses, from concerts to installations. The new pavilion theater serves simultaneously as a theater stage, experimental performance space, and lecture room with movable seating, augmented by an operable wall to an exterior garden which provides additional audience capacity. The renovation creates an environment where students can explore the links between performance, community service, and diverse artistic traditions from across the globe.

库夫曼大厅是世界艺术与文化系的新校舍。该建筑的前身意大利罗马式建筑建于1932年，起初作为妇女健身中心，后在1992年北岭地震中严重受损。这一历史建筑，作为原校园的核心部分之一，经过改建之后成为一个最先进的表演场地，其中包括了一个可容纳300人的剧院、一个户外花园剧场馆、五个舞蹈排练室、多媒体实验室、办公室和教室。

在这个占地8,779平方米的建筑中，主要表演空间和练习区的灵活性加强了教师、来访的艺术家和学生之间的互动。非正式的流通空间为音乐会和流通设施区提供了大量的弹性空间。新剧场馆还可作为戏剧舞台、实验表演空间、报告厅之用，一个通往室外花园的开闭式间壁可提供额外的席位。改建后的建筑将大大拉近学生和表演、社区服务、多样化的全球艺术传统之间的距离。

University of California, Los Angeles

GLORYA KAUFMAN CENTER FOR WORLD ARTS & CULTURES

加州大学洛杉矶分校

库夫曼世界艺术与文化大厅

洛杉矶 LOS ANGELES

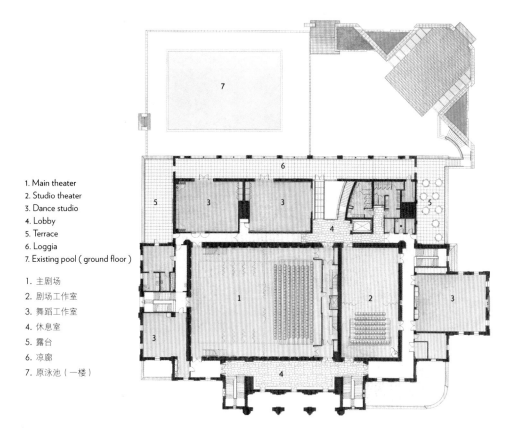

1. Main theater
2. Studio theater
3. Dance studio
4. Lobby
5. Terrace
6. Loggia
7. Existing pool (ground floor)

1. 主剧场
2. 剧场工作室
3. 舞蹈工作室
4. 休息室
5. 露台
6. 凉廊
7. 原泳池（一楼）

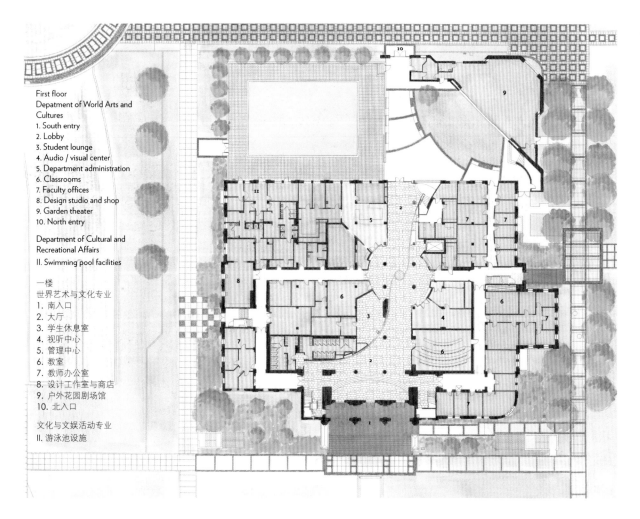

First floor
Depatment of World Arts and
Cultures
1. South entry
2. Lobby
3. Student lounge
4. Audio / visual center
5. Department administration
6. Classrooms
7. Faculty offices
8. Design studio and shop
9. Garden theater
10. North entry

Department of Cultural and
Recreational Affairs
II. Swimming pool facilities

一楼
世界艺术与文化专业
1. 南入口
2. 大厅
3. 学生休息室
4. 视听中心
5. 管理中心
6. 教室
7. 教师办公室
8. 设计工作室与商店
9. 户外花园剧场馆
10. 北入口

文化与文娱活动专业
II. 游泳池设施

A new street passes
through the building linking
historic elements with
the new garden theater.

一条新的通道穿过建筑，
将历史性的元素与新的花
园剧场串联起来。

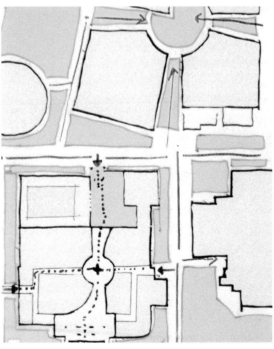

The old first floor locker room is transformed into an active gallery through movement, light and program.

底层旧的衣柜间，借着活动、灯光，改变成一个展览馆。

The former woman's gym
becomes a transformable
high tech theater.

旧的女子健身房改建成新
的高科技剧院。

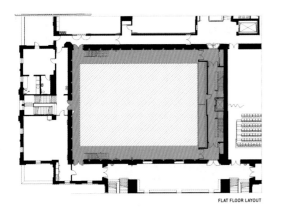

FLAT FLOOR LAYOUT

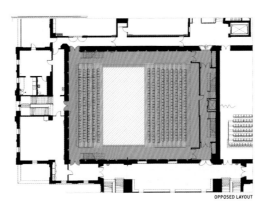

OPPOSED LAYOUT

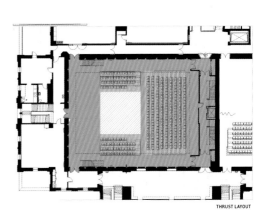

THRUST LAYOUT

The new theater has
multiple configurations
including proscenium, arena
and flat floor performance.

新剧院，包括前台、舞台
和平面地板性能的多种
配置。

The new garden theater is sized for performance and practice and can be open or closed as desired.

新的花园剧场为演出及练习而设计，开关自如。

圣巴巴拉市

SANTA BARBARA

曼泽尼特村，这个可容纳800名学生的本科生公寓综合建筑经过改造后转变成一个立体的格状建筑群，各宿舍大楼间衔接自然。在太平洋和潟湖校园的环抱中，新曼泽尼特村设置了一系列户外空间，从入口贯穿中央广场一直向建筑的三个方向进行延伸，所形成的休闲空间与远处的水景相通。

该建筑群楼层均为三、四层，三个联成一组，可容纳40至60名学生。每一个围绕一个垂直公共区进行布局，该公共区中囊括了入口、洗衣房、休息室、厨房和学习室。从公共区延伸出来的门厅中设置的双人间或单间套房中配备了可容纳四人的浴室。

三个额外的村庄设施中囊括了个人或团体的生活配套空间。它们分别为卡里略餐饮中心、德安萨资源中心和诺玛·派隆纳多功能厅。卡里略餐饮中心为学生营造了温馨、惬意的就餐环境；德安萨资源中心设有行政办公室、会议室和小型研讨室；而诺玛·派隆纳多功能厅则设置了两个大型会议室和学生休闲空间。

建筑的设计崇尚简约、清晰的理念，强调细节和色彩的运用。精心选用的色调不仅对建筑的每个空间进行区分，同时与每个独立区域相得益彰。白色的宿舍将令建筑群更为统一，而鲜艳的色彩则象征着室内的勃勃生机。

Manzanita Village, an 800-bed undergraduate student housing complex, developed as a three-dimensional "social-plaid" – provides spaces both within and without that encourage dynamic interaction between residents. Placed on a promontory overlooking the Pacific Ocean and the Campus Lagoon, the new village is defined by a series of outdoor spaces extending from entry courts through the Central Plaza to the three housing quads that shape recreational spaces that open to spectacular views of the water beyond.

Three and four story houses – three linked pairs per quad, accommodate between 40 and 60 students. Each house organizes around a vertical social magnet comprised of entries, laundries, lounges, kitchens, and study rooms. Extending from the social core are thoughtfully scaled hallways that group double and single rooms with bathrooms that serve four students each.

Support spaces for student life—both for the individual and groups—are found in three additional village facilities. Carrillo Dining Commons provides a variety of settings for student activity all with the support of a rich dining experience. The De Anza Resource Center houses administrative offices, meeting spaces and smaller study rooms. The Loma Pelona Multi-purpose Hall provides two large flexible meeting rooms and student recreation space.

The buildings are designed as simple, clear volumes with meaningfully placed details and colors. Color was orchestrated, not only to define special moments on the buildings, but also to anchor each quad to its location on the site. The white of the resident houses serves to unify the village, while the intensely colored commons buildings symbolically announce the vibrant activity within.

University of California, Santa Barbara

MANZANITA VILLAGE STUDENT HOUSING

美国加州大学圣巴巴拉分校
曼泽尼特村学生公寓

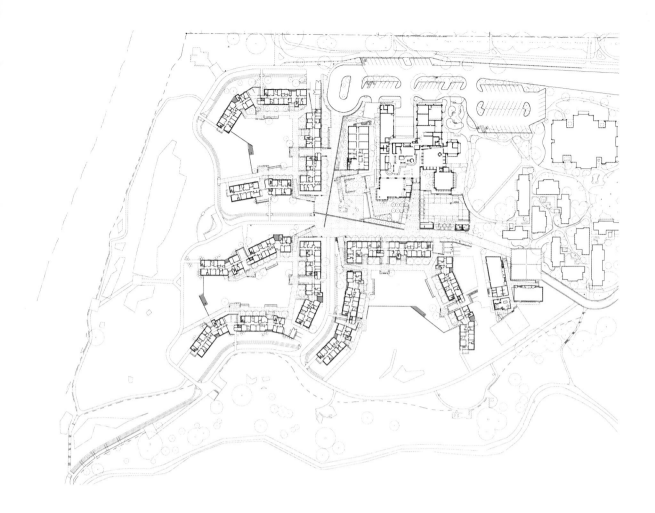

Through careful responses to orientation, detailing and choices of supporting technical systems, the buildings are quietly supportive of sustainability goals. Sun-shading on the southern and western exposures reduce heat gain while building configurations maximize natural ventilation. Landscaping responsibly manages water-use through the use of reclaimed irrigation water while bio-swales and permeable surfaces regulate surface run-off on this highly sensitive site.

通过准确的定位，配套技术体系的精心安排，该建筑将可持续的设计理念贯穿始终。南部和西部的遮阳设施成功地避免了强光的暴晒，并有利于加强室内通风效果。通过对洼地和雨水径流的巧妙处理，使水源得以重复利用，对植物进行灌溉。

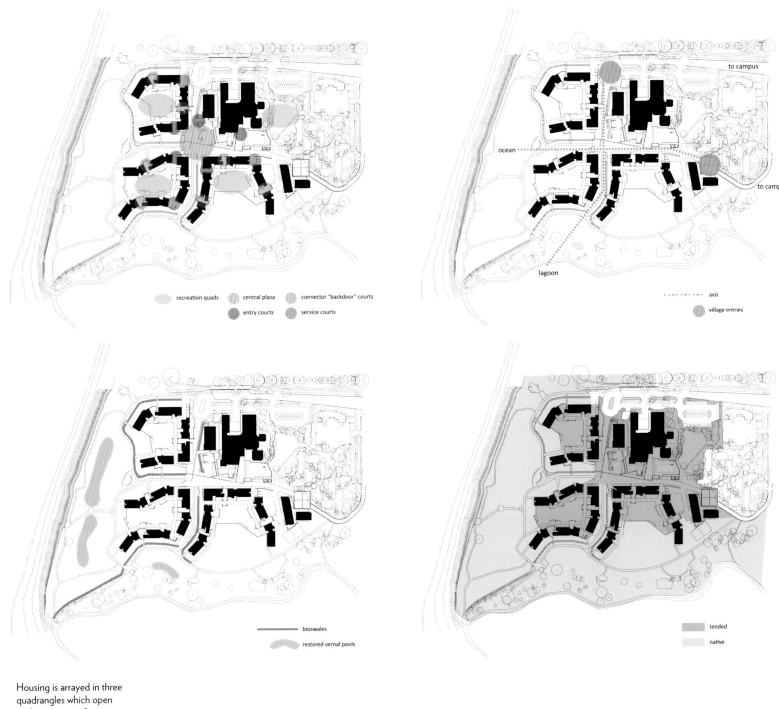

recreation quads   central plaza   connector "backdoor" courts

entry courts   service courts

ocean

to campus

to campus

lagoon

axis

village entries

bioswales

restored vernal pools

tended

native

Housing is arrayed in three
quadrangles which open
to the ocean yet frame an
urban plaza at their center.

宿舍以三个向着海洋的三
合院形式安排,并在它们之
间形成一个都市广场。

　　　　　　　　UC SANTA BARBARA MANZANITA VILLAGE STUDENT HOUSING　　美国加州大学圣巴巴拉分校曼泽尼特村学生公寓

UC SANTA BARBARA MANZANITA VILLAGE STUDENT HOUSING　美国加州大学圣巴巴拉分校曼泽尼特村学生公寓

温哥华市

VANCOUVER

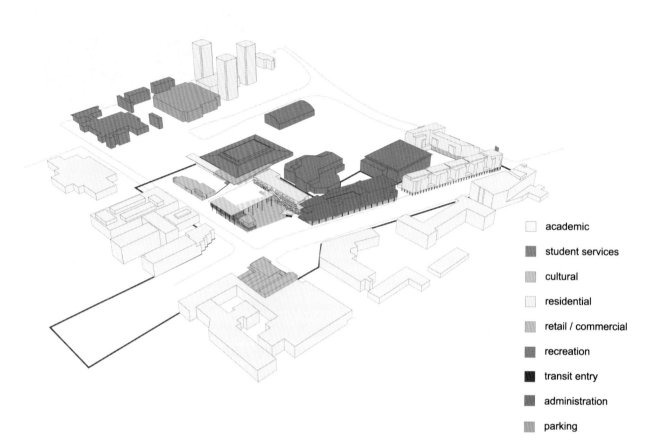

The new University
Boulevard supports a rich
mix of uses, multiple modes
of transportation, and
connects to the existing
campus fabric.

新的大学林荫大道提供了
多项功能交通用途,并与现
有校园密切连接。

academic

student services

cultural

residential

retail / commercial

recreation

transit entry

administration

parking

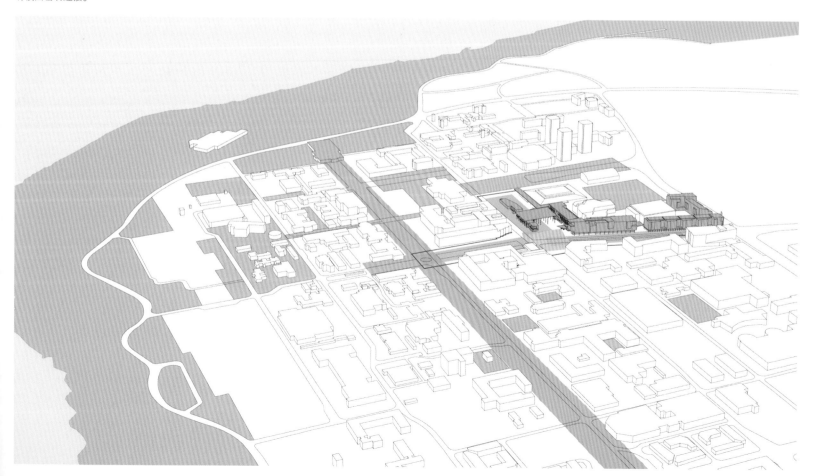

该总体规划的主旨是在大学周围创建一个林荫大道，为学校构建一个迷人的"门户"，吸引世界学子的目光。其周围的建筑群之间衔接自然，理想的室内环境能够满足学生的多种需求，并促进学生、教师及员工之间的沟通，并与气候和环境和谐共融。从林荫大道东侧延伸出的部分是一个生态示范区，通过种植本地物种以实现蓄水和净化空气的目标。

这个占地7.2公顷的开放空间能够满足各种活动的需要，无论是朋友小聚还是大型聚会，此处均是理想场所。两个新建筑中将设置一系列零售空间，为新公共空间"大学广场"的建立提供有利条件。该广场位于一个地下中转站之上，从中转站穿过一个露天中庭可到达广场之上。大学广场上集中了主要开放空间，纵横交错的通道和区域彰显了此处作为社交枢纽的独特地位。

The vision for the master plan of a new University Boulevard Neighborhood is to establish a flagship "gateway" that will welcome the world to the university. The neighborhood is effective on various scales—harmonious buildings and programs create a powerful sense of entering and inhabiting a creative district, while housing is designed to accommodate varied needs of individuals. Memorable places nurture interaction for students, faculty, and staff, as well as connecting to climate and context. The eastern extension of University Boulevard is an ecological demonstration of water collection and purification using native species.

Positively configured open spaces on the 7.2-hectare site support myriad activities, from serendipitous encounters to celebratory gatherings. Two new buildings, which will accommodate a mix of retail uses, contribute to the formation of a new public open space called "University Square". The square is positioned over an underground transit station, which can be accessed through an open-air atrium on the square. Major open spaces converge at University Square, where the weaving of paths and districts is celebrated, creating a vibrant social hub.

加拿大不列颠哥伦比亚大学
林荫大道参赛设计

University of British Columbia, Canada
UBC UNIVERSITY BOULEVARD COMPETITION

university boulevard

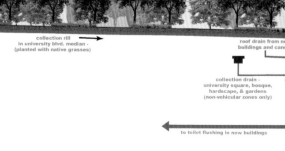

collection rill
in university blvd. median -
(planted with native grasses)

roof drain from ne
buildings and cano

collection drain -
university square, bosque,
hardscape, & gardens
(non-vehicular zones only)

to toilet flushing in new buildings

Water and landscape based
on northwestern ecology are
designed to clean and recycle
rainfall and site drainage.

水与景观是针对美洲西北生
态而设计，目的是清理和
利用回收雨水和基地排水。

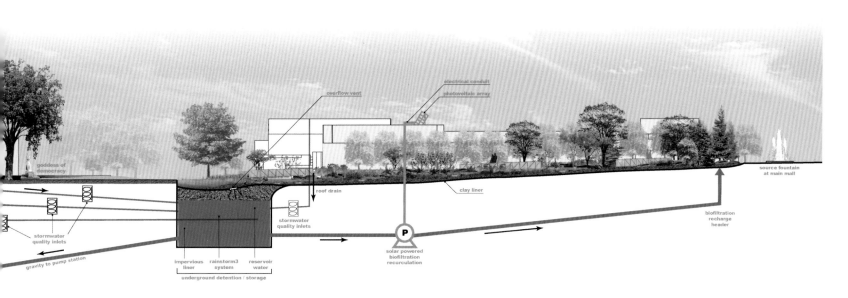

goddess of
democracy

overflow vent

electrical conduit

photovoltaic array

roof drain

clay liner

source fountain
at main mall

stormwater
quality inlets

stormwater
quality inlets

gravity to pump station

impervious
liner

rainstorm3
system

reservoir
water

underground detention / storage

P

solar powered
biofiltration
recirculation

biofiltration
recharge
header

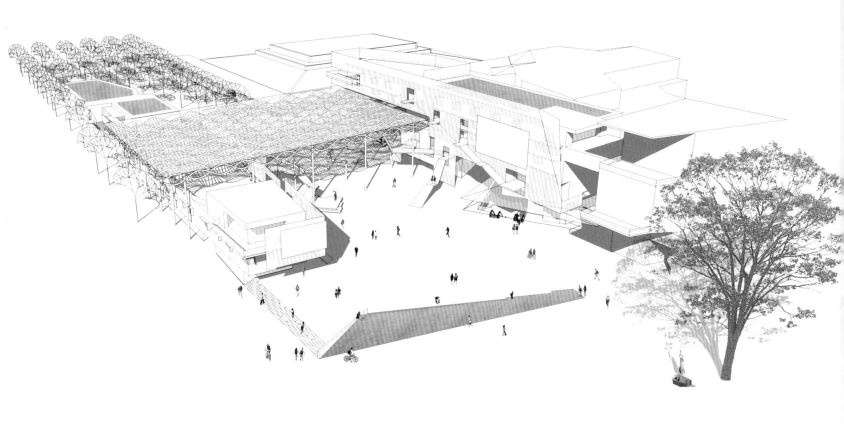

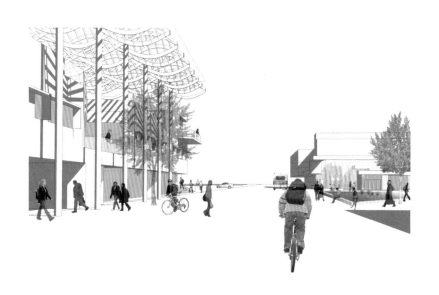

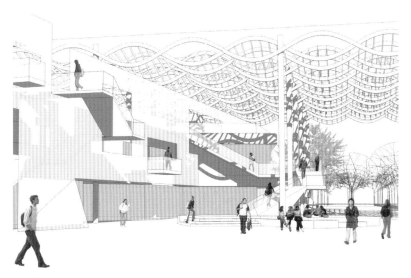

都柏林市

DUBLIN

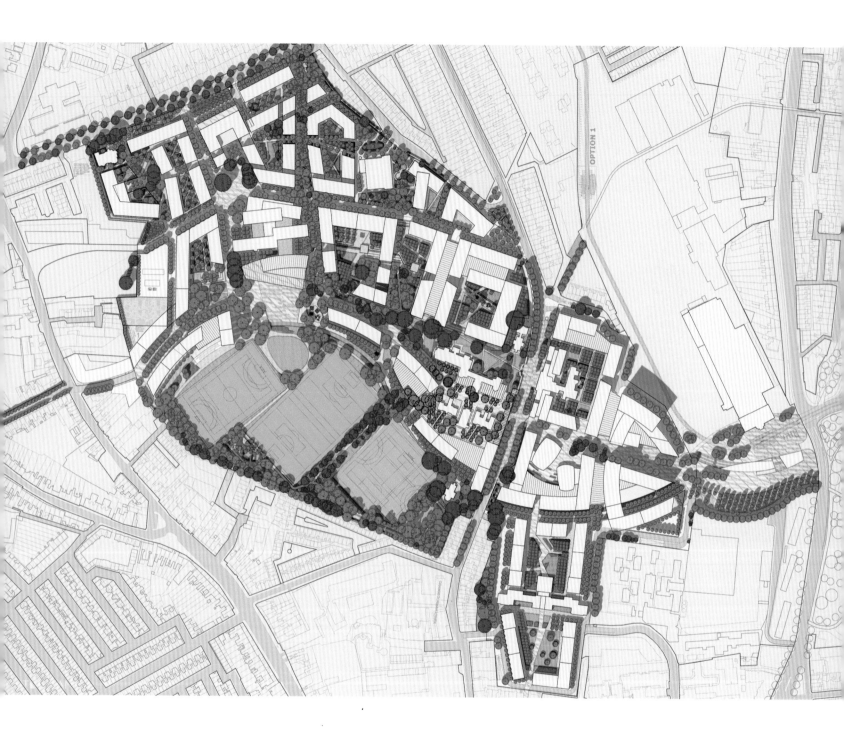

OPTION 1

爱尔兰都柏林Grangegorman总体规划方案旨在为都柏林理工学院和爱尔兰国家医疗保健服务中心设计一个新的可持续性校园环境，并保留这里悠久的历史背景，加强这一地区同城市环境之间的联系。文化花园将校园中的旧式建筑和新式建筑有机衔接了起来。该设计将为校园提供世界一流的创新型便利设施，并通过现代手法将传统的学院建筑风格进行完美诠释。

一条贯穿东西方向的步行大道上融入了许多条绿化带。该规划在校园中设置了两个主要活动中心：一处是图书馆广场，这个广场面向西侧开放，是校园的"心脏"部位。另一处是艺术论坛，旁边设有剧院、博物馆和展览画廊。而一条"主路"将校园内各处重要地点连接了起来，主路旁边通往各个建筑的"小径"绿草茵茵，生机盎然。一系列南北景观带呈径向延伸，与都柏林理工学院和爱尔兰国家医疗保健服务中心各入口相衔接。学生公寓和文化设施位于运动场边，从这里可以远眺市区景象和都柏林山脉景色。

The Grangegorman master plan creates a vibrant campus for the Dublin Institute of Technology (DIT) and Health Service Executive (HSE) by responding to the site's rich historical context and strengthening connections to the existing urban fabric. All of the standing "protected structures" within the site have been preserved and are connected to the new buildings through a Cultural Garden. The design offers world-class, innovative facilities for both DIT and HSE, enhancing their identity and image by employing a contemporary interpretation of traditional collegiate quads.

A major east-west pedestrian path seamlessly integrates with several significant green belts and circulation axes in the area. Within the campus, the master plan is focused on two centers of activity: Library Square, which serves as the "campus heart" toward the west, and the more public-oriented Arts Forum to the east, which is lined with theaters, museums and exhibition galleries. A formal "urban path" links the significant destinations on the campus while its counterpart—a "landscaped path"—provides a casual means of pedestrian circulation. A series of north-south landscape "fingers" extend radially to provide direct access to the separate DIT and HSE districts. Student housing and amenities are woven through the site along a sinuous landscape path at the edge of the sports pitches, looking out onto the city and Dublin Mountains beyond.

都柏林理工大学

Grangegorman
总体规划

Dublin Institute of Technology

GRANGEGORMAN
MASTERPLAN

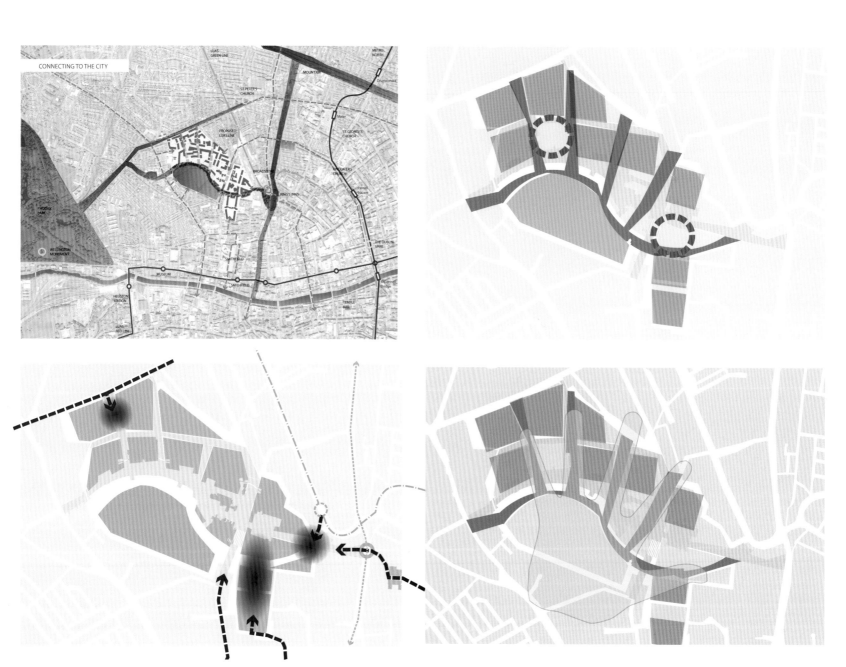

The serpentine pedestrian
spine connects two
social hearts, professional
programs, and North
Dublin neighborhoods.

蜿蜒的步道连接了两个
社区核心，专业学术区
及北都柏林社区。

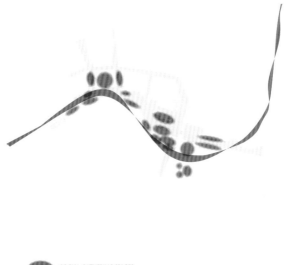

SOCIAL GATHERING SPACES

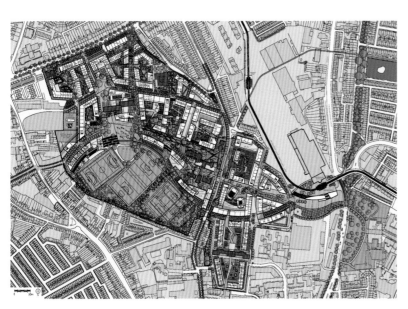

Possible Luas Stop

Possible Access

Possible Access

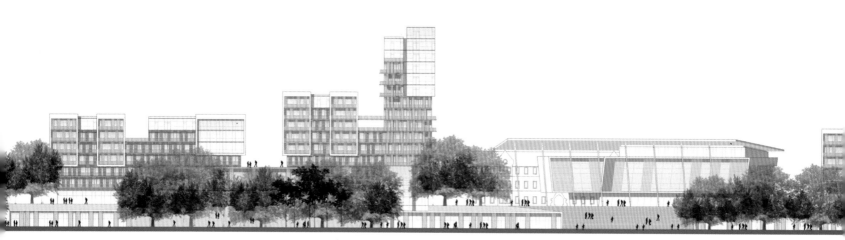

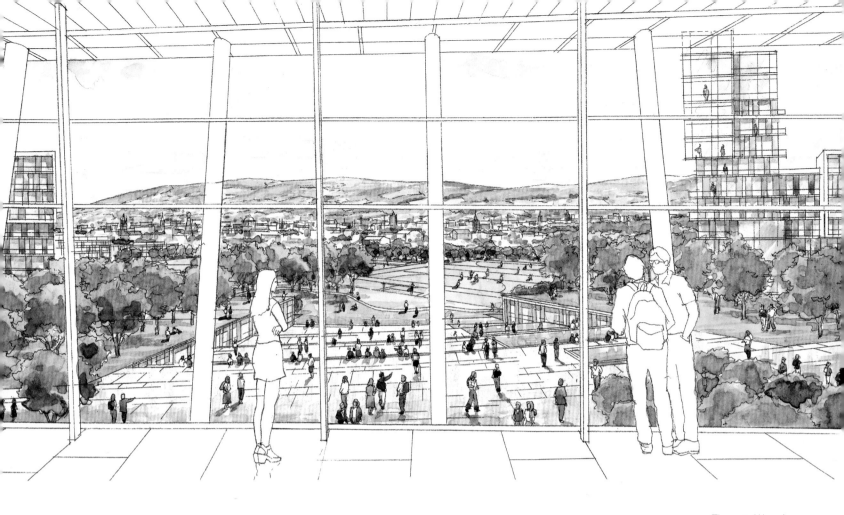

The central library's panoramic terrace looks south to the Liffey River and the Dublin Mountains.

中央图书馆的观景露台向南看到都柏林的利菲河及后方的山景。

总体规划与住宅：

MASTER PLANNING AND HOUSING

目前，我们国际建筑项目的重点是住宅及综合建筑的设计。我们的客户也遍及全世界，包括大开曼岛、马尼拉、马尔默、成都、第比利斯等不同背景的国家和地区。设计在获得市场认可的同时，更注重与项目所在地环境背景、地区文化及气候的协调，尤其是采用独特的建筑形式、城市空间和景观设计彰显社区的独特性。此外，对于亚洲日趋增长规模和密度的项目设计，我们将这些设计元素也融入其中，其成效相信在不久即将显现出来。

The principal focus of our international practice continues to be residential and mixed-use development. Working with a spectrum of enlightened developer clients we have sought to create whole-cloth places of community, in such diverse settings as Grand Cayman, Manila, Malmö, Chengdu, and Tbilisi. The work is pragmatic in terms of the marketplace—but idealistic in seeking authentic responses to urban context, regional culture, and climate. We search for patterns of community, richly expressed in a varied repertoire of built form, urban space, and landscape. The increasing scale and density of projects in Asia have indeed put these principles to the test, and the results are yet forthcoming—presented in this volume as a work-in-progress.

住宅与住宅设计

我们对住房和城市规划建筑设计的价值观和原则通过两个截然不同的实践实现了跨越式发展：量身定做的独栋住宅和欧洲社会住房。与独栋住宅客户的合作经验，令我们受益匪浅。独特的建筑外观、与气候的和谐共处、多样化的居住空间、简约宁静的室内环境等为打造优秀的住宅提供了有利条件，同时也是我们最为关注的。

我们在泰格尔港总体规划中首次采用了以社区为导向的设计方法，之后在德国勃兰登堡州的一系列项目中也同样运用了这一方法。这一德国社会住房方案系列项目中涉及了250至5000个住宅单位不等。这些项目的设计起初作为参赛作品，随后通过与城市规划师，景观建筑师和客户进行合作得以完成。

HOUSES AND HOUSING

The values and principles we bring to housing and urban development have evolved through two extremely divergent practices: custom single-family homes, and European social housing. Working with house clients helped us understand a range of issues that might apply to all residential clients—even the anonymous ones. Regional identity, expressive response to climate, multiple scales of habitation, and a degree of simplicity or serenity that enables inhabitants to "read into" and add to the character of the setting—to make it their home—all became deeply important to us.

Our particular approach to housing as community-oriented planning first emerged with our Tegel Harbor Master Plan, and later with a series of projects in the former East German state of Brandenburg. Projects ranging from 250 to 5,000 units offered opportunities under Germany's "social housing" program—a unique partnership of public and private financing that peaked in the 1990's. While these projects began as design competitions, their further development became a process of collaboration with city planners, landscape architects, and our clients.

从早期现代主义中学习

社会住房是20世纪早期现代主义构想的关注重点，社区在20世纪八九十年代扮演了重要角色，其传奇项目工程包括由布鲁诺·陶特设计的汤姆叔叔的小屋和布里茨马蹄社区等，这些建筑的某些设计理念至今仍为适用并得以传承，诸如可持续发展的原则：建筑朝向和采光，规模的适中，建筑与开放空间的平衡。

另外一个经典的案例是对柏林周围地区传统城镇和郊区的社区设计。这些早期的以交通为导向的社区以商业、教育和公共场所形成的自然层次结构为特征。随着基础设施的升级，这些内部郊区社区仍然具有高度可持续性。

LEARNING FROM EARLY MODERNISM

Social housing was central to the formulation of early 20th century modernism, and the siedlung became paradigmatic for our work throughout the 1980's and 90's. Legendary pioneering works such as Onkel-Toms-Huette and the Britz Hufeisen Siedlung by Bruno Taut and others established principles that today would be seen as sustainable: building orientation and spacing for daylight, with efficient residential units whose modest size was compensated by a generous balance of building and open space.

The other great paradigm for our purposes was the siedlung's complement—the classic repertoire of traditional towns and green suburbs in and around Berlin. These early transit-oriented communities featured a natural hierarchy of public places activated by commercial, educational, and civic functions. With a few infrastructural upgrades, these inner-suburb communities are still highly sustainable.

EXPANDING CHOICES

A further influence on the Berlin/Brandenburg projects was California—or at least the sunny, free-spirited impression of Southern California that prevailed among our clients. Even the toughest, most bottom-line oriented developers looked to us for qualities distinctly missing in most public housing projects: warmth, color, surprise, and most importantly freedom of choice. While social housing requirements and economics tended to endless repetition, we shaped and combined the limited range of unit types into a variety of formats—small villas, town house courts, mews, and perimeter block patterns that framed gardens, streets, and squares. Inhabitants were offered options—both where to dwell and where to gather. The deepest principles that emerged in projects such as Tegel Harbor and Karow Nord—which we seek to apply to all our housing—are community and diversity.

SCALES OF HABITATION

There is a fractal-like, recursive continuity in human settlements—with nested scales of boundaries, networks, centers, and gatherings. Viewed from satellites, African villages gather circular huts in circular arrangements; Western cities place rectilinear spaces within cubic shells within patchworks of orthogonal grids. At the experiential level, a private window seat looks onto a garden, just as a cafe looks onto a square. We inhabit rooms, edges, centers, passages, and landscapes, both large and small. Organic, historic towns offer just such a gradient—a repertoire of intermediate places that enrich the transition between public and private—giving us the diversity of choice.

On a grand scale our Serendra Housing in Manila operates like a Spanish baroque villa. At the center a foyer of retail shops provides a mixer for visitors and residents of the project. Flanking this central hall are two great rooms—garden courts framed by 6–12 story blocks of condominiums, their balcony-lined walls sliding in and out in steps and undulations. These green rooms are "furnished" with clubhouse pavilions and swimming pools. At the outer edges are the tallest elements—residential towers that offer views out and beyond the sprawling urban development of Fort Bonifacio to the landscape surrounding the city.

扩大选择

影响柏林/勃兰登堡项目的另外一个因素是加州,或者可以说是南加州阳光、自由奔放的印象。在这里,建筑即使缺少了其他地区公共建筑中必不可少的魅力、色彩、惊喜等品质,也不能缺少自由气息。为应对复杂多变的社会住房需求和经济形式,我们将有限的单位类型转变为各种形式——小别墅、乡镇联排小屋、车房及构成花园、街道和广场的周边建筑等。居民们可在此居住和集会。在泰格尔港和卡罗诺德的项目中,最重要也是最深刻的设计原则是将社区化和多样性完美融入到每个建筑之中。

居住尺度

人类住宅具有零散的循环连续性的特点。从卫星上看,非洲的民居呈圆形布局;西方城市中的立方体建筑则采用直线型排列。从经验角度上讲,一个靠窗的座位能够将下方的花园景致尽收眼底,其视觉体验与从一个咖啡厅遥看广场雷同。无论面积大小,房间、边界、中心、通道和风景均是我们居住空间中不可或缺的部分。结构完整的历史城镇也同样具有梯度之美,巧妙地利用过渡空间实现公共空间与私人空间的自然衔接。

马尼拉的Serendra住宅犹如一栋西班牙巴洛克式别墅。位于中央门厅的零售商店为到访者和居住者提供了一个丰富的综合性空间。中央大厅的两端设有两个由6-12层公寓建筑构建出的园区,建筑的阳台呈阶梯状排列,充满动态之感。这些绿色的客房均配有会所和游泳池。最外围的最高建筑是住宅大楼,能够将博尼法乔堡的城市景观尽收眼底。

连接城市
自然景观

衔接和连续性将新建区域和发展区与其周围环境融为一体，并从视觉角度将景观和城市以外地区联系在一起。在接手一个新项目之初，设计遇到的第一个问题可能是资金问题，也可能是选址依据等问题。答案应该是该项目所在地的独特性，独特的地域性是设计的出发点。

甚至于一个高密度社区的成功设计亦可得益于对其周边环境的参考。重庆春森彼岸的滨河位置不单单是一个简单的设计背景，同时更是设计的原因所在：事实上，该项目的总体目标是为居民营造一个优美的滨水居住空间。不仅仅关乎景色，同时涉及该规划的整体构造、为居民和访客打造的河滨广场等。该项目在中国颇受关注，其蜿蜒迂回、错落有致的排列与嘉陵江湍湍的水流遥相呼应。6-12层楼及塔楼建筑在波光粼粼的水面上投下清晰的倒影，二者交相辉映，美不胜收。

住房建设的核心目的是为人们提供住宅空间。即使再小的房屋规划也可以看作是公共场所的陪衬或框架。圣莫尼卡市区住宅建筑为历史性市政厅、县法院、市立会议厅、新公园提供了城市背景。同时，从该建筑中能够欣赏到开放绿地至太平洋和市区码头以外的景致。多样化的城市公共建筑、娱乐区、商业区等形成了一个在城市结构上，几乎能媲美欧洲的南加州小城镇。

CONNECTIONS TO URBAN NATURAL CONTEXT

Connection and continuity allow new districts and developments to partake of their surroundings—to expand visually into the landscape or the city beyond. When approaching a new site, the first question for design—possibly for financing as well—is simply "why build here?" The answer should say something about the special opportunities of the site—opportunities that can and must inform the design at the deepest level.

Even the most brutally high-density development can benefit from the specifics of its setting. Chun Sen Bi An's riverfront site in Chongqing is not simply a context—it is rather a pretext: indeed the whole purpose of the project is to bring the inhabitants to the experience of the waterfront. This is not simply a matter of views, but of the whole shaping of the plan, and the provision of a grand, 5th-story waterfront esplanade for residents and visitors. The project has become famous in China specifically because its many towers are not lined up in a grid—they twist and turn as if caught in the Jialing river's currents. The river flow is further mirrored in the curves of 6—12 story housing that mediates the scale of the towers while shaping a series of gardens.

While housing has a central function of its own—residence—it also comprises the principal building material of the city. Even smaller housing developments can take on special importance as liners and frames for public places. Santa Monica's Civic Center Housing helps to establish an urban surround for the historic City Hall, a county courthouse, the civic auditorium, and a new park. In return the project enjoys a beautiful prospect across open green space to the Pacific Ocean and the Municipal Pier beyond. Its urban connections have to do with linking diverse civic, recreational, and commercial functions, forming a remarkably urban—almost European—hybrid of place for a southern California town.

NARRATIVE STRUCTURE AND CHOREOGRAPHY

Just as urban projects, like houses, have entrances, great halls, secondary rooms, and openings out to places beyond, they can also tell a story. The front door of our master planned town center, Camana Bay New Town on Grand Cayman Island, is a retail street, lined with two-story arcades and loggias, shaded by moveable canopies and animated by visitors, palm trees, water sculptures, graphics, and festive multi-colored lighting at night. Cross streets extend laterally past interior courtyard gardens, through breezeways and porches, and out to the edges of the blocks.

At the center the procession leads from a new tree-lined boulevard up the shopping street to a new waterfront lined with restaurants, overlooked by apartments and hotel rooms. The waterfront itself opens onto a lagoon with schools and houses on the opposite shore. This narrative of unfolding, leading, opening, and connecting gives a sense of grander scale and continuity than Camana Bay's seven or eight blocks would otherwise imply. The density of events, details, colors, and textures breaks up the unified character that a newly built development inevitably poses (fig. 1).

叙述结构和编排　　与城市综合项目类似，住宅中同样设有入口、大厅、出口等，每一个场所均能够讲述一个故事。位于大开曼岛上的卡玛纳湾新城的前门是一条零售街道，两旁设有两层楼的商场和凉廊，可移动檐篷能够为人们有效遮蔽强光，棕榈树、水雕塑、彩绘以及喜庆多彩色夜灯将此处装点得美轮美奂。十字街道呈横向延伸经过内部庭院花园之后，穿过通风廊和门廊，最后抵达建筑的边界。

在中央地带，这种布局从一个绿意盎然的林荫大道经过购物街最后一直延伸至新建的滨水区，其两端林立的餐厅，与上方的公寓和酒店房间遥遥相对。滨水区与潟湖相通，其对岸设有学校和住宅。这种伸展、导向、开放和衔接过程凸显出项目规模的宏大和持续性。活动、细节、色彩、质地打破了单调、统一的风格，一个独具匠心的特色建筑无疑将成为人们关注的焦点。（图1）

fig. 1

设计流程与
对真谛的探索

从任何标准来看，卡玛纳湾都是一个与众不同的项目。我们的设计团队从参赛到总体规划直至初步设计，大约历经14年之久。虽然时间很长，我们和客户对建筑的标准并没有因此而动摇，其精湛的设计手法和细节令我们联想到另一个环境制造者——迪士尼幻想工程。

当然，环境并不是建筑的全部主题。空间构造的设计灵感源自两种源泉。一种是大开曼岛的气候与建筑的历史特征，即建筑与佛罗里达群岛新市镇的联系。第二个设计灵感是可持续性，强调空间的历久弥新，建筑与艺术和景观的衔接。气候和耐久性这两个原则是卡玛纳湾的设计语言。

材料经过认真探讨和测试，才得以采用，以应对独特的海洋环境。空间强调自然通风。零售顾问对西棕榈滩这样的综合性项目进行了全面考察和研究。我们的设计伙伴，奥林顾问公司的景观建筑师，也对材料进行了谨慎筛选。虽然14年看似很长一段时间，卡玛纳湾真正的设计时间并不算长，毕竟传统的建筑风格和城市化至少需要几百年才能实现。

相较于卡玛纳湾，商业建筑设计则较为匆忙。幸运的是，先前的设计经验可以对这种短时间的项目设计提供有力的帮助。但是，无论项目规模和设计时间长短，我们仍旧致力于住房和城市规划建筑的设计，能够为住户营造温馨的居住空间，为团体构建惬意、舒适的公共空间，我们乐此不疲。

DESIGN PROCESS AND THE SEARCH FOR AUTHENTICITY

By any standards Camana Bay is a highly unusual project. Our team's efforts from competition to master plan to early design and through construction span over 14 years. During this period our client's commitment to quality did not erode—indeed it was accented: the level of craft and detail reminds us of another great maker of environments—Disney Imagineering.

Yet the environment is not arbitrarily "themed". The fabric of place is created out of two great passions. One is the climate of Grand Cayman and the kind of architecture it has historically fostered—an architecture with significant links to the towns of the Florida Keys. A second passion has been sustainability—simply to build to last, with equal concern for architecture, art and landscape. With these two principles—climate and longevity—the language of Camana Bay slowly unfolded through iteration after iteration.

Materials were explored and tested—many rejected as inadequate in the marine environment. Details of urban design were subjected to computer-based wind studies, with the goal of meaningful natural cooling. Retail consultants thoroughly researched the most relevant comparisons to mixed-use precedents, like West Palm Beach, with long histories of success. Landscape architects, our colleagues at Olin Partnership, were on the project long enough to use select materials they and our clients had established in local nurseries years before construction. While 14 years may seem like a long time, the essence of the Camana Bay design process has been an effort to evolve in a few years what traditional architecture and urbanism has taken centuries to achieve: an authentic way of building in a specific place.

In comparison to Camana Bay, more typical commercial projects are designed on a fast-track, driven by shorter-term economics. Fortunately, the lessons learned from such a remarkable urban laboratory can be relevant to other, less time-intensive efforts. But regardless of the process imposed by scale or schedule, we remain committed to housing and urban development that is devoted to the experience of the inhabitants, and to the celebration of place and community.

马尔默市

MALMÖ

探戈住宅项目对密度和可持续性的综合运用堪称是住宅项目设计的成功典范。作为2001年Bo-01欧洲住宅展览的一部分，该项目中设置了27个租赁单元，每一个单元的平面布局各具特色，均能够透过开阔的玻璃窗口欣赏到中央花园园景。简约、低调的建筑风格与周围的城市建筑自然融为一体。在内部，生机勃勃的彩色单体建筑围绕庭院进行微妙地转动，仿佛舞者轻盈的舞姿，也是该建筑名称的由来。

每个单元的客厅在建筑中扮演重要角色。从花园中"借入"一部分空间到室内，将室内空间从视觉角度进行延伸，营造通透、开阔之感。此外，玻璃墙体成功将室外景致与室内相结合，淡化了内外空间的界限。连接住宅核心和户外庭院的桥梁横跨于湿地之上，与周围景观自然融为一体。

该建筑采用了最先进的信息技术和可持续设计理念。每个单元均设计了一个独特的"智能墙"：一个木板隔墙创造了多样化布局的条件。这个"智能墙"与探戈住宅的电力和能源使用率检测仪相连接。屋顶表面覆以草皮和光电板，能够对室温进行有效调节，同时为大楼提供足够的能源供给。

The Tango Housing project is unprecedented in its successful synthesis of density and sustainability. Created as a part of the 2001 Bo-01 European Housing Exhibition, it includes 27 rental units, each with its own unique floor plan that allows a view of the central landscaped garden through generously glazed towers. The exterior perimeter of the structure relates to the surrounding urban fabric with its simple yet sophisticated elevations. On the interior, the playful and vibrantly colored individual building masses turn slightly as they step around the courtyard in a dance-like movement that inspired the project's name.

The living room of each unit occupies part of a tower, "borrowing" space from the garden while making the units feel more spacious. To the same effect, entire walls of glass open onto the garden, allowing the units to literally flow into the landscape. Bridges link the residential cores to the outdoor courtyard, passing above an expanse of marshy land that reflects the flora of the nearby sound.

The building offers an array of state-of-the-art sustainability and information technology features. Each unit is fitted with a specially designed "intelligent wall": a dividing wood panel that houses several functional attributes in a modular design that allows for various plan layouts. The wall is also connected to Tango's custom technology network, which monitors the details of power and energy use throughout the day. The roof surfaces are covered with grass and photovoltaic panels that provide passive heating and cooling for the building and produce more than 100% of the building's energy needs.

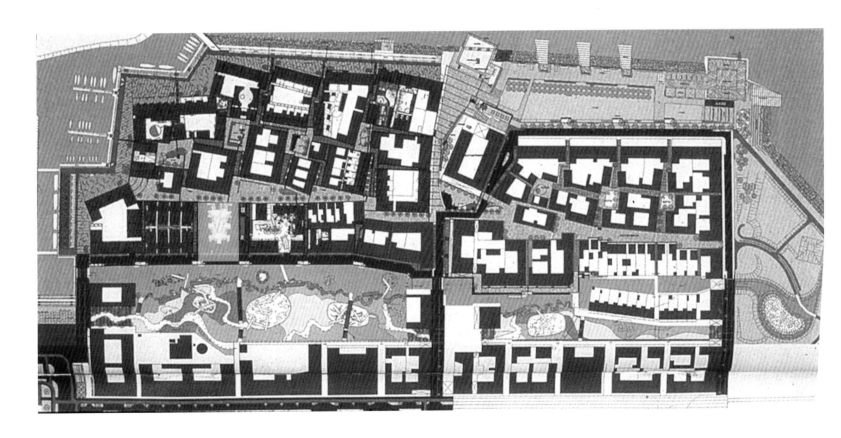

瑞典，马尔默

探戈Bo01住宅设计展览

Malmö, Sweden

TANGO BO01 HOUSING EXHIBITION

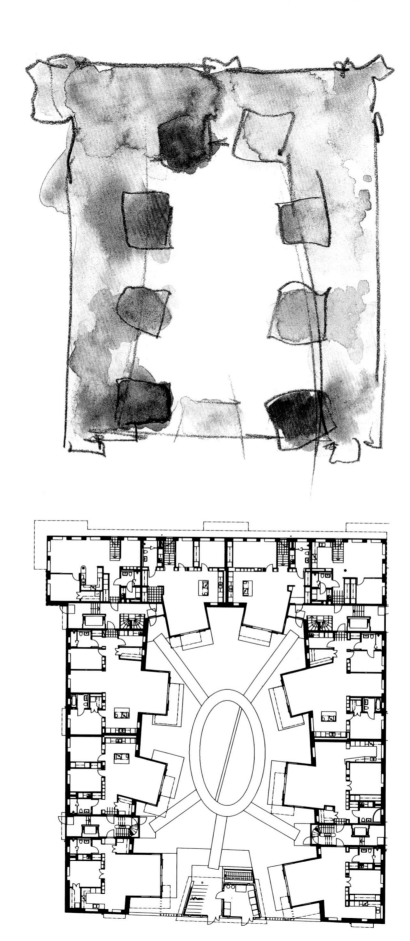

TANGO BO01 HOUSING EXHIBITION 探戈BO01住宅设计展览

TANGO BO01 HOUSING EXHIBITION 探戈BO01住宅设计展览

圣莫尼卡市
SANTA MONICA

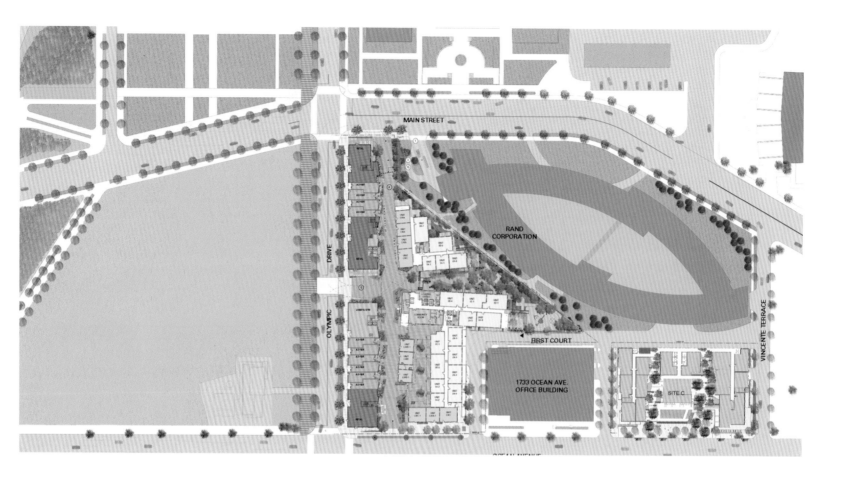

A mix of affordable and
market housing creates the
fine grain of walkable streets
and lanes.

以不同的经济房型及市场需
求房型住宅，营造出一个精
致的行人步道及小径。

圣莫尼卡社区位于圣莫尼卡市中心，占地12,141平方米，集325个住宅单元、零售网点、开放空间于一体。该项目毗邻市政厅和法院以及酒店、商业建筑和拟建的公园。该总体规划旨在平衡和优化设计元素的配置，加强建筑与周围环境的衔接。

在圣莫尼卡这个高密度城市，交通、停车、建筑高度限制等问题在设计中扮演的角色越来越重要。该建筑在对周围环境进行周密考察之后，以城市结构为设计背景，打造了一个风格独特的可持续发展社区，获得公众的好评，该项目为全国其他地区的综合性社区建设提供了示范作用。

Santa Monica Village is a synthesis of 325 housing units, retail outlets, and open spaces, located on a three-acre site in the heart of Santa Monica's Civic Center. The site is centrally located—adjacent to the town City Hall and Courts, hotels, commercial structures, and a proposed garden park. The master plan for this development addresses this spectacular context by balancing and optimizing the configuration of programmatic elements to foster a sense of neighborhood.

In a city of Santa Monica's density, the issues of traffic, parking, and building height limits become increasingly critical. A well-organized community input process played a valuable role in resolving different views and helped to give the project an identity that is rooted in its Santa Monica context. With the ambitious housing strategy program set by the City and the commitment to building a sustainable community, this development can serve as a remarkable prototype for mixed-income living nationwide.

加利福尼亚州，圣莫尼卡市
圣莫尼卡社区住宅

Santa Monica, California,
SANTA MONICA VILLAGE

SANTA MONICA

RETAIL 110
582 SF

UP

Unit 101 (2/1)
766 SF

Unit 102 (2/1)
766 SF

Unit 103 (3/2)
1014 SF

GAS MTRS

LAUNDRY
113 SF

ELEVATOR
SHAFT

TRASH
ROOM &
CHUTES

COMMUNITY ROOM
1133 SF

DN

Unit 104 (3/2)
1012 SF

OVERHEAD GARAGE DOOR

Unit 106 (3/2)
1002 SF

GARAGE
ENTRY

UP

DN

C4 ZONE

TRASH STAGING
ROOM
250 SF

Unit 105 (3/2)
1043 SF

Affordable housing on
a small site creates a
rich variety of units and
community uses.

经济型的住宅设计在这
不大的基地上创造出不
同的房型及社区功能。

该项目旨在为圣莫尼卡非营利性机构社区于笔克大道和28号大街交口处创建经济适用型住宅。这一综合性城市项目中设有33个住宅单元以及下方的零售店和围绕活动庭院布局的社区空间。该项目的建立将为住户、周边地区及城市生活注入勃勃生机，通过亲切的城市立面设计，使笔克大道和28号大街重新绽放活力。

建筑的体量呈阶梯式设计，由二层至四层不等。位于北侧立面的断点为行人提供了入口，并巧妙地将繁忙的笔克大道街景引入到内部庭院之中。在28号大街一侧的立面，一个两层的建筑作为社区活动室之一，打破了建筑的巨大体量所带来的沉重、单调之感，并将海风引入到室内，从而加强空间的通风。建筑以一层作为根基，上层采用分层凹凸的外墙板设计手法以降低建设成本。墙壁上的花纹窗户呈纵向和横向或环形设置，确保空间内部光线的充足。建筑材料的选用遵循简约、淳朴的原则，以彩色水泥板为主。

庭院的设立有效促进了社区之间的交流，将桥梁、通道和楼梯巧妙地衔接在一起，匠心独运。与笔克大道入口处同侧的社交中心，位于庭院的中央，而庭院则由社区活动室、洗衣房、主楼梯、电梯和儿童游乐场等空间所环绕。

This project provides 100% affordable housing at the corner of Pico Boulevard and 28th Street for the nonprofit organization Community Corporation of Santa Monica. This mixed-use urban project accommodates 33 units above active retail and community space organized around an engaging courtyard. The project strives to contribute to the life of its residents, neighbors and the City, by providing a pedestrian-friendly urban facade to enliven the corner of Pico and 28th streets.

The building is configured as an ensemble of stepped volumes ranging from two to four floors. A break in the urban facade on the north provides pedestrian access and engages the interior courtyard with the street life along Pico. On the 28th Street facade, a two-story volume accommodating a community room helps to break down the mass of the building and allows the ocean breeze to create naturally ventilated spaces. The architectural design emphasizes economy by using a layering approach of projected and recessed planes, with the ground floor expressed as a strong base. The walls are punched with a pattern of windows articulated as vertical, horizontal or wrapped openings. The simple palette of materials includes multicolored cement board panels.

The courtyard optimizes social interaction and incorporates a playful array of bridges, walkways and stairs. Aligned with the entrance from Pico Boulevard, a social hub is created at the heart of the courtyard surrounded by the community room, laundry, main stairs and elevator that surround a children's play area.

加利福尼亚州，圣莫尼卡市

笔克大道2802号住宅

Santa Monica, California

2802 PICO HOUSING

圣莫尼卡市
SANTA MONICA

这个位于百老汇大街606号的六层综合性建筑为圣莫尼卡市区增添了一道魅力景观。通透式的外观设计能够确保空间四面通透，与周围环境自然融为一体。建筑位于两条街道的交叉口，立面富于变幻，与所在街区的格调相得益彰。北侧的一层空间设置了若干零售区，为行人的出入提供便利；西侧则主要为住宅区，采用外墙退缩式设计手法，确保空间的私密性。中央庭园中设有娱乐室、健身房、休息室等便利设施。

该建筑包括53个单元，面积从65平方米至93平方米不等，并伴有几套两层阁楼公寓户型，其中一部分的单元将指定为经济型平民住宅。私人露台有效地加强了室内的采光和通风，令空间时刻沐浴在温暖的阳光下，来自海洋的清风则能够促进空间的空气流通，令室内时刻空气清新。建筑的两侧，顶端错落有致的阳台和玻璃凸窗将楼上空间进行有机衔接，并巧妙地优化了观景廊空间，人们于此能够将圣莫尼卡山脉和太平洋美景尽收眼底。屋顶上的太阳能光电板能够为建筑提供额外的能源供给，符合城市可持续发展方针的要求。

606 Broadway animates a revitalized urban area of Santa Monica with a memorable, six-story, mixed-use infill development. The porous design is open on all sides to the surrounding neighborhoods and integrates seamlessly with community life. The project design responds to the different characteristics of the two bordering streets, reflecting and reinforcing their identity within the urban fabric. The north side of the project is retail-oriented along the ground floor and supports pedestrian activity, while the west side of the building has a more residential quality and is set back from the street for a sense of privacy. Amenities include a recreation room, an exercise facility, and a lobby area that is oriented toward the central garden court.

The 53 units range in size from 700 to 1000 sf, with some two-story loft apartments, of which a percentage is designated affordable housing. The light-filled units have large private balconies that create an open feel and welcome ocean breezes into the apartments. On both sides of the building, the upper floors are articulated by a syncopated rhythm of balconies and glassy bays that optimize the view corridors toward the Santa Monica Mountains and Pacific Ocean. Photovoltaic panels provide an additional energy source for the building and meet the City's sustainability guidelines.

COURTYARD

Market rate apartments are given a sense of dignity and identity through the weaving of scales and materials.

专为房屋市场设计的公寓利用不同的尺度与材质创造出高尚的风格。

加利福尼亚州，圣莫尼卡市
百老汇大街606号住宅

Santa Monica, California,
606 BROADWAY HOUSING

天津市

TIANJIN

天津新河总体规划，占地250公顷，在人造湖岛屿周围创建一系列建筑。每个住宅区的设计风格由其中设置的住宅大楼风格和周围的环境条件而定。多样化的住宅类型、休憩用地、设施和娱乐等空间大大丰富了住户的生活。

住宅楼宇间的公共空间部分，诸如户外表演空间、博物馆、图书馆、剧场、游乐场、幼儿园、商场、展馆、茶馆等为住户提供了最佳休闲去处。住宅空间的尺度丰富多样，休憩用地和水景、建筑体量和高度以及建筑之间的距离设计均衡，公共广场及散步广场共同打造了宁静的庭院。

The Tianjin Xin-He masterplan, located on a 250-hectare site, designates a series of themed neighborhoods on islands within a man-made lake. The character of each neighborhood is defined by the types of residential buildings it contains, as well as the surrounding environmental conditions. The lives of the residents are enriched by the variety of housing types, open spaces, amenities, and recreational opportunities.

Neighborhood-scaled amenities are interspersed within the residential blocks to allow for convenient, walkable access. These include a range of outdoor performance spaces, a museum, a library, and a theater, as well as playgrounds, kindergarten schools, retail spaces, pavilions, and tea houses. Designed at multiple scales of habitation, open spaces and water features, building massing and heights, and the space between buildings are carefully balanced to frame vistas, animate public plazas and promenades, and create serene courtyards.

中国，天津

天津新河总体规划

Tianjin, China

TIANJIN XIN-HE
MASTERPLAN

Neighborhood
Retail Area

500 m
5 minutes

500 m
5 minutes

500 m
5 minutes

500 m
5 minutes

500 m
5 minutes

500 m
5 minutes

Outdoor Market
Retail Street

Shopping Center

Community Retail /
Markets

亲和的人性尺度
Intimate Human Scale

Vehicular Access

Vehicular Access

Vehicular Access

Main Pedestrian Access

入口
Gateway Elements

入口和地标
Gateways and Landmarks

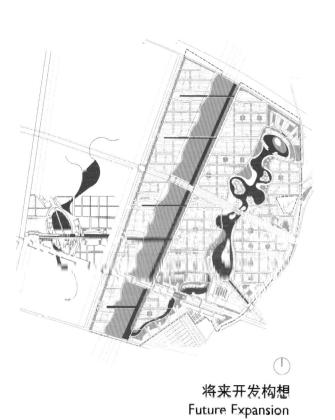

将来开发构想
Future Expansion

延续性的流动
Continuous Movement

大连市

DALIAN

A stony pedestrian path
meanders down from the
hilltop terrace to a retail
center at the shore.

石板行人步道从山顶露台
蜿蜒至岸边商业中心。

琥珀湾度假村位于中国主要港口城市大连外围的辽东半岛之上。依山傍水，背靠千山山脉，西邻渤海，东面黄海。该建筑糅合了传统的风水理念，设有10间别墅，58,000平方米的联体别墅、公寓单元、会所、娱乐中心和零售店。琥珀湾度假村将成为以与自然相和谐为重点的中国沿海住宅规划的典范。建筑有效利用地形特征，最大限度地开放空间以降低建筑的密集度。

The Amber Bay Resort is a located on a spectacular site on the Liaodong Peninsula, outside the leading port city of Dalian, China. The serene site is backed by the Qianshan Mountain range and bordered by the Bohai Sea to the west and the Yellow Sea to the east. This breathtaking peninsula location provides views and access to an expansive beach toward the southwest, and to a picturesque ravine leading to a more secluded beach to the northeast. The siting protectively embraces the project in the tradition of Feng Shui. The project will include ten villas; 58,000 square meters of townhouse and condominium units; clubhouse/recreational amenities; and retail components. Amber Bay Resort will create a new paradigm for coastal residential development in China by focusing on respect for the land and harmony with nature. This is achieved through a design that maximizes the sense of openness and reduces the apparent density by closely relating the building masses to the existing geography.

中国，大连
琥珀湾度假村

Dalian, China
AMBER BAY RESORT MASTERPLAN

AMBER BAY RESORT MASTERPLAN　琥珀湾度假村

马尼拉

MANILA

Serendra总体规划占地121,406平方米，集商业和住宅功能于一体，专为年轻专业人士和新家庭打造。该项目围绕一个零售广场和中央景观地带进行布局，这两部分同时将两个住宅区进行衔接。空间外观设计巧妙，匠心独运的通道和精致的入口有效增强了人们的互动。

该项目为避免重复之感，巧妙地将建筑进行迂回式设计，并在建筑之间打造了通风廊，使优美的景观贯穿于整个建筑。在每一个扇形区域、衔接自然的景观和水景中均设置了休闲和娱乐设施。日托中心、健身中心、网球场、羽毛球和壁球馆以及游泳池的设立大大丰富了住户的生活。这个坐落于马尼拉地区的现代化高级中心将为该地的未来住宅规划提供良好的示范作用。

The Serendra masterplan is located on a 30-acre site and synthesizes commercial and residential uses for young professionals and new families. The project is organized around a Retail Plaza and central Landscape Spine, which flow together and unify the two residential sectors. The artful shaping of spaces, paths of movement, and qualities of entry work together to support creative interaction at multiple scales.

The design avoids a feeling of repetition by allowing the blocks to curve in a sinuous fashion and breaking them at intervals with breezeways, which allow for a multitude of vistas throughout the entire site. Within each sector, a series of connected landscape and water features accommodate a wide variety of leisure and recreational activities. A number of amenities, such as a daycare center, fitness facilities, multi-purpose courts for tennis, badminton and racquetball, and pool areas, are provided to enrich the lives of residents. The project's benefits to the larger Manila region establish this area as a modernized, well-equipped center that will serve as an excellent precedent for future residential development in the region.

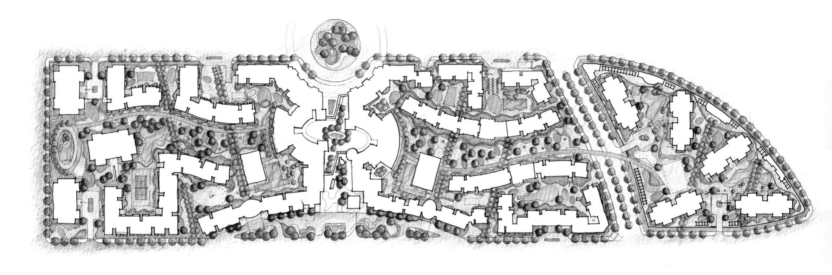

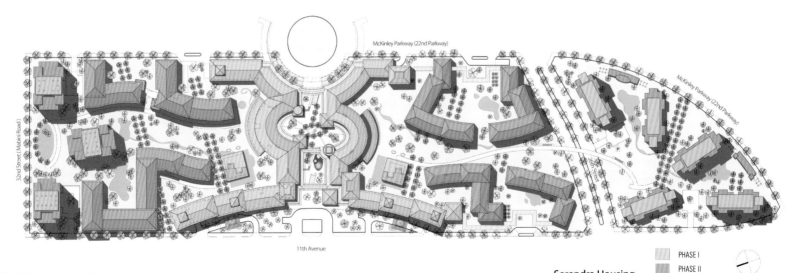

Park-like gardens provide an urban oasis of serenity and security.

公园般的社区花园,提供了一个宁静安全的城市绿洲。

Serendra Housing
Manila, The Philippines

PHASE I
PHASE II
PHASE III

0   50 m

菲律宾，马尼拉市，博尼法西奥堡区
Serendra总体规划

Fort Bonifacio City, Manila, The Phillipines
SERENDRA MASTERPLAN

SERENDRA MASTERPLAN SERENDRA总体规划

成都市

CHENGDU

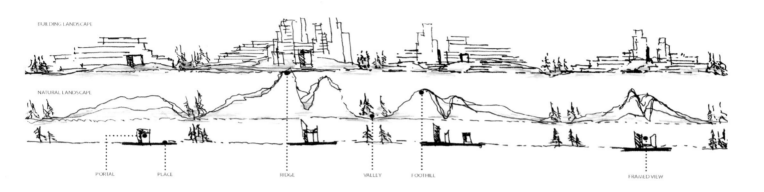

BUILDING LANDSCAPE

NATURAL LANDSCAPE

PORTAL   PLACE   RIDGE   VALLEY   FOOTHILL   FRAMED VIEW

The hilly landscape becomes
a metaphor for shaping
multiple scales of habitation
and community.

多样化的住宅和社区外观
设计与丘陵景观相得益
彰。

麓湖新城位于成都历史中心的正南端，周围绿草茵茵、生机盎然，与远处的梯田果园交相辉映。为体现成都的水文化特点，该建筑与所在地区的低地新湖相互交织。原绿化带和扩建的景观为建筑提供了优良的环境背景。工作、娱乐和生活区共享新湖正面，并通过波状的快速道、优雅的桥梁、开阔的人行道和自行车车道、巴士和水上的士有机衔接在一起。

总体规划旨在创建一个风格独具的社区，每部分空间根据地形特征和湖边景致而风格各异。光线和水景对建筑类型产生了很大影响。无论是别墅、联体别墅，还是中高层建筑或超高层建筑均被景观花园、游憩区、会所、人行道和自行车道和滨水大道所围绕。

建筑与景观的和谐一致是该项目的特点所在。自然丘陵和山脉、梯田式耕地、水和土地之间的相互作用为建筑营造了完美的环境背景。每一个特色区域景观都是建筑的创作灵感源泉之一，在建筑的整体设计中扮演重要角色。

Located due south of Chengdu's historic center, the new town of Luxe Lakes occupies verdant land characterized by flat flooded fields interwoven amongst low, evenly spaced hills crowned with woods and terraced orchards. Consistent with Chengdu's reputation as a region focused on water with a relaxed lifestyle, the new city—a garden city—will be intimately intertwined with a new lake created within the lowlands of the site. The native land is honored through preservation of significant green belts and the extensive landscaping forming the context for the built environment. Work, play and live districts all share extensive lake frontage and will be interconnected through gracefully contoured roadways, elegant bridges, extensive pedestrian and bicycle trails, shuttle buses and water taxis.

The master plan envisions the development of a collection of neighborhoods, each defined by the special nature of its relationship to the land's topography and the water of the lake. Access to the sun and views of the lake greatly influenced placement of the wide variety of housing types—from villas and townhouses to mid-rise and high-rise options—all set within a generous landscape of parks, community gardens, recreational areas, club houses, foot and bicycle paths and waterfront promenades.

The harmony of the built environment and landscape represents the essence of the unique character of the project. This is manifested in an evocation of the most beautiful of the regional landscape characteristics including: the vertical movement of natural hills and mountains, the terraced forms of cultivated land, the interaction between water and land. Each of these characteristics provides inspiration for the principles and architectural organizations that underlie and unite all parts of the project.

中国，成都
麓湖新城总体规划

Chengdu, China
LUXE LAKES MASTERPLAN

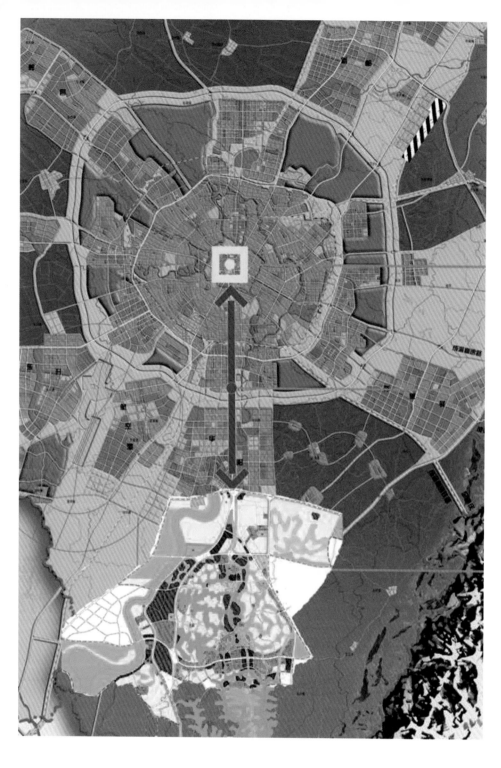

The master plan for Luxe Lakes is in stark contrast to the more typical approach to high-density residential projects in which there is often great repetition and therefore little real choice for the prospective tenant or owner. United by a shared material palette, the choreography of building forms and materials, a shared commitment to creating a sustainable environment and a rich and varied landscape, this new town will embody a set of distinct identities and characters that enable residents to identify with the unique place in which they live. Although this initial collection of neighborhood parcels appears to be a small selection of the new town's total area, it embodies a significant exploration of the character and program to be found throughout and provides a strong model for development in the years to come.

麓湖的总体规划与其他典型的高密度住宅项目不同，传统的住宅项目多重复性，租户或业主很少有机会拥有个性化住宅设计。该项目通过运用相似的色调、个性化的建筑模式和材料，打造一个可持续发展的环境和丰富多姿的景观，为住户提供一个独一无二的个性化居住空间。尽管该项目只是城市总面积的一小部分，然而其与众不同的特性和对空间设计方案的重要探索将成为未来几年建筑规划的成功典范。

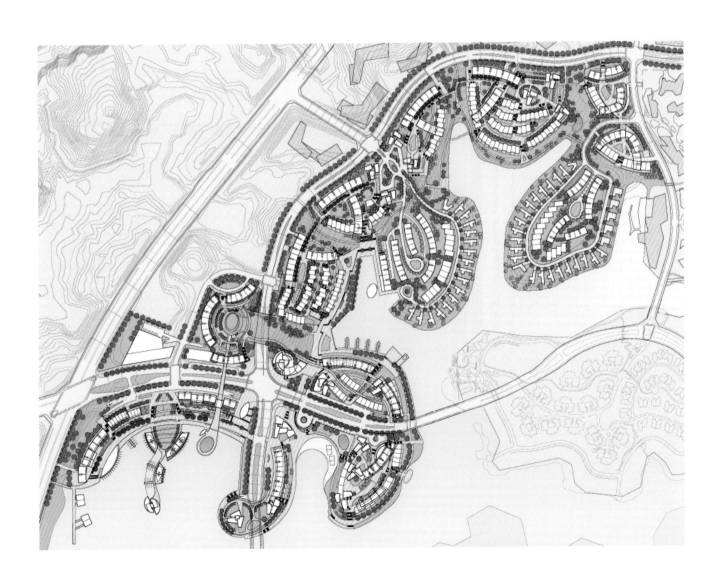

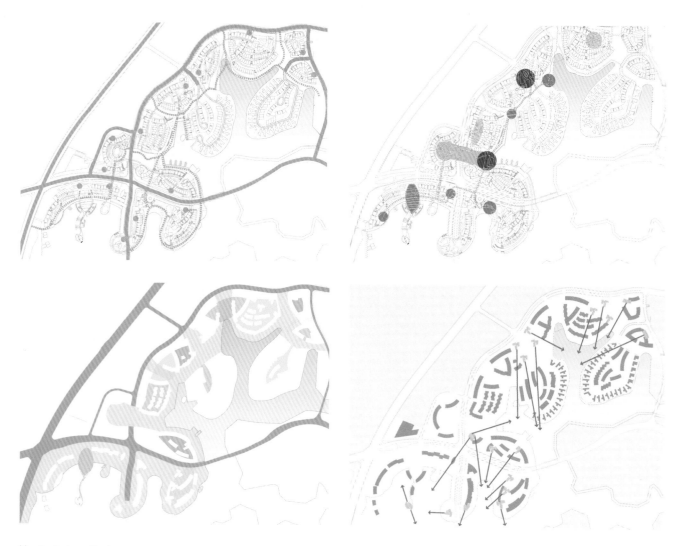

Housing is shaped in plan
and section to frame views,
connect to water and reflect
the surrounding topography.

住宅群的设计考虑到景观
与水的连接及地形环境的
融合。

LUXE LAKES MASTERPLAN 麓湖新城总体规划

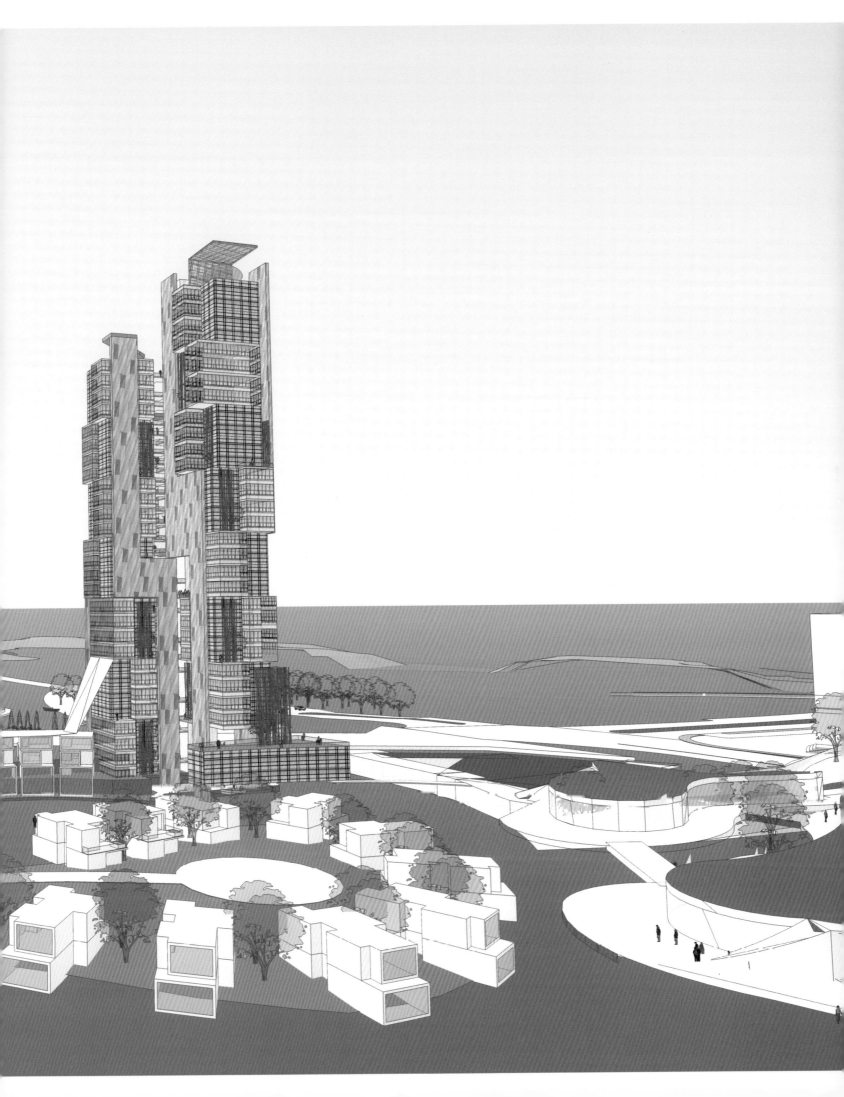

9号地块的总体规划包括地标性节能建筑、长形建筑和别墅的创建。

创新的"热带大楼"
该建筑采用可持续设计理念，结合当地热带气候，通过设置"空中花园"加强室内空气的净化，降低空调使用率，并将室外自然景观自然引入到室内。30层大楼的中心设有通风廊，确保室内空气清新。空中花园作为户外聚集区位于楼层较高的地方，温度和湿度均明显低于地面。

建筑材料结合屏幕、檐篷、悬梁、棚架和悬臂式托架为建筑提供有效遮荫，墙壁上种植的竹子和藤蔓植物有效加强了与自然环境的连接。可持续设计元素还包括屋顶上的太阳能光伏板以及地热供暖系统。

与自然的和谐相处
纵横交错的嵌壁式体量打造了充满动感的建筑外立面。虚实空间的巧妙搭配犹如积木游戏，光影交汇令建筑富于变化，十分引人注目。在每座大楼的顶部均设有别致的阁楼。

低层长形建筑和别墅延续了大楼"交织"的特征，并增添了较多的雕塑感。位于滨水区的零售店、餐饮店、多功能厅和俱乐部与大楼融为一体。景观设计提高了住宅的环境质量，由水路分开的一系列小岛屿经由东侧的公路自然衔接在一起。

Our conceptual design for Parcel 9 of the Master Plan creates a landmark ensemble of energy-efficient towers, lower bar buildings and villas.

Innovative "Tropical Towers"
The iconic towers incorporate optimal sustainable strategies that respond to the tropical climate. The design creates a vertical movement of "sky garden" units that minimize the need for heating and air conditioning, while maximizing views to the outstanding natural surroundings. Central to the design of the 30-floor towers are their "perforations"—openings through the building that allow breezes to blow freely over sky gardens. These cut-outs naturally cool and ventilate the building while the sky gardens place the outdoor gathering areas on higher floors, where the heat and humidity are significantly lower than at ground level.

The architectural materials incorporate screens, canopies, overhangs, trellises and cantilevered bays to provide shade, while green walls planted with bamboo and creeping vines strengthen the connection to the natural environment. Sustainable elements also include the use of photovoltaic panels on the roof, and geothermal heating/cooling.

Harmony with Nature
The tower facades are animated by a dynamic sense of movement—a "weaving" character of projected and recessed volumes to provide a strong identity for the buildings. Creating an architectural version of the game of Jenga, the "in-and-out" pieces form a distinctive rhythm of solids and voids, light and shadow, that serves to enrich and modulate the large scale of the towers. At the top, each tower is marked by special "sky penthouse units".

The low-rise bar building and villas on the Parcel 9 site incorporate the same "weaving" character comparable to the towers, but with a more sculptural treatment. Public amenities including retail, restaurant, function rooms, and a clubhouse has been closely integrated with the towers on the waterfront. The landscape design enhances the quality of residential living on a lake and lagoon, by shaping a series of islands separated by waterways and connected by a road from the east.

Gardens are integrated at entry levels to allow for ventilation and vertical integration of the landscape.

入口处的开放式花园有助于通风,并体现垂直式空中花园。

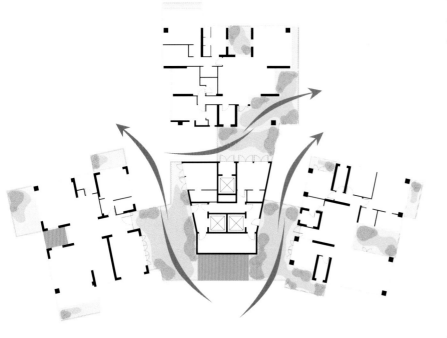

中国，成都
麓湖9号地块大楼

Chengdu, China
LUXE LAKES
PARCEL 9 TOWERS

重庆
CHONGQING

The prominent natural conditions of the Chongqing area served as inspiration for the 13.8-hectare Chun Sen Bi An master plan. 3000 units of housing enjoy sweeping views and direct access to the waterfront and sloped river banks.

    A formal axis in the center of the site represents the urban, public realm of the project, pulling the pedestrian flow from the city down to the river. This axis is animated by a grand flight of steps that echo the traditional street-stairs of the region. Retail shops are located on both sides of this central spine, adding to the lively urban character of the space. In contrast, an informal path, representing the more private and intimate realm of the project, meanders across the site from east to west. This smaller route echoes the winding, ancient pedestrian path between the docklands and the upper town that has been used for hundreds of years.

重庆地区的自然条件为这个占地13.8公顷的春森彼岸总体规划提供了设计灵感。3000套住房依水而设，其独特的地理优势无疑将为住户营造温馨、浪漫的居住空间。

项目规划的中心部分，设计风格较为庄重，代表传统的城市公共空间，将来自市区的人流引向水边。核心附近的梯阶与当地传统的街道交相呼应。两侧林立的零售商店为该区域增添了无限活力。相反，一个象征私密空间的小径蜿蜒迂回，从项目的东侧一直延伸至西侧，与连接具有百年历史的码头和城区之间的行人古道相得益彰。

Chongqing, China

CHUN SEN BI AN
HOUSING MASTERPLAN

中国，重庆

春森彼岸住宅总体规划

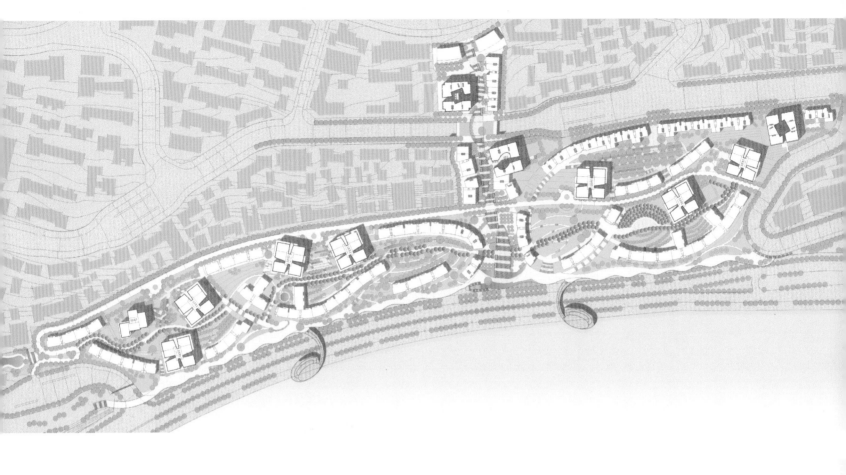

台北市　TAIPEI

内湖高档住宅大厦由两个占地48,000平方米的住宅大楼构成，共设136个住宅单元，地理位置优越，与台北美国在台协会遥遥相对。该建筑群分为如下几个部分：建筑的底层采用了独特的石墙结构将建筑牢牢固定于地面，彰显庄重之感。建筑的中央部分设置的预制混凝土板搭配可移动窗口，满足了结构和观景的需要。楼上空间受城市规模的影响成梯级状设计，令空间富于变化。建筑顶端的大型玻璃隔间犹如城市上方的一盏明灯，为城市注入了无限活力和生机。

公共广场、宁静的花园和喷泉在炎热夏日为空间注入了一丝清凉。从西南露台汩汩流淌下来的水景流经低处的大堂花园直至入口广场和落客区。一个开放空间将上方广场衬托得格外宽敞、通透，同时，将自然光线引入到大堂、游泳池和地下停车场。上方广场经由大堂花园之上的天桥与西南露台自然衔接，而大堂花园外部则罩以大型双层玻璃天棚。

The Nei-Hu High End Residential Towers provide 136 units of housing within two 48,000 sqm residential towers that are located on a well-connected site directly across from the future American Institute in Taipei. The building mass is divided into sections: the base and lower floors are strengthened with prominent stone walls that anchor the buildings to the ground and enhance the sense of formal presence. The middle portions of the buildings are animated by an interplay of prefabricated concrete panels with shifting windows, which fulfill both structural and view requirements. The stepped massing of the upper floors relates to the scale of the city while providing a varied and intriguing silhouette. The tower tops are the lightest element, characterized by large glass bays that act as luminescent lanterns.

A series of public plazas, serene gardens and cooling fountains provide refreshing shade in the hot, humid climate. A series of water features has a hidden origin in the southwest terrace and cascades down through the lower lobby garden to greet residents and visitors at the entry plaza and drop-off area. The Upper Plaza is amplified by a generous opening that brings light down into the lobby, swimming pool and parking area below. This Upper Plaza is connected to the southwest terrace by a pedestrian bridge over the main lobby garden, which features a grand, double-angled glass canopy.

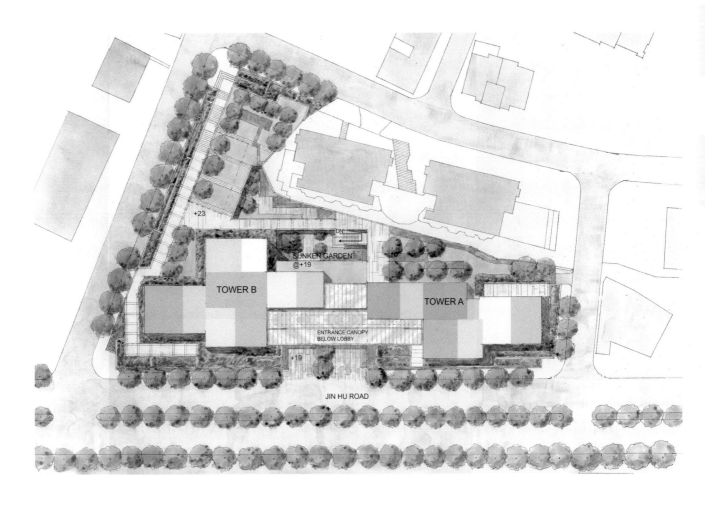

Taipei, Taiwan

NEI-HU HIGH END RESIDENTIAL TOWERS

台湾，台北市

内湖高档住宅大厦

NEI-HU HIGH END RESIDENTIAL TOWERS 内湖高档住宅大厦

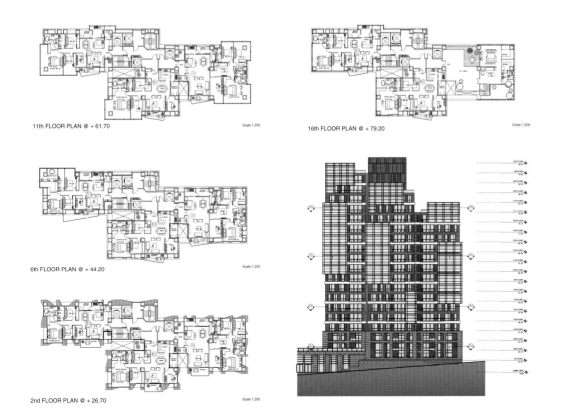

11th FLOOR PLAN @ + 61.70   Scale 1:200

16th FLOOR PLAN @ + 79.20   Scale 1:200

6th FLOOR PLAN @ + 44.20   Scale 1:200

2nd FLOOR PLAN @ + 26.70   Scale 1:200

337

澳门市 MACAU

澳门度假村为人们提供一个奢华的家庭住宅区的同时，还设置了酒店、零售店、休闲区等空间，以彰显其作为度假和娱乐胜地的独特身份。一个向北的优雅椭圆形开口与莲花的形象相得益彰，与醒目的标志性建筑相通。在这个占地50,181平方米的空间中，公共场所、运动跑道、入口区的设置大大促进了居民之间的沟通和互动。一个中央潟湖扮演了社交和娱乐中心的角色，三个湖中浮岛为空间增添了无限意境，营造出浪漫、惬意的氛围，与度假村的特征相得益彰。一个公共行人大道将中央潟湖进行环绕，并在景观、观景平台、桥梁和亭台楼阁的衬托下越发生动，活力四射。

可持续发展、环保理念一直贯穿整个建筑的设计，绿色草皮屋顶和集成光伏系统以及微型涡轮机发电系统将这一设计理念彰显得恰到好处。水节约方式涉及生物过滤、废水管理、地面径流处理等全球性节水战略。郁郁葱葱的原生植物和棚架及檐篷为空间在热带气候下提供了有效遮阳，并加强自然通风。

The Concordia Macau resort creates a luxurious, family-oriented residential district while offering hotel, retail, and leisure facilities to celebrate the area's famed identity as a resort and entertainment destination. An elegant oval opening to the north evokes the image of a lotus blossom and is anchored by taller landmark buildings that serve as gateways to the project. Public spaces, paths of movement, and qualities of residential entry on this spectacular 12.4-acre site work together to encourage social interaction among residents. A Central Lagoon serves as the social and recreational heart of the project, with three floating "islands in a lake" which evoke a fantasy setting and enhance the project's resort atmosphere. A public pedestrian promenade encircles the Central Lagoon and is animated with landscaping, viewing terraces, bridges, and pavilions.

Sustainable, ecologically-friendly features are optimized throughout the project, ranging from green sod roofs and integrated photovoltaic systems to micro-turbines that generate on-site power. Water conservation methods include bio-filtration, wastewater management, and a global strategy that utilizes waterfalls and grading to keep water in constant motion. Lush native plants, trellises and canopies provide shade, while screens facilitate natural ventilation in the hot and humid tropical climate.

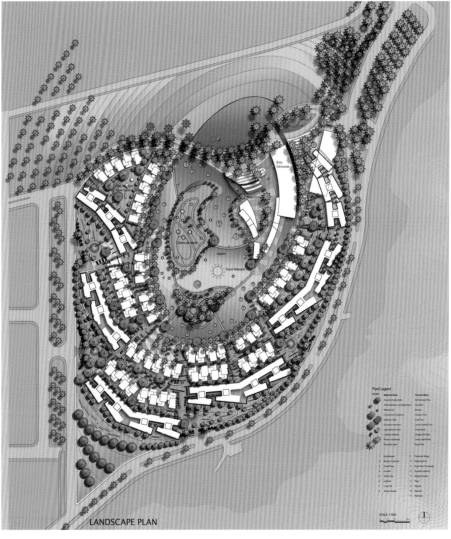

LANDSCAPE PLAN

中国，澳门
澳门度假村规划

Macau, China
CONCORDIA MACAU RESORT DEVELOPMENT

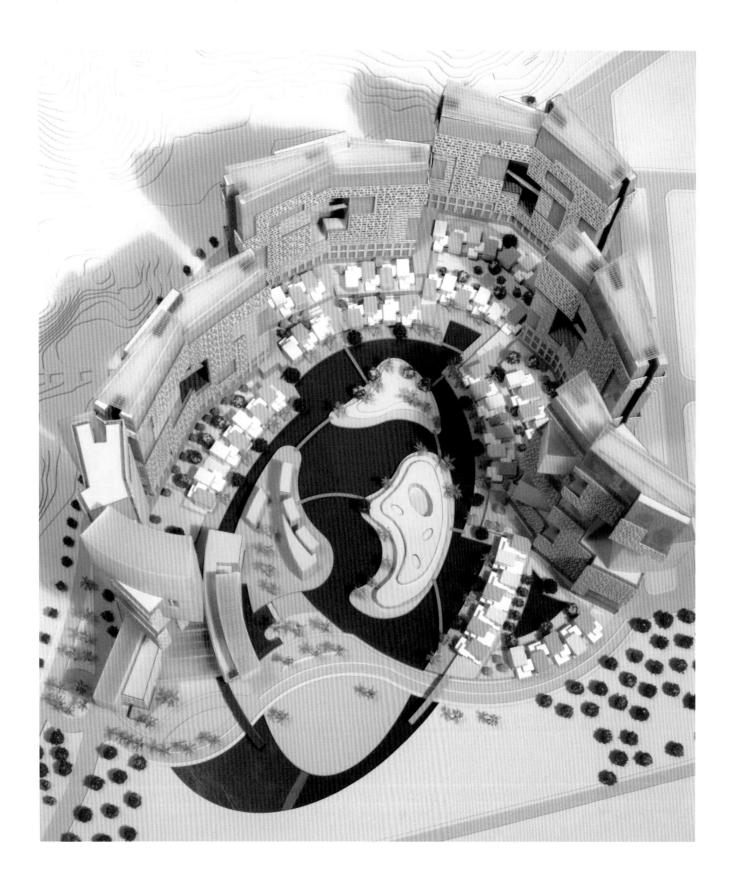

CONCORDIA MACAU RESORT DEVELOPMENT 澳门度假村规划

第比利斯市

TBILISI

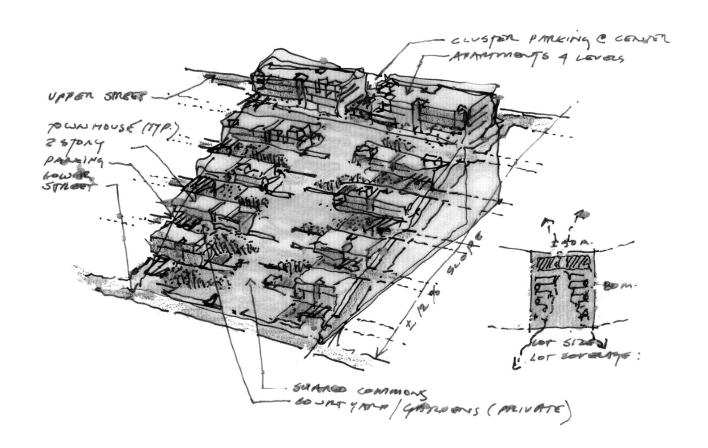

CLUSTER PARKING @ CENTER
APARTMENTS 4 LEVELS

UPPER STREET

TOWNHOUSE (TYP.)
2 STORY
PARKING
LOWER
STREET

12% SLOPE

±50 M.
80 M.

LOT SIZES
LOT COVERAGE:

SHARED COMMONS
COURTYARD/GARDENS (PRIVATE)

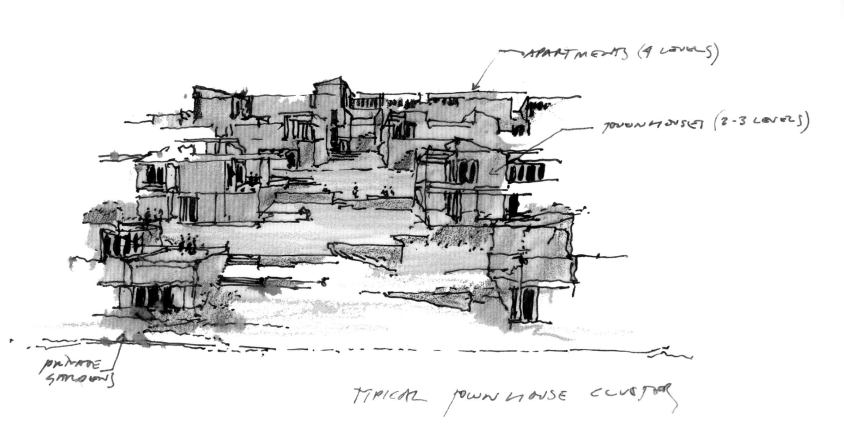

APARTMENTS (4 LEVELS)

TOWNHOUSES (2-3 LEVELS)

PRIVATE
GARDENS

TYPICAL TOWNHOUSE CLUSTER

344

Lisi Lake's sheltered gardens are equal in scale and importance to the residences themselves.

李斯湖住宅花园的尺度相同,并显现了对居民的重要性。

格鲁吉亚或许是也或许不是葡萄酒的诞生地,但它绝对是生产葡萄酒的国家,那里的居民大多崇尚户外生活。位于李斯湖附近的地区风景如画,其中一处景观经过几十年的过度放牧而急需修复。客户要求该项目的设计不仅要完成对原景观的修建,同时也要尊重格鲁吉亚的生活方式,通过住宅规划将当地的传统与国际标准设计和结构相结合。

第比利斯的设计和总体规划为人们提供了丰富多彩的住宅类型,包括大型别墅、联排别墅和公寓等。该地区地形较为复杂,乡间小路错综交织。在山下,湖水为周围的会所、马术中心、美国私立学校注入了勃勃生机。山顶之巅是格鲁吉亚东正教教堂。每个住宅类型的设计方案均强调建筑与景观的融合,对冬季东风的遮挡以及空间的贯通。随着季节的变化,住户能够轻松地从住处到达露台和私人花园。

Georgia is in many ways the Tuscany of Eastern Europe. It may or may not be the birthplace of wine—but it is definitely wine country, and a place where people take joy in outdoor living. The lands around Lisi Lake form a picturesque rural setting, and a landscape in need of restoration after many decades of overgrazing. Our clients saw the opportunity to restore not only the hillsides: the project aims to revive the entire concept of Georgian lifestyle with a unique development of houses and housing, combining the best of local tradition with international standards of design and construction.

The design and master plan that emerged from our workshops in Tbilisi presents a broad spectrum of residential "types"—from grand villas to townhouses and flats—arranged in a series of patterns on the hillsides. The site's many topographic domains are traversed and linked by a soft network of country lanes. At the base of the hills, the lake is the scene of a small village, complete with a clubhouse, an equestrian center, and a private "American Schoo". At the top of the highest hilltop is a Georgian Orthodox Chapel. Each of the house schemes seeks to provide lovely vistas, shelter from easterly winter winds, and the promise of intimate family life that flows easily from dwelling to terrace to private garden, in time with the seasons.

格鲁吉亚,第比利斯市
李斯湖住宅设计

Tbilisi, Georgia
LISI LAKE HOUSING

345

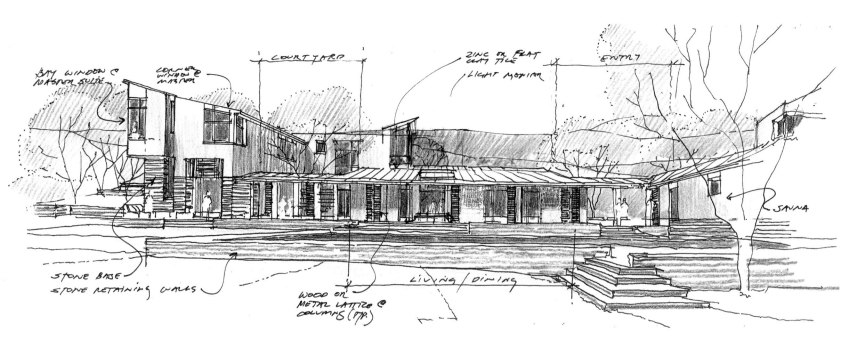

旧金山市

SAN FRANCISCO

水印大楼是一个设有130个住宅单元的22层高楼建筑，坐落于旧金山恩巴克德罗，占地面积约为2,023平方米。因毗邻旧金山湾，地理位置显赫，备受瞩目。塔楼呈外墙退缩式设计，突窗和阳台外凸，强调建筑物的垂直度，同时确保所有公寓内均能够欣赏到室外景致。此外，外墙退缩式设计还为单间、双人间、三人间卧室的打造提供了有利条件。

土壤条件决定了停车位设于基台的上方。建筑的地基形状与周围建筑保持和谐统一，其独特的设计构思也巧妙地融入到塔楼之中。塔楼明亮、通透的特征与阳台上的玻璃栏杆以及淡色玻璃和金属拱肩一直延续到布莱恩特/比尔区附近，石墙结构的嵌壁式入口、窗口、开孔衬托出底层的美感。

The Watermark is a 130-unit 22-story high-rise project on a half-acre site on San Francisco's Embarcadero. The design considers the site's spectacular setting on the San Francisco Bay, at the confluence of varying urban districts and their respective scales. The building's tower form is articulated with step-backs which, along with projecting bays and balconies, emphasize the slender verticality of the building while affording maximum view opportunities for all apartments. The step-backs also accommodate the mix of one, two and three-bedroom and penthouse units.

Soil conditions dictated that parking be accommodated in a three-story above grade podium structure. This building base is shaped to relate to the scale of surrounding buildings, and its expression is carefully integrated with the tower. The light, transparent nature of the tower, with its glass balcony balustrades and light-colored spandrels of glass and metal, is brought down into the base at the monumental Bryant/Beale corner, while cast-stone walls punctuated with recessed entries, windows, and openings articulate the base walls.

San Francisco, California

WATERMARK TOWER CONDOMINIUMS

加利福尼亚州，旧金山市

水印住宅大楼

大开曼群岛

GRAND CAYMAN

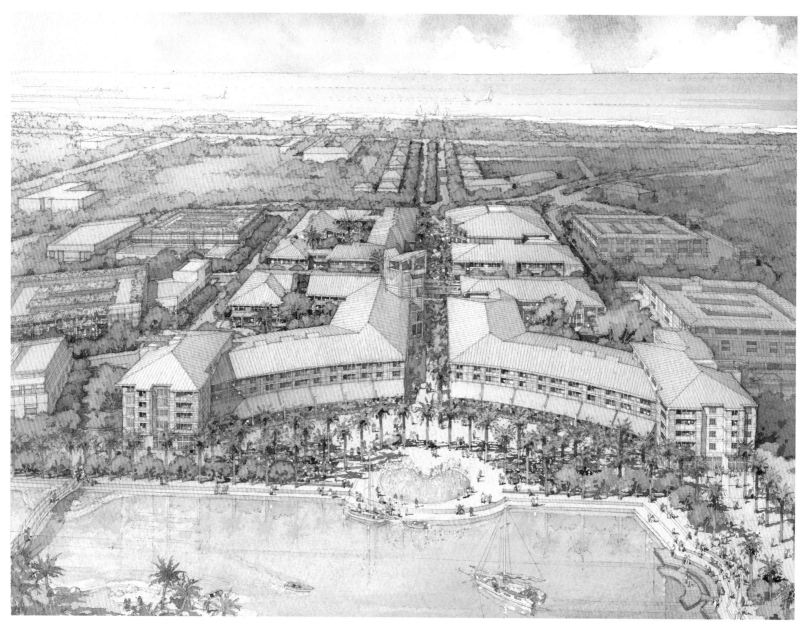

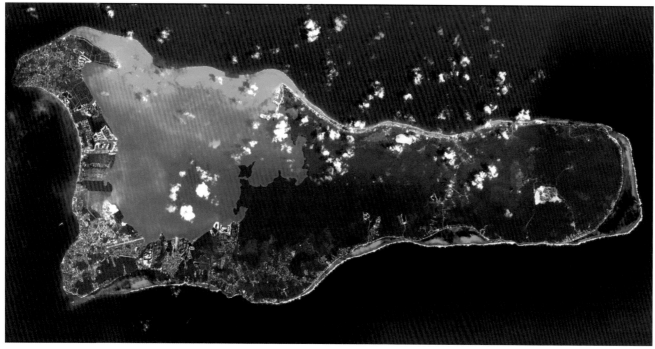

开曼湾作为大开曼岛社区建设的成功典范,由最初的参赛获奖作品、四村总体规划方案最终转变成一个充满活力的城市中心。摩尔·乐伯·约德建筑事务所在该项目的总体规划和室内设计中担任设计总监。这个以行人为导向的社区综合规划项目涉及景观的建设和办公、停车场、零售店、住宅和娱乐等空间的建立,其风格和结构与之前岛屿的社区项目形成鲜明对比。交织的檐篷街道、公园、景观区、室内连接通道、行人散步广场和城市广场为岛屿打造了一个真正的步行环境。

每个新村皆体现了对简约、独特的空间的向往,庭院与小径交织在一起,如画的美景不禁令人心驰神往。各空间因功能不同而规模各异。建筑规划在"控制"机动车辆的同时,也为行人提供了优良的步行环境。行人和慢机动车道以及自行车道为蓬勃发展的城市新村注入了勃勃生机。

Conceived as an antidote to the rapid, auto-oriented growth on the small island of Grand Cayman, Camana Bay has grown from a competition-winning, four-village master plan into a vibrant town center that is quickly becoming the communal heart of the Island. Moore Ruble Yudell provided a wide range of design leadership from master planning through building and interior design within a highly collaborative design process. Development of the new mixed-use, pedestrian oriented community included an intimate weaving of landscaped environments with office, parking, retail, residential and entertainment structures providing a considerable contrast to previous growth on the Island. The network of shaded streets with destination parking structures, landscaped courts, inter-connecting passages, pedestrian arcades and urban plazas provide the Island's only true walking environment.

Each new village will embody the desire for clear, memorable spaces interwoven with courts and paths of surprise and discovery. These various spaces will be configured to create a hierarchy of scales— grand to intimate, as well as a range of experiences from civic to private. The Villages will create pedestrian friendly environments while allowing "tempered" traffic on most streets. The harmonious mix of pedestrians with slow auto traffic, while bicycles will produce the vitality found in thriving urban villages.

Four neighborhoods are linked from ocean to bay creating the armature for a walkable community.

介于大海与海湾之间的四个不同社区,由优良步行街道串联起来。

英属西印度群岛,大开曼群岛
开曼湾总体规划

Grand Cayman, British West Indies
CAMANA BAY MASTERPLAN

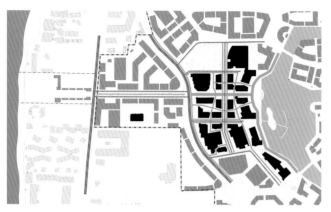
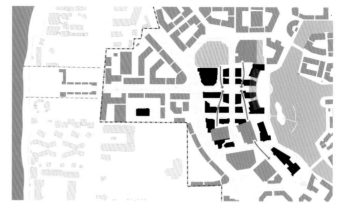

The town center is developed with a fine grain of streets, pedestrian paths and courtyards to create a rich diversity of places. Buildings and open space are shaped for shading and to capture prevailing breezes.

由街道、人行步道及庭园组成一个多元化的市区中心，设计所有建筑及广场时，均考虑到最佳的遮阳及通风效果。

JUNE 21ST

The retail facade on the first floor receives 2 hours 20 minutes of sun which is the least for the year.
The office facade at the second floor receives 1 hour 20 minutes of sun light.

MARCH 21ST
SEPTEMBER 21ST

During the spring and autumn months the sun exposure of the first floor retail facade increases up to 2 hours 40 minutes.
The second floor office facade receives 1 hour 45 minutes of sun light.

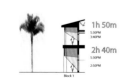

DECEMBER 21ST

During the winter months the retail facade receives up to 2 hours and 40 minutes of sun light, which is similar to the equinox.
The second floor office facade receives 1 hour 50 minutes of sun light.

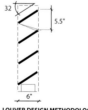

LOUVER DESIGN METHODOLOGY
SCALE 1"=1'

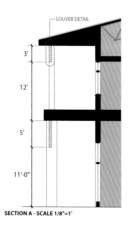

SECTION A - SCALE 1/8"=1'

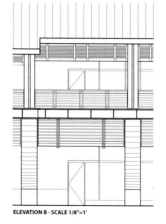

ELEVATION B - SCALE 1/8"=1'

WEST FACING FACADES

Shading concept:

West facing facdes are exposed to low sun angles in the afternoon hours. Arcades and balconies along with deeper louvers protect window openings.

Second storey:

The office facades at the second storey are shaded by the gallery setback and a band of 3' deep louver. Window sills are at 3'.

First storey:

The retail facades on the first floor are shaded by the arcade setback and a 5' deep louver.

Computer studies helped optimize shading and ventilation for all parts of the town center.

利用电脑为城市中心设计出最佳的遮阳及通风方式。

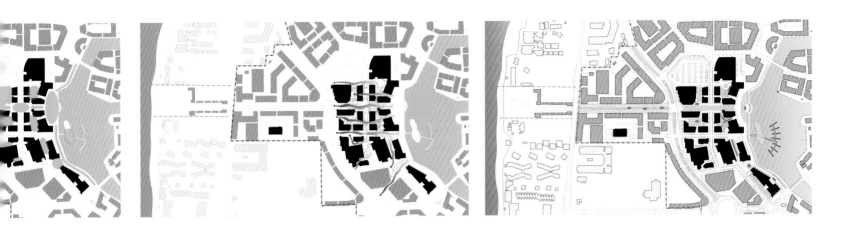

大开曼群岛
GRAND CAYMAN

作为未来几十年规划构想的首期设计，城市中心的建立为新社区的质量和环境效应树立了典范。该建筑在利用当地气候条件和历史条件的基础上，形成了独一无二的设计风格。特殊定制的照明设备、马赛克艺术、水景、精致的建筑细节和源自当地环境的色彩运用将空间烘托得美轮美奂。

强烈的自然光线、较高的湿度和较为集中的降雨为设计带来了诸多挑战。建筑结构巧妙，独特的庭院设计能够加强空间自然通风，遮阳设备诸如拱形游廊、百叶窗、屏幕、张拉薄膜结构以及伸缩遮阳篷的设置时刻确保空间舒适、怡人。来自当地或加勒比海的建筑材料和色彩的应用有效改善了热岛效应。一个中央动力厂房、蓄水区以及原生植物的设置为实现可持续发展目标提供了有利条件。

开曼湾的设计理念也同样适用于世界各地城市地区的建设。丰富而多样化的空间设计能够为行人营造活泼、生动的环境氛围，从而实现和谐与多样化的平衡。所有的设计元素：建筑、景观、图案、照明、喷泉和街道设施在新市镇的建设中扮演了不可或缺的角色。开曼湾的设计经验证明，一个真正的现代社区的成功建设，与其所在地的历史、文化和气候元素密不可分。

Envisioned as the first phase of a multi-decade build-out, the Town Center sets the example for the new community's quality and environmental responsiveness. Architectural expressions have grown from an understanding of the Island's climate and history without replication of inappropriately borrowed styles. Custom lighting, integrated mosaic art, extensive water features and a wide variety of architectural details and colors, inspired by the local environment, contribute to the Town's sense of Place.

The challenge of the intense sun, high humidity and sudden torrential rains of this tropical environment focused the design's response to include structures and courtyards shaped to enhance cooling easterly breezes, extensive use of an array of sunshading devices including arcades, louvers, screens, tensioned fabric structures and retractable fabric awnings. The careful choice of local or Caribbean sourced materials and colors mitigate the heat-island effect while the development of a central utility plant, creation of rain-water collection cisterns and the extensive use of native, non-invasive planting all contribute to sustainability goals.

The experience of Camana Bay, often found in the most highly regarded urban locations around the world, is rich and varied supporting a lively pedestrian life intended to find a balance of harmony and variety. All the elements of design—architecture, landscape, graphics, lighting, fountains, and street furniture—contribute to the richness of the new town. This experience is at the core of the sense of community—authentic and contemporary grown with respect to the history, culture and climate of the place.

英属西印度群岛，大开曼群岛

开曼湾城市中心

Grand Cayman, British West Indies

CAMANA BAY TOWN CENTER

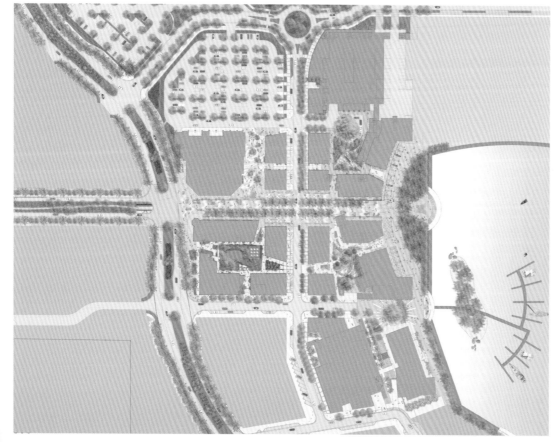

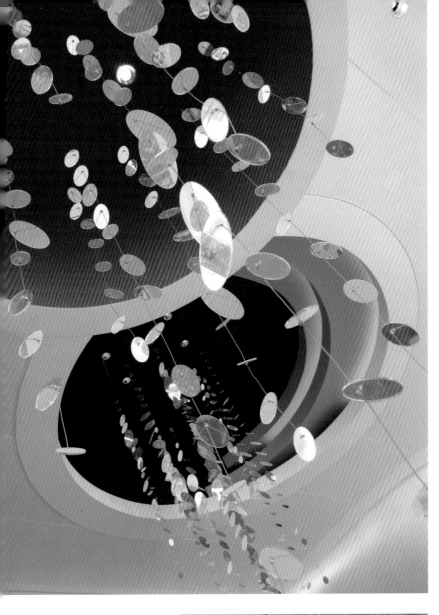
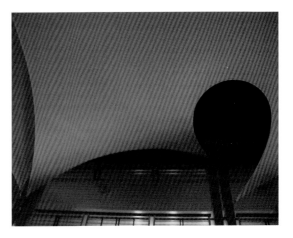

Moore Ruble Yudell principals and partners (*from left*):
Mario Violich, Buzz Yudell, Jeanne Chen, Neal Matsuno, John Ruble,
Michael Martin, Krista Becker, Stanley Anderson, James Mary O'Connor

建筑事务所信息
STUDIO PROFILE

Buzz Yudell, FAIA
Partner

Buzz Yudell's passion for architecture grew out of a synthesis of artistic and social concerns. While at Yale College, his work in sculpture was complemented by exploration of sciences and humanities. Graduate studies at the Yale School of Architecture expanded these boundaries to a range of scales from small construction in situ to community participation and urban design. Here, he began his long association with Charles Moore. In 1977, Buzz, Charles and John Ruble formed Moore Ruble Yudell, a partnership based on shared humanistic values and a celebration of collaboration within the office and beyond to their clients and communities.

Buzz has collaborated intensively with John to expand the firm's expression and expertise to include campus, cultural, civic, residential and commercial architecture. Together they have led the firm as pioneers in planning and architecture for sustainable communities. Working in Europe for over thirty years, Buzz and John bring advanced approaches to sustainable architecture to numerous projects in the United States.

Buzz has led project design on a broad array of community and civic projects including the Steger Student Life Center at the University of Cincinnati, Manzanita Village Housing at the University of California, Santa Barbara, the Camana Bay town master plan, Grand Cayman, and master planning for new towns in Germany. Master planning and new buildings for campuses include UCLA, UC Berkeley, Dartmouth College, Massachusetts Institute of Technology and California Institute of Technology. Buzz has helped the firm achieve international recognition for its residential architecture and the honor of many years as one of AD 100 (Architectural Digest's 100 Top Firms worldwide).

Throughout his career, Buzz has found teaching, writing, and community service to be critical in the evolution of both the theoretical and cultural role of architecture in shaping and celebrating place and community. He has taught at Yale, University of California, Los Angeles, University of Texas, Austin, and was honored to hold the distinguished Howard Friedman Chair of Architecture at University of California, Berkeley.

In 2006, Buzz and John's leadership was recognized when the firm received the National American Institute of Architects Firm Award, the highest honor that can be bestowed to an American architecture firm.

In 2007 Buzz Yudell and John Ruble received the 2007 American Institute of Architects Los Angeles Gold Medal Award.

John Ruble, FAIA
Partner

John Ruble, FAIA began his career as architect and planner in the Peace Corps, Tunisia, where a profound experience of culture, climate, and place provided lasting influences on his work. At the University of California, Los Angeles, he studied and associated with Charles Moore. In 1977, John, Charles, and Buzz Yudell formed Moore Ruble Yudell.

Since co-founding Moore Ruble Yudell, John Ruble has collaborated with his partners on a broad spectrum of residential, academic, cultural and urban design work. As Partner-in-Charge, he has helped realize some of the firm's best-known international work, including Moore Ruble Yudell's competition winning design for the United States Embassy in Berlin and the National AIA Honor award-winning Comprehensive Master Plan for the University of Washington, Tacoma.

With architecture degrees from University of Virginia and the University of California, Los Angeles School of Architecture and Urban Planning, John has been active in teaching and research, leading graduate design studios at UCLA and Cornell University. Together with Buzz Yudell, John is the 2007 American Institute of Architects Los Angeles Gold Medal recipient.

James Mary O'Connor, AIA
Principal

Born in Dublin, Ireland, James Mary O'Connor came to Charles Moore's Master Studios at University of California, Los Angeles in 1982 as a Fulbright Scholar. James received his Diploma in Architecture from the Dublin Institute of Technology, his Bachelor of Science in Architecture degree from Trinity College, Dublin, and his Master of Architecture from UCLA. He joined Moore Ruble Yudell in 1983.

As Principal-in-Charge, James has provided design leadership for large-scale residential, academic and mixed-use urban projects. International work has become a focus, with large-scale housing and planning projects in Malmö, Sweden, Manila, Philippines , and several areas of China. James is Principal-in-Charge of all the firm's Asian projects.

In China, the current Master Plan for the COFCO Eco-Valley Agricultural Production and Exhibition Center outside Beijing envisions a state-of-the-art sustainable project that will be one of the first net zero-carbon project of its kind in the world. The landmark Science Park Towers headquarters building for Time-Medical Inc. in Taizhou, China, incorporates state-of-the-art sustainable, environmentally-friendly and information-technology features to create an outstanding precedent for future live/work developments in Taizhou's "Medical City. " A current prominent academic project is the Grangegorman Urban Quarter Master Plan in Dublin, Ireland, creating a new campus for Dublin Institute of Technology (DIT) in the historic core of the city.

James has a special interest in projects with a strong sustainability component, as reflected in his work on the award-winning Santa Monica Civic Center Parking Structure, one of the first buildings of its kind to be LEED-Certified in the United States, and the "Village" housing development nearby. The highly-sustainable Tango Building for the innovative Bo01 Housing Exhibition in Malmö, Sweden has received numerous awards for design excellence, and was selected as The Year's Building 2001 in Sweden.

Over the past twenty years, James has taught design studios, lectured, and been invited as guest critic at universities around the world. James was recipient of the AIA Young Architect Award in 2007.

Jeanne Chen, AIA
Principal

The focus of Jeanne Chen's work has been on many campuses across the country and she enjoys the challenges of working with multiple constituents who form the university client group and who often see the project from their own unique perspective. Jeanne believes that listening is the first step of responsive design.

Jeanne brings over twenty years of experience from campus planning, programming, through design and construction to the project with her most recent projects at Dartmouth College (LEED® Gold and Silver Certified) and the expansion of the Sloan School at MIT which is on track for LEED® Gold Certification. Currently, she is working on the Student Community Center at the University of California Berkeley which began with our developing a strategic master plan for the adaptive reuse, new construction and revitalization of the southwest campus district.

Jeanne's ability to advance and develop the broad vision of each project while attending to client needs and technical details has made her successful in leading complex institutional projects, including the firm's largest civic project, the Robert E. Coyle United States

Courthouse in Fresno, California. The design of the courthouse both represents the open and public face of our judicial system while addressing stringent security and circulation criteria.

Krista Becker, AIA, LEED® AP
Principal

Krista Becker graduated magna cum laude from the University of Southern California with on-site studies in Paris and Rome. Her ability to lead and coordinate complex project teams and tackle challenging project programs with attention to design, schedule and budget as made her a strong influence in the advancement of Moore Ruble Yudell's management approach.

As the Principal-in-Charge for the recently completed United States Embassy in Berlin, the American Institute in Taipei, College of Arts and Sciences South Lawn Project at University of Virginia, and the Santa Monica Public Library, she has emphasized skillful communication and understanding, earning the confidence of some of the firm's most discerning client groups.

Her unique understanding of the Embassy program requirements, design excellence and strong project management skills has contributed to several recent state department commissions including; Santo Domingo, Dominican Republic New Embassy Compound; The Hague, The Netherlands New Embassy Compound; Helsinki, Finland New Embassy Addition and Renovation; Beirut, Lebanon new Embassy and Housing Compound and the Seoul, Korea New Embassy and Housing masterplan.

In addition to project management and design, Krista brings over twenty years of specialty program planning knowledge and experience. She is responsible for the flexible, efficient and functional space program layouts of several complex civic and academic buildings, including embassy programs.

Krista Becker is an active member of the American Institute of Architects and a guest lecturer at University of California Los Angeles Professional Practice in Architecture and Construction Management programs.

Michael S. Martin, AIA
Principal

Mario J. Violich, AIA, ASLA
Principal

With a background in landscape architecture and architecture, Mario's professional and academic experiences blur the traditional boundaries between building and landscape. Mario received his Bachelor of Landscape Architecture degree at the University of California, Berkeley in 1983, followed by his Master of Architecture degree in 1989 from the University of California, Los Angeles. He joined Moore Ruble Yudell the same year.

Mario's design leadership has influenced a broad spectrum of projects at Moore Ruble Yudell, ranging from master planning, to mixed-use urban projects, to institutional buildings, to numerous single-family homes and gardens. His design approach is rooted in the exploration of the interdisciplinary nature of the design process.

As Principal, Mario has been in charge of many of the firm's residential projects, including the recently completed Moir House in Carmel and the Ruddell House in Kauai. Mario's award-winning projects include the Joseph A. Steger Student Life Center at the University of Cincinnati, Ohio and the Beth El Synagogue in Berkeley, California. In addition to his broad interdisciplinary professional experience, Mario has also been an instructor at the Department of Landscape Architecture at UCLA Extension since 1993 and an associate teacher with Adjunct Professor Buzz Yudell at UCLA and UC Berkeley.

After spending his senior year studying architectural design in Europe, Michael graduated with honors from the University of Illinois, Urbana-Champaign in 1976. Having gained significant professional experience developing architectural projects in numerous states and in Europe, he extended his study of both architectural and urban design, earning a Master of Architecture II degree in 1993 from the School of Architecture and Urban Planning at the University of California, Los Angeles.

In over thirty years of study and practice, Michael has led a wide variety of project types and scales. Informing each has been his keen interest in sustainable design which grew from early work in Colorado including the exploration of innovative passive energy-use reduction strategies while on staff with John Denver's Windstar Foundation and culminating with the design of Amory and Hunter Lovins' first headquarters for the Rocky Mountain Institute in Snowmass, Colorado.

Extending beyond a background of experience that ranges from low income and migrant farm worker housing and single family residences to large commercial and institutional projects such as Canary Wharf in London and the World Bank in Washington, D.C., Michael's work at Moore Ruble Yudell has focused on large-scale, multi-building academic and commercial projects, as well as, master planning and urban design. While there is a diversity of projects that fall under his leadership, all benefit from a range of design explorations that seek authentic and appropriate solutions. This approach has successfully guided a new town development in the Cayman Islands, an academic complex in Hong Kong and mixed-use master planning in China, as well as, numerous projects throughout the United States.

Within the context of his broad experience, Michael has developed an expertise in the field of facilities for scientific research and teaching, enjoying both the rigor and creativity required in developing functional, humane and exciting homes for this community. He recently completed the French Family Science Center, a laboratory complex of new and renovated facilities for five scientific departments at Duke University, and is currently undertaking the programming and design for the new Bioengineering Laboratory at the University of California, Santa Barbara.

In addition to project involvement, Michael's leadership extends to being head of Moore Ruble Yudell's Research and Sustainability focus group and his participation as co-chair of Moore Ruble Yudell's Standards and Quality Control Group. Michael is a member of the American Institute of Architects and was Adjunct Professor in Design at Woodbury University in 1997.

Neal Matsuno, AIA, LEED® AP
Principal

Neal Matsuno joined the firm shortly after graduating from University of Southern California in 1984. While leading projects, Neal is recognized for combining design sensitivity with skills in technical coordination throughout the design process. Neal is the Principal-in-Charge of large-scale projects involving multiple user groups, and detailed program requirements, such as the Sloan School of Management Massachusetts Institute of Technology, Claremont McKenna College Master Plan, as well as detailed historical transformation of the recently completed Glorya Kaufman Hall Center for World Arts and Cultures at UCLA.

Neal's areas of special expertise include architectural lighting design, and he has won numerous lighting design awards for his work. Neal has had major responsibility for lighting design and technical detailing for projects including the MIT Sloan School of Management, UCLA Glorya Kaufman Hall, the California Center for the Arts, Escondido, Law Library at University of California, Los Angeles, and the firm's residential projects.

Stanley has taught in the Interior Architecture Department at the School of the Art Institute of Chicago and California College of Arts and Crafts.

Tina Beebe

Stanley Anderson, AIA, IIDA
Associate Principal
Director, Interior Design Studio

Stanley Anderson graduated with honors and received his Bachelor of Architecture degree from the College of Architecture and Design at Kansas State University in 1985. An Associate Principal with Moore Ruble Yudell, Stanley specializes in Interior Architectural projects and has led the Interior Design Studio since joining the firm in 2004. Stanley has worked on a number of different project types, including commercial, residential, institutional, and academic. Recent and current projects include the United States Embassy in Berlin, Germany, the US Embassy in Santa Domingo, and the Camana Bay cinema, office and residential buildings in the Cayman Islands.

Stanley believes strongly in the relationship between architecture and interior design, and understands that although interior design can act separately from the architecture in which it is contained, it is most successful when it acknowledges its envelope and takes cues from its surrounding exterior environment. He also believes the basic purpose of all interior design solutions is to organize its parts and improve the functional, aesthetic and psychological experience of space.

Tina Beebe received her MFA from the Yale School of Art and Architecture. Working with Charles Moore as a student, Tina joined his firm in Essex, Connecticut and subsequently came to California to work with him in 1976. She also worked in the office of Charles and Ray Eames, learning much from her great friend and mentor, Ray Eames. As resident colorist and interior designer for Moore Ruble Yudell, Tina has integrated these influences with her extensive travel experiences to inform her choices for custom color and material palettes on commercial, institutional, and residential projects. She has provided consulting services for many distinguished U.S. and international-architecture firms in the United States and abroad.

Tina's practice has expanded to combine her design and color abilities to include the design of gardens for residential and commercial settings gardens. As plant material inspires her color palette, color evokes ideas for whole gardens, which in turn complement and enhance the color and materials of architecture. This unique approach is exemplified in her color and landscape design for the award-winning Tango Housing at the Bo01 Exhibition in Malmö, Sweden. Tina has successfully applied principles of color and landscape at an extraordinary range of scales, from her own houses and gardens in Malibu, Santa Monica, and The Sea Ranch, California, to the coloring of whole townscapes at Karow-Nord, Berlin.

Books by Moore Ruble Yudell

Moore Ruble Yudell with Glaserworks. *Arc of Interaction*. Philadelphia: ORO Editions, 2008

Anderton, Frances, Robert Campbell and Shouzhi Wang. *Moore Ruble Yudell Report/2007*. Beijing: AADCU, 2007

Moore Ruble Yudell with SWECO FFNS Arkitekter AB. *Innovation in Sustainable Housing: Tango*. New York: Edizioni Press, Inc., 2005

Ruble, John and Buzz Yudell. *Moore Ruble Yudell: Making Place*. Sydney: Images Publishing Group, 2004

Ruble, John. "Libraries/Learning Centers." In *Building Type Basics for College and University Facilities*, edited by David J. Neuman , New York: John Wiley & Sons, 2003

Koffka, Adrian and Wendy Kohn, eds. *Moore Ruble Yudell: Building in Berlin*. Sydney: Images Publishing Group, 1999

Riera Ojeda, Oscar, James Mary O'Connor and Wendy Kohn. *Campus & Community: Moore Ruble Yudell Architecture and Planning*. Rockport Publishers, Inc., 1997

Riera Ojeda, Oscar and Lucas H. Guerra, eds. *Moore Ruble Yudell: Houses and Housing*. AIA Press, 1994

Steele, James, ed. *Moore Ruble Yudell*. Academy Editions, 1993

Books featuring Moore Ruble Yudell projects

Images Publishing, *21st Century Houses: 150 of the World's Best*. Sydney: Images Publishing Group, 2010

Images Publishing, *100 Country Houses*. Sydney: Images Publishing Group, 2009

Dickhoff, Anne, *Outdoor Rooms II*. Massachusetts: Quarry Books, 2006 (Yorkin House, Malibu, California)

Beaver, Robin (ed.). *100 More of the World's Best Houses*. Sydney: Images Publishing Group, 2005

Trulove, James Grayson and Il Kim, eds. *New American Additions and Renovations*. New York: Watson-Gupkill Publications, 2001 (Gilbert House, Los Angeles, California)

Yee, Roger. *Educational Environments*. New York: Visual Reference Publications, Inc., 2002 (Hugh and Hazel Darling Law Library Addition, UCLA)

Residential Spaces of the World, Volume 5. Sydney: Images Publishing Group, 2002 (Yorkin House, Malibu, California)

Slessor, Catherine. *See-Through Houses: Inspirational Homes and Features in Glass*. London/New York: Ryland Peters & Small, 2001 (Yorkin House, Malibu, California)

Trulove, James Grayson and Il Kim, eds. *New American House 3*. New York: Watson-Gupkill Publications, 2001 (Dodici Giardini, Pacific Palisades, California)

Hardenbergh, Don and Todd S. Phillips, eds. *Retrospective of Courthouse Design 1991-2001*, 2001 (United States Courthouse and Federal Building, Fresno, California)

Cyberspace: the World of Digital Architecture, Australia: Images Publishing, 2001 (Sunlaw Power Plant)

Crisp, Barbara. *Human Spaces*. Massachusetts: Rockport Publishers, Inc., 2001 (Nishiokamoto Housing, Kobe, Japan)

Goslee Power, Nancy and Susan Heeger. *The Gardens of California: Four Centuries of Design from Mission to Modern*. Clarkson N. Potter, Inc., 2000 (Yudell-Beebe House, Malibu, California)

Langdon, Philip, *American Houses*. New York: Stewart Tabori & Chang, 1997 (Marine Street House, Santa Monica, California)

Riera Ojeda, Oscar, ed. *The New American House*. Whitney Library of Design, 1995 (Yudell-Beebe House, Malibu, California)

Ferguson, R. *Urban Revisions: Current Projects in the Public Realm*. MIT Press, 1994

Webb, Michael and J. Carter Brown. *Architects House Themselves: Breaking New Ground*. The Preservation Press, 1994

Sanoff, Henry. *School Design*. New York: Van Nostrand Reinhold, 1994

Steele, James. *Museum Builders*. Academy Editions/ Ernst & Sohn, London, 1994 (Hood Museum; Hollywood Museum, California; and St. Louis Art Museum, Missouri)

Toy, Maggie, ed. *World Cities: Los Angeles* London: Academy Editions and Berlin: Ernst + Son, 1994

Johnson, Eugene J. *Charles Moore Buildings and Projects 1949–1986*. New York: Rizzoli, 1986 (varoius)

Street-Porter, Tim. *Freestyle*. New York: Stewart Tabori & Chang, 1986

参考文献
SELECTED BIBLIOGRAPHY

2010

Chicago Athenaeum/Europe American Architecture
Award 2010: Grangegorman Master Plan,
Dublin Institute of Technology, Ireland

World Architecture Festival, Future Residential
Housing Highly-Commended Award: Chun Sen Bi
An Housing Master Plan, China.

American Institute of Architects California Council
Honor Award for Urban Design 2010: UC Berkeley
Sproul Student Community Center

American Institute of Architects California Council
Merit Award 2010: Santa Monica Civic Center
Parking Structure

National Center for State Courts Citation,
Retrospectives of Courthouse Design 2001-2010:
Robert E. Coyle United States Courthouse

Pacific Southwest Regional winner of The Office
Building of the Year (TOBY), Government
Category: Robert E. Coyle United States Courthouse

2009

World Architecture Festival, Future Projects–
Masterplanning Highly–Commended Award:
Grangegorman Master Plan, Dublin Institute
of Technology, Ireland

AIA California Council Merit Award: Grangegorman
Master Plan, Dublin Institute of Technology, Ireland

AIA Santa Barbara Merit Award 2009: Manzanita
Village housing, University of California,
Santa Barbara

American Institute of Architects California
Council Merit Award: Santa Monica Civic Center
Parking Structure

2008

Architecture Foundation of Los Angeles AFLA
Design Green Awards Honor Award: Santa Monica
Civic Center Parking Structure

Chicago Athenaeum American Architecture Award:
Santa Monica Civic Center Parking Structure

AIA California Council Design Awards "Savings By
Design": Santa Monica Public Library

Boston Society of Architects Campus Planning Award:
Dartmouth College North Campus Plan

AIA/LA 2008 Design Award: Santa Monica Civic
Center Parking Structure

SEGD 2008 Design Award (Society for Environmental
Graphic Design): Santa Monica Civic Center
Parking Structure

Westside Urban Forum Westside Prize: Santa
Monica Village

Xang Ten Yo Outstanding Residential Community
Award: Longhu Chun Sen Bi An

Chongqing Outstanding Planning Design Award:
Longhu Chun Sen Bi An

2007

**American Institute of Architects Los Angeles Gold
Medal 2007: Buzz Yudell, FAIA and John Ruble,
FAIA**

American Institute of Architects Academy of
Architecture for Justice, Justice Facilities Review
2006-2007: Robert E. Coyle United States
Courthouse

GSA Design Excellence Honor Award for Architecture:
Robert E. Coyle United States Courthouse

Chicago Athenaeum American Architecture Award:
Santa Monica Public Library

New American Architecture 2007 Exhibition, Kimball
International, New York: Santa Monica Public Library

Boston Society of Architects Sustainability Award and
Build Boston Exhibition: Santa Monica Public Library

Society of Campus and University Planners/AIA
Merit Award for Excellence in Architecture for
Renovation or Adaptive Reuse: Glorya Kaufman
Hall, University of California, Los Angeles

Los Angeles Business Council Preservation Award, 37th
Annual Los Angeles Architectural Awards: Glorya
Kaufman Hall, University of California, Los Angeles

AIA Santa Clara Valley Honor Award: Horace Mann
Public Elementary School

United States Institute for Theater Technology,
PQ2007 Architecture & Technology Exhibition,
Prague, Czechoslovakia: Clarice Smith Performing
Arts Center, University of Maryland, College Park

United States Institute for Theater Technology,
PQ2007 Architecture & Technology Exhibition,
Prague, Czechoslovakia: Glorya Kaufman Hall,
University of California, Los Angeles

California Preservation Foundation Preservation
Design Award: Glorya Kaufman Hall, University
of California, Los Angeles

Glass Association of North America Design in Glass
Award: Santa Monica Civic Center Parking Structure

所获奖项及展览
SELECTED AWARDS AND EXHIBITIONS

2006

American Institute of Architects National Firm Award

National AIA Honor Award: Joseph A. Steger Student Life Center, University of Cincinnati

National AIA Urban & Regional Award: University Boulevard, University of British Columbia, Vancouver

American Institute of Architects Academy of Architecture for Justice, Citation: Robert E. Coyle United States Courthouse

Calibre Award for Environmental Leadership: Santa Monica Public Library

SCUP/AIA-CAE Merit Award: University Boulevard, University of British Columbia, Vancouver

Royal Architectural Institute of Canada National Urban Design Award/ Vancouver Award: University Boulevard, University of British Columbia, Vancouver

Chicago Athenaeum American Architecture Award: Robert E. Coyle United States Courthouse

Westside Urban Forum Westside Prize: Glorya Kaufman Hall Center for World Arts & Cultures, University of California, Los Angeles

Los Angeles Architectural Awards, Sustainable category: Santa Monica Public Library

International Interior Design Association Calibre Award for Environmental Leadership: Santa Monica Public Library

Pre-cast Institute Design Award: Santa Monica Public Library

Southern California Development Forum Honor Award: Santa Monica Public Library

McGraw Hill California Construction Best 06, Best Civic/ Redevelopment: Santa Monica Public Library

Berkeley Design Advocates Award of Excellence: Congregation Beth El

2005

AIA/LA Merit Award: Joseph A. Steger Student Life Center, University of Cincinnati

University Boulevard Competition, First Prize: University Boulevard, University of British Columbia, Vancouver

AIA California Council Merit Award: Joseph A. Steger Student Life Center, University of Cincinnati

AIA Ohio Design Award: Joseph A. Steger Student Life Center, University of Cincinnati

Educational Facilities Design Award of Merit, AIA Committee on Architecture for Education (CAE): Joseph A. Steger Student Life Center, University of Cincinnati

Educational Facilities Design Award of Merit, AIA Committee on Architecture for Education (CAE): Horace Mann Public Elementary School

Benjamin Moore HUE Award for Residential Interiors

Westside Urban Forum Westside Prize: 606 Broadway Housing

Precast Concrete Award 2005: Robert E. Coyle United States Courthouse

2004

AIA Cincinnati Honor Award: Joseph A. Steger Student Life Center, University of Cincinnati

AIA California Council Merit Award 2004: Horace Mann Elementary School

AIA/LA NextLA Citation: Chun Sen Bi An Housing, Chongqing

Westside Urban Forum Westside Prize: Santa Monica Civic Center Parking Structure

CMACN & AIA California Council Concrete Masonry Honor Award: Horace Mann Elementary School

2003

National AIA Honor Award: Bo01 "Tango" Housing

AIA California Council Honor Award: Bo01 "Tango" Housing

Colorado Springs Partnership in Community Design: Russell T. Tutt Science Center, Colorado College

Gröna Gårder Vilda Grännar award (landscaping/ habitat): Bo01 "Tango" Housing

2002

Council for New Urbanism Charter Award: New Campus Master Plan & Phase I, University of Washington Tacoma

Excellence on the Waterfront Honor Award: Bo01 "Tango" Housing

2001

Årets Stadsbyggnadspris (The Year's Building 2001): Bo01 "Tango" Housing

2000

"Bo01 'Tango' Housing at the Swedish Pavilion at Mostra Internazionale," La Biennale di Venezia, Venice, Italy: Bo01 "Tango" Housing

Dartmouth North Campus Plan Competition, First Prize: Dartmouth College

1999

American Institute of Architects Honor Award for Urban Design: New Campus Master Plan & Phase I, University of Washington Tacoma

1998

American Institute of Architects Honor Award: Powell Library, University of California, Los Angeles

1997

AIA/ALA Library Buildings Award: Powell Library, University of California, Los Angeles

Los Angeles Business Council Award: Powell Library, University of California, Los Angeles

Los Angeles Conservancy Award: Powell Library, University of California, Los Angeles

1996

U.S. Foreign Building Operations, National Design Competition, First Prize: United States Embassy, Berlin, Germany

California Governor's Historic Preservation Award: Powell Library, University of California, Los Angeles

IIDA Edwin F. Guth Memorial Award of Excellence for Interior Lighting Design: California Center for the Arts

Lumen West Award for Lighting Design: California Center for the Arts

1995

American Concrete Institute, Winner Architectural
Category: Walter A. Haas School of Management,
University of California, Berkeley

United States Institute for Theater Technology Merit
Award: California Center for the Arts

Stucco Manufacturers Association Bronze Award for
Architectural Excellence: California Center
for the Arts

1994

American Institute of Architects (AIA)/American
Association of School Administrators, Citation:
Walter A. Haas School of Management, University
of California, Berkeley

AIA California Council/National Concrete Masonry
Association Award of Merit: Microbiology Research
Facility, University of California, San Diego

GE Edison Award of Merit: California Center for
the Arts

1993

AIA National Interior Architecture Award of
Excellence: Church of the Nativity

State of Maryland, National Design Competition,
First Prize: Maryland Center for Performing Arts,
University of Maryland, College Park

1992

AIA California Council Firm of the Year Award, 1992

Architectural Design Honor: First Church of Christ,
Scientist

AIA California Council Honor Award: Yudell/Beebe
House, Malibu

Interiors Magazine 13th Annual Interiors Awards, Best
in Institutional Design: Church of the Nativity

Interfaith Forum on Religion, Art and Architecture
International: Church of the Nativity

AIA California Council Urban Design Award: Plaza
Las Fuentes

AIA SW Oregon Chapter First Place, Peoples'
Choice Awards: University of Oregon
Science Complex

AIA Southwestern Oregon Chapter Citation Winner:
University of Oregon Science Complex

California Institute of Technology, Invited Design
Competition, First Place: Avery House

Arge Karow (Berlin) International Design Competition,
First Prize: Karow-Nord Master Plan

Taiwan National Invited Design Competition, First
Prize: Dong-Hwa University Master Plan

1991

AIA San Diego Chapter Honor Award: Church
of the Nativity, Rancho Santa Fe

AIA California Council National Honor Award:
First Church of Christ, Scientist

AIA/Sunset Magazine Western Home Awards Award
of Merit, 1991-1992: Yudell/Beebe House, Malibu

American Wood Council National Honor Award:
First Church of Christ, Scientist

1990

AIA Los Angeles Honor Award: Humboldt Library

AIA/American Library Council National Design Award:
Humboldt Library

1989

AIA California Council Merit Award: House on Point
Dume (Anawalt House)

1988

AIA National Honor Award, 1988: Tegel Harbor
Housing

AIA California Council Honor Award: Tegel
Harbor Housing

AIA California Council Honor Award: Carousel Park

1987

City of Santa Monica Mayor's Commendation,
October: Carousel Park

Waterfront Center Excellence on the Waterfront
Honor Award: Carousel Park

State of California Department of Rehabilitation
Architectural Design Awards Program, "Building
a Better Future Honor Award": Carousel Park

1984

AIA National Honor Award: Parish of St. Matthew

AIA California Council Merit Award: Parish of
St. Matthew

AIA Los Angeles Chapter Merit Award: Parish of
St. Matthew

1981

Architectural Record House of the Year: Rodes House

Santa Monica Pier Design Charrette, First Prize:
Carousel Park

1980

Tegel Harbor International Design Competition,
West Berlin, First Prize: Tegel Harbor Master
Plan, Germany

1977–1979
Rodes House
Los Angeles, California

1979–1983
Parish of Saint Matthew Episcopal
Church
Pacific Palisades, California

1980–1985
Kwee House
Singapore

1981–1983
Marine Street House
Santa Monica, California

1981–1988
Tegel Harbor Housing
Berlin, Germany

1982
Parador Hotel
San Juan Capistrano, California

1982–1989
San Antonio Art Institute
San Antonio, Texas

1983–1987
Saint Louis Art Museum, West Wing
Renovation and new Decorative Arts
Galleries
Saint Louis, Missouri

1983–1989
Plaza Las Fuentes Mixed-use
Development
Pasadena, California

1984–1987
Inman House
Atlanta, Georgia

1984–1988
Humboldt Bibliothek
Berlin, Germany

1984–1993
Bel Air Presbyterian Church
Los Angeles, California

1984 Competition; 1984–1987
Carousel Park at Santa Monica Pier
Santa Monica, California

1985–1988
Anawalt House
Malibu, California

1985–1989
Church of the Nativity
Rancho Santa Fe, California

1985–1989
Science Complex Master Plan
University of Oregon, Eugene

1986–1988
Peter Boxenbaum Arts Education
Center
Crossroads School
Santa Monica, California

1986–1989
First Church of Christ Scientist
Glendale, California

1986–1995
Cellular and Molecular Medicine,
East and West Wings
University of California, San Diego

1987–1995
Walter A. Haas School of Business
University of California, Berkeley

1987–1989
Yudell/Beebe House
Malibu, California

1987–1994
California Center for the Arts
Escondido, California

1988–1995
Chemistry Building
University of Washington
Seattle, Washington

1988–1996
Nishiokamoto Housing
Kobe, Japan

1988–1996
Powell Library Seismic Renovation
University of California, Los Angeles

1988–2002
Potatisåkern Housing and Villas
Malmö, Sweden

1990
Bolle Center Competition
Berlin, Germany

1990–1993
Villa Superba
Venice, California

1991
Friedrichstadt Passagen Competition
Berlin, Germany

1991–1994
Schetter House
Pacific Palisades, California

1991–1998
Berliner Strasse Housing
Potsdam, Germany

1991–2003
New Campus Master Plan
University of Washington Tacoma
Tacoma, Washington

1992–1995
Campus Master Plan
Dong–Hwa National University
Hwa–Lien, Taiwan

1992 competition; 1992–1994
Peek & Cloppenburg Department Store
Leipzig, Germany

1992 competition; 1992–1996
Avery House
California Institute of Technology
Pasadena, California

1992 competition; 1992–1999
Karow–Nord Housing
Berlin-Weissensee, Germany

1992 Competition; 1993–1998
Kirchsteigfeld Housing
Potsdam, Germany

1992–1994
Walrod House
Berkeley, California

1992–1996
Avery Center
California Institute of Technology
Pasadena, California

1992–1998
Hugh & Hazel Darling Law Library
Addition
University of California, Los Angeles

1993–2000
Bahnhof Westseite Master Plan
Göttingen, Germany

1993–1998
Sherman M. Fairchild Library of
Engineering and Applied Science
California Institute of Technology
Pasadena, California

1994 Competition; 1994–2001
Clarice Smith Performing Arts Center
University of Maryland, College Park

1994–2003
Wasserstein House
Santa Barbara, California

1995–1997
Kartanesí Winter Resort Hotel
Uludag, Turkey

项目设计年表
PROJECT CHRONOLOGY

1995–1998
Percival/Westbrook House
Newport Beach, California

1995–1999
Shmuger/Hamagami House
Pacific Palisades, California

1995 competition; 1996–2008
United States Embassy
Berlin, Germany

1996–1997
Groth House (project)
Mustique, St. Vincent and the
Grenadines

1996–1997
Peg Yorkin House
Malibu, California

1996–1998
Elizabeth Moore House
Orinda, California

1996–1998
Gilbert House Remodel
Los Angeles, California

1996–1999
Graalfs House
Berlin, Germany

1996–1999
Tiergarten Dreieck Housing and
Mixed-Use
Berlin, Germany

1996–2002
Regatta Wharf Housing at Jackson's
Landing
Pyrmont, Sydney, Australia

1996–2010
Camana Master Plan and Town Center
Grand Cayman, Cayman Islands

1998–2006
Robert E. Coyle US Courthouse
Fresno, California

1997–1998
Miramar Villas (project)
Istanbul, Turkey

1997–1998
Nautilus Residences
Yesilyurt, Turkey

1997–1999
Baas/Walrod House
The Sea Ranch, California

1997–1999
Göttingen Office Building
Göttingen, Germany

1997–2001
Yudell/Beebe House
The Sea Ranch, California

1997–2002
Fairmont Towers Hotel Addition
San Jose, California

1997–2002
Interdisciplinary Sciences Building
University of California, Santa Cruz

1997–2002
Manzanita Village and Carrillo
Commons
University of California, Santa Barbara

1997–2005
Congregation Beth El
Berkeley, California

1998
House for the Next Millennium
(project)
House Beautiful magazine

1998–2000
Disney Imagineering GC3 Master Plan
Glendale, California

1998–2003
Horace Mann Elementary School
San Jose, California

2001–2003
East Campus District Plan/SHASS/
Dewey Library/Sloan School
of Management
Massachusetts Institute of Technology
Cambridge, Massachusetts

2005–2010
Sloan School of Management
Massachusetts Institute of Technology,
Cambridge

1998–2003
Russell Tutt Science Building
Colorado College, Colorado Springs

1998–2002
Physical Sciences Building
University of California, Santa Cruz

1999–2001
Tango Bo01 Housing Exhibition
Malmö, Sweden

1999–2002
New Science Building
University of Washington Tacoma
Tacoma, Washington

1999–2002
Falkenberg House
Woodside, California

1999–2004
Joseph A. Steger Student Life Center
University of Cincinnati, Ohio

1999–2005
Glorya Kaufman Hall, Center for World
Arts and Cultures
University of California, Los Angeles

2000–2003
Halprin House
The Sea Ranch, California

2001–2005
Watermark Tower Condominiums
San Francisco, California

2001–2002
Inclusion Area D Faculty Housing
Master Plan
University of California, Santa Cruz

2001–2007
606 Broadway Housing
Santa Monica, California

2001–2003
Amgen Laboratories, Administration,
and Dining Complex
Longmont, Colorado

2001–2002
North Campus District Plan
Dartmouth College
Hanover, New Hampshire

2002–2006
Kemeny Hall & Haldeman Centers
Dartmouth College
Hanover, New Hampshire

2002–2006
McLaughlin Cluster Student Housing
Dartmouth College
Hanover, New Hampshire

2003–in progress
Class of 1954 Dining & Social
Commons
Dartmouth College
Hanover, New Hampshire

2001–2007
Santa Monica Civic Center Parking
Structure
Santa Monica, California

2001–2006
Livermore House
Carmel, California

2002
United States Air Force Memorial
Competition
Arlington, Virginia

2003–2006
The French Family Science Center
Duke University
Durham, North Carolina

2003–2012
Serendra Housing and Retail Center
Manila, The Philippines

2002–2005
Santa Monica Public Library
Santa Monica, California

2002–2008
Ruddell House
Kauai, Hawaii

2003–in progress
Tianjin Xin-He Housing
Tianjin, China

2002–2004
Western Asset Plaza
Pasadena, California

2003–2006
John Brooks Williams
Natural Sciences Center
St. Edward's University
Austin, Texas

2003–in progress
American Institute in Taiwan
Taipei, Taiwan

2004–2010
Chun Sen Bi An Housing
Chongqing, China

2004–2005
West Village Master Plan
University of California, Davis

2004–2008
Moir House
Carmel, California

2004–2006
Maguire House
Santa Barbara, California

2005
University Boulevard Urban Design
Competition
University of British Columbia,
Vancouver

2005
North Houses Study
California Institute of Technology
Pasadena, California

2005–2006
Law-Business Connection
University of California, Berkeley

2005–2006
Boalt Hall Reading Room Renovation
University of California, Berkeley

2005–in progress
Santa Monica Civic Center Village
Santa Monica, California

2005–2010
College of Arts and Sciences South
Lawn Project
University of Virginia
Charlottesville, Virginia

2005–in progress
Nei-Hu Housing
Taipei, Taiwan

2005–in progress
Amber Bay Resort Development
Dalian, China

2005
Jinghua Retail Shopping Center
(project)
Yangzhou, China

2005–2007
Santa Monica Civic Center
Parking Structure
Santa Monica, California

2006–2008
Park Place Mixed-Use/Master Plan
Irvine, California

2007–2008
Loma Pelona Multi-Purpose Center
University of California, Santa Barbara

2006
Baxter Hall Study
California Institute of Technology
Pasadena, California

2007–2008
NBC/Universal Backlot Master Plan
Universal City, California

2007–in progress
Walston House
Beverly Hills, California

2007
Chinese University of Hong Kong
Master Plan
Hong Kong, China

2007–2008
Maguire Aviation
Van Nuys, California

2007–in progress
Two Integrated Teaching Building
Chinese University of Hong Kong
Hong Kong, China

2007–in progress
Grangegorman Masterplan
Dublin Institute of Technology
Dublin, Ireland

2007–2009
Jules Stein Eye Institute Expansion
Studies
University of California, Los Angeles,
California

2007–in progress
Saint John's Health Center
South Campus Master Plan
Santa Monica, California

2007–2009
Wilson House Interiors
Malibu, California

2007
Livermore Courtyard, Guest House,
and Woodside Remodel
Carmel, California

2008
Graduate School of Management
Library
St. Petersburg University
St. Petersburg, Russia

2008–2010
Yudell/Beebe House
Santa Monica, California

2008–2009
Lisi Lake Residential Development
Tbilisi, Georgia

2008–in progress
Student Community Center
University of California, Berkeley

2008–in progress
United States Embassy, The Hague
The Hague, The Netherlands

2008–in progress
Umbach/Gunderson House
The Sea Ranch, California

2008–in progress
Campus Land Use Planning and
Feasibility Study
University of California, Los Angeles,
California

2008–in progress
United States Embassy, Seoul
Seoul, South Korea

2008–in progress
Community Corporation Housing
Santa Monica, California

2009–in progress
Golden Sea Lake Master Plan and
Housing
Beijing, China

2009–in progress
Claremont McKenna College Master
Plan and Landscape
Claremont, California

2009–in progress
Takahashi Penthouse
Los Angeles, California

2009–in progress
United States Embassy
Beirut, Lebanon

2009–in progress
United States Embassy
Santo Domingo, Dominican Republic

2009
United States Courthouse
Design/Build Competition
Bakersfield, California

2009–in progress
Saint Mary's College Library
Moraga, California

2010–in progress
Zellerbach Hall
University of California, Berkeley
Berkeley, California

2010–in progress
Bioengineering Building
University of California, Santa Barbara
Santa Barbara, California

2010–in progress
New Santa Clarita Courthouse
Santa Clarita, California

2011–in progress
EOFCO Eco-Valley
Agricultural Production and Exhibition
Center
Beijing, China

2011–in progress
University of California, Santa Barbara
Faculty Club Renovation & Expansion
Santa Barbara, California

2011–in progress
University of California, Los Angeles
WIN-GEM Building
and Engineering VI Building
Los Angeles, California

The Master Plan for COFCO
Agricultural Eco-Valley, Beijing

RUDDELL HOUSE
Client: Steven and Merlyn Ruddell
Partners: Buzz Yudell, John Ruble
Principal-in-Charge: Mario Violich
Project Team: Ross Morishige, Alberto Reano
Color and Materials: Tina Beebe, Kaoru Orime
Interior Design: Stanley Anderson
Landscape Design: Mario Violich

MAGUIRE BEACH HOUSE
Client: Robert Maguire III
Partners: Buzz Yudell, John Ruble
Principal-in-Charge: Stanley Anderson
Project Team: Amy Sklar, Sepi Salehirad, Kinneret Atia, Charlotte Thomas,
    Philippe Arias
Executive Architect: Bob Easton Architects

MOIR HOUSE
Client: Paul and Becky Moir
Partners: Buzz Yudell, John Ruble
Principal-in-Charge: Mario Violich
Project Team: Tim Eng, Alberto Reano
Landscape Design: Mario Violich
Interior Design: Stanley Anderson, Kinneret Atia, Amy Sklar

LIVERMORE HOUSE
Client: Anonymous
Partners: Buzz Yudell, John Ruble
Principal-in-Charge: Mario Violich
Project Team: Tim Eng, Alberto Reano
Color and Materials: Tina Beebe, Kaoru Orime
Landscape Design: Mario Violich
Interior Design: Audrey Alberts Design

YUDELL/BEEBE HOUSE
Client: Buzz Yudell & Tina Beebe
Partner: Buzz Yudell
Associate: Clay Holden
Project Team: Martin Saavedra, Neal Matsuno, Alberto Reano
Color and Materials: Tina Beebe, Clay Holden
Interior Design: Tina Beebe
Renderings: Takuji Mukaiyama
Models: Mark Grand

SANTA MONICA PUBLIC LIBRARY
Client: The City of Santa Monica
Partners: John Ruble, Buzz Yudell
Principal-in-Charge: Krista Becker
Associates: Clay Holden, Haekwan Park
Project Team: Michael de Villiers, Richard Destin, Bob Dolbinski, Carissa Shrock,
    Oscar Pineda, Bernardo Frias, JT Theeuwes, Martin Saavedra, Simone Barth,
    Krista Scheib, Gerardo Rivero, Henry Lau
Color and Materials: Tina Beebe, Kaoru Orime
Landscape Architect: Pamela Burton & Co.
Interior Furnishings: Clara Igonda
Renderings: Shimahara Illustrations
Models: Mark Grand
Artist: Carl Cheng

SANTA MONICA CIVIC CENTER PARKING STRUCTURE
Client: The City of Santa Monica
Partners: John Ruble, Buzz Yudell
Principal-in-Charge: James Mary O'Connor
Associate: Halil Dolan
Project Team: Tim Feigenbutz, Haruyuki Yokoyama, Tony Tran,
    Pooja Bhagat, Simone Barth
Color and Materials: Tina Beebe, Kaoru Orime
Landscape Architect: Melendrez Design Partners
Associate Architect: International Parking Design, Don Marks, Dirmali Botejue,
Models: Mark Grand, Halil Dolan
Lighting Consultant: Francis Krahe & Associates
Artist: Mark Lere

ROBERT E. COYLE U.S. COURTHOUSE, FRESNO
Client: General Services Administration
Partners: John Ruble, Buzz Yudell
Principal-in-Charge: Jeanne Chen
Associate: Bob Dolbinski
Project Team: Chris Hamilton, Tim Eng, Ross Morishige, Roger Lopez
Color and Materials: Tina Beebe, Kaoru Orime
Landscape Architect: Pamela Burton & Co.
Executive Architect: Gruen Associates, Mike Enomoto, Debra Gerod
Renderings: Doug Jamieson
Models: Mark Grand, Vely Zajek
Artists: Doug Hollis & Anna Valentina Murch

U.S. COURTHOUSE, BAKERSFIELD
Client: General Services Administration
Partners: John Ruble, Buzz Yudell
Principal-in-Charge: Jeanne Chen
Associate: Bob Dolbinski
Project Team: Laurie Groehler, Kaoru Orime, Andrew Kao, Ken Kim
Sustainability Consultant: Buro Happold
Landscape Architect: Pamela Burton & Co.
Models: Mark Grand

项目资讯
PROJECT CREDITS

UNITED STATES EMBASSY, BERLIN

Client: United States Department of State, Office of Overseas Building Operations
Partners: John Ruble, Buzz Yudell
Principal-in-Charge: Krista Becker
Associate: Adam Padua
Project Team: Bernardo Frias, JT Theeuwes, Carissa Shrock, Oscar Pineda,
    Jerome Chang, Therese Kelly, Tiffany Pang, Joan Young, Matt Blake,
    Matt Vincent, Vely Zajec, Chris Bach, Tony Tran, Tim Feigenbutz, Mark Grand,
    Clay Holden, Michael S. Martin
Color and Materials: Tina Beebe, Kaoru Orime
Interior Design: Brayton + Hughes, Stanley Anderson, Yana Khudyakova
Landscape Architect: Olin Partnership
Technical Architect: Gruen Associates, Debra Gerod, Jill Wagner
Renderings: Doug Jamieson
Models: Model Concepts, Inc.

UNITED STATES EMBASSY, SANTO DOMINGO

Client: United States Department of State—Office of Overseas Building Operations
Partners: John Ruble, Buzz Yudell
Principal-in-Charge: Krista Becker
Associates: JT Theeuwes, Don Yamami
Project Team: Jed Bunkowski, Bob Dolbinski, Bernardo Frias, Haekwan Park,
    Carissa Shrock, Martin Saavedra, Tarry Chung, Laurie Groehler,
    Alexander Acemyan, Clay Holden, Richard Destin, Ken Kim
Interior Design: Stanley Anderson, Kinneret Atia
Landscape Architect: Pamela Burton & Co.
Models: Mark Grand

AMERICAN INSTITUTE IN TAIWAN

Client: United States Department of State—Office of Overseas Building Operations
Partners: John Ruble, Buzz Yudell
Principal-in-Charge: Krista Becker
Associates: JT Theeuwes, Don Yamami
Project Team: Martin Saavedra, Adam Padua, Tarry Chung, Bernardo Frias,
    Carissa Shrock, Alberto Reano, Jed Bunkowski
Interior Design: Stanley Anderson, Kinneret Atia, Sepi Salehirad
Models: Model Concepts, Inc.

UNIVERSITY OF CALIFORNIA, SANTA BARBARA
BIOENGINEERING BUILDING

Client: University of California, Santa Barbara
Partners: John Ruble, Buzz Yudell
Principal-in-Charge: Michael S. Martin
Collaborating Principal: Krista Becker
Associate: Chris Hamilton
Project Team: Anthony Wang, Jed Bunkowski, Tarry Chung, Laurie Groehler,
    Daniela Oberherr Hammond
Landscape Architect: Suding Design
Renderings: Al Forster
Models: Mark Grand

UNIVERSITY OF CALIFORNIA BERKELEY,
STUDENT COMMUNITY CENTER

Client: University of California, Berkeley
Partners: Buzz Yudell, John Ruble
Principal-in-Charge: Mario Violich
Collaborating Principal: Jeanne Chen
Associate: Richard Destin
Project Team: Adam Padua, Simone Barth, Ken Kim, Eric Tecza
Landscape Architect: CMG
Renderings: Al Forster
Models: Mark Grand

UNIVERSITY OF CALIFORNIA BERKELEY,
LAW BUSINESS CONNECTION

Client: University of California, Berkeley
Partners: Buzz Yudell, John Ruble
Principal-in-Charge: Mario Violich
Collaborating Principal: Krista Becker
Project Team: JT Theeuwes, Adam Padua, Erin Hillhouse,
    Carissa Shrock, Chris Hamilton, Richard Destin, Simone Barth,
    Ben Foster, Darin Morris, Takuji Mukaiyama, Oscar Pineda
Color and Materials: Tina Beebe, Kaoru Orime
Interior Design: Stanley Anderson
Landscape Architect: Olin Partnership
Renderings: Al Forster
Models: Model Concepts, Inc.

UNIVERSITY OF CINCINNATI,
JOSEPH A. STEGER STUDENT LIFE CENTER

Client: University of Cincinnati
Partners: Buzz Yudell, John Ruble
Principal-in-Charge: Mario Violich
Associate: Adam Padua
Project Team: Bob Dolbinski, Alberto Reano, Ted Kane, Alexis Bennett,
    Ross Morishige
Color and Materials: Tina Beebe, Yana Khudyakova, Kaoru Orime
Landscape Architect: Hargreaves Associates
Executive Architect: Glaserworks, Art Hupp, Michael Maltinsky, Evan Eagle
Models: Mark Grand, Don Hornbeck

UNIVERSITY OF VIRGINIA,
COLLEGE OF ARTS AND SCIENCES SOUTH LAWN PROJECT

Client: University of Virginia
Partners: John Ruble, Buzz Yudell
Principal-in-Charge: Krista Becker
Associate: Adam Padua
Project Team: Don Yamami, JT Theeuwes, Simone Barth, Carissa Shrock,
    Jason Voss, Sun Lee, Alex Martinson, Darin Morris, Alberto Reano, Mario Violich
Interior Design: Stanley Anderson, Kinneret Atia
Landscape Architect: The Office of Cheryl Barton and Walter Hood
Technical Architect: Glaserworks, Art Hupp, Michael Maltinsky
Models & Renderings: Model Concepts, Inc.

DUKE UNIVERSITY, FRENCH FAMILY SCIENCE CENTER

Client: Duke University
Partners: John Ruble, Buzz Yudell
Principal-in-Charge: Michael S. Martin
Associate: Chris Hamilton
Project Team: Anthony Wang, Simone Barth, JT Theeuwes, Matthew Vincent,
   Vely Zajec, Tiffany Pang, Oscar Pineda, Frank Maldanado, Therese Kelly,
   Stanley Anderson
Color and Materials: Kaoru Orime, Yana Khudyakova
Landscape Architect: Olin Partnership
Executive Architect: Hillier Group, Steve Gifford, Jim Theodore
Models: Mark Grand

DARTMOUTH COLLEGE, NORTH DISTRICT CAMPUS PLAN

Client: Dartmouth College
Partners: Buzz Yudell, John Ruble
Principal-in-Charge: Jeanne Chen
Associate: Bob Dolbinski
Project Team: Kaoru Orime, Ross Morishige
Executive Architect: Bruner/Cott & Associates, Leland Cott, Lynne Brooks
Models: Mark Grand

DARTMOUTH COLLEGE, KEMENEY HALL & HALDEMAN CENTER

Client: Dartmouth College
Partners: Buzz Yudell, John Ruble
Principal-in-Charge: Jeanne Chen
Associate: Bob Dolbinski
Project Team: Laurie Groehler, Wing-Hon Ng, Simone Barth, Ross Morishige,
   Martin Saavedra
Color and Materials: Tina Beebe, Kaoru Orime, Yana Khudyakova
Lighting Collaboration: Neal Matsuno
Interior Design: Stanley Anderson, Kinneret Atia, Yana Khudyakova
Landscape Architect: Richard Burke Associates
Executive Architect: Bruner/Cott & Associates, Leland Cott, Lynne Brooks
Renderings: Al Forster
Models: Mark Grand

DARTMOUTH COLLEGE, MCLAUGHLIN CLUSTER STUDENT HOUSING

Client: Dartmouth College
Partners: Buzz Yudell, John Ruble
Principal-in-Charge: Jeanne Chen
Associate: Bob Dolbinski
Project Team: Laurie Groehler, Simone Barth, Chris Jonick, Mark Grand
Color and Materials: Tina Beebe, Kaoru Orime, Yana Khudyakova
Interior Design: Stanley Anderson, Kinneret Atia, Yana Khudyakova
Landscape Architect: Richard Burke Associates
Executive Architect: Bruner/Cott & Associates, Leland Cott, Lynne Brooks, Dan Raih
Renderings: Al Forster

CHINESE UNIVERSITY OF HONG KONG, TWO INTEGRATED TEACHING BUILDING

Client: Chinese University of Hong Kong
Partners: John Ruble, Buzz Yudell
Principal-in-Charge: Michael S. Martin
Associate: Anthony Wang
Project Team: James Mary O'Connor, Philippe Arias, Katie Peterson,
   Annie Shu, Halil Dolan, JT Theeuwes
Color and Materials: Kaoru Orime
Executive Architect: Andrew Lee King Fun and Associates, Peter Lui, Ellis Leung,
   Ricky Tsang
Renderings: Philippe Arias

ST. PETERSBURG STATE UNIVERSITY, GRADUATE SCHOOL OF MANAGEMENT LIBRARY

Client: SetlCity Development & Graduate School of Management,
   St. Petersburg State University
Partners: John Ruble, Buzz Yudell
Principal-in-Charge: Neal Matsuno
Associate: Clay Holden
Project Team: Matthew Henry, Philippe Arias
Color and Materials: Clay Holden
Renderings: Josh Ashcroft
Executive Architect: Studio 44

UNIVERSITY OF CALIFORNIA, SANTA CRUZ PHYSICAL SCIENCES BUILDING

Client: University of California, Santa Cruz
Partners: John Ruble, Buzz Yudell
Principal-in-Charge: Michael S. Martin
Associate: Wing-Hon Ng
Project Team: Erin Hillhouse, Alberto Reano,
   Murat Sanat, Ada Mancilla
Color and Materials: Tina Beebe
Landscape Architect: Joni L. Janecki & Associates Inc.
Executive Architect: Anshen + Allen, S.F., Gregory Blackburn, Marissa Tweedie
Models: Mark Grand, Vely Zajec, Matt Vincent

TIME-MEDICAL INC, TOWERS

Client: Time Medical Inc.
Partners: John Ruble, Buzz Yudell
Principal-in-Charge: James Mary O'Connor
Associate: Halil Dolan
Project Team: Kaoru Orime, Takuji Mukaiyama, Toru Narita,
   Matasaburo Murakami, Nozomu Sugawara, Tony Tran
Models: Takuji Mukaiyama, Toru Narita, Matasaburo Murakami, Nozomu Sugawara
Renderings: Eric A. Tecza

MASSACHUSETTS INSTITUTE OF TECHNOLOGY, SLOAN SCHOOL OF MANAGEMENT

Client: Massachusetts Institute of Technology
Partners: Buzz Yudell, John Ruble
Principal-in-Charge: Neal Matsuno
Collaborating Principal: Jeanne Chen
Landscape Design: Mario Violich and Halvorson Design
Associate: Wing-Hon Ng
Project Team: Bob Dolbinski ,Tarry Chung, Laurie Groehler,
    Daniela Oberherr Hammond, Haekwan Park, Heather Hunt
Color and Materials: Tina Beebe, Kaoru Orime
Interior Design: Stanley Anderson, Kinneret Atia
Executive Architect: Bruner Cott & Associates, Leland Cott, Lynne Brooks,
    Dan Raih, Robert Peirce
Models: Mark Grand

HORACE MANN ELEMENTARY SCHOOL

Client: San Jose Unified School District and The Redevelopment
    Agency of the City of San Jose
Partners: John Ruble, Buzz Yudell
Principal-in-Charge: James Mary O'Connor
Associate: Adam Padua
Project Team: Alberto Reano, Lisa Belian, Ed Diamante, Roger Lopez,
    Martin Saavedra, Tony Tran
Color and Materials: Tina Beebe, Kaoru Orime
Landscape Architect: Pamela Burton & Co.
Executive Architect: BFGC Architects Planners Inc., David Cartnal
Models: Mark Grand, Matthew Vincent, Vely Zajec, Lance Collins
Renderings: Al Forster

UNIVERSITY OF CALIFORNIA, LOS ANGELES, GLORYA KAUFMAN CENTER FOR WORLD ARTS AND CULTURES

Client: University of California, Los Angeles
Partners: Buzz Yudell, John Ruble
Principal-in-Charge: Neal Matsuno
Associate: Erin Hillhouse
Project Team: Richard Destin, Kaoru Orime, Martin Saavedra, Marc Schoeplein
Color and Materials: Tina Beebe, Kaoru Orime
Landscape Architect: Fong, Hart, Schneider
Models: Mark Grand

UNIVERSITY OF CALIFORNIA, SANTA BARBARA, MANZANITA VILLAGE

Client: University of California, Santa Barbara
Partners: Buzz Yudell, John Ruble
Principal-in-Charge: Michael S. Martin
Associate: Richard Destin
Project Team: Laurie Groehler, Alberto Reano, Ted Kane, Oliver Matla,
    Stephen Penhoet, Katherine Yi, Izzet Motola, Murat Sanal, David Ellien,
    Roger Lopez, Angel Gabriel, Adrian Koffka, Alexis Bennett
Lighting: Neal Matsuno
Color and Materials: Tina Beebe, Kaoru Orime
Landscape Architect: Katherine Spitz and Associates
Executive Architect: DesignARC, Michael Holliday, Steve Carter, Bruce Bartlett
Renderings: Al Forster, Tony Tran
Models: Mark Grand, Don Hornbeck, Josh Lunn, Vely Zajec, Michael O'Bryan,
    Dirk Schorner

UNIVERSITY OF BRITISH COLUMBIA, UNIVERSITY BOULEVARD COMPETITION

Client: University of British Columbia
Partners: Buzz Yudell, John Ruble
Principal-in-Charge: Jeanne Chen
Associate: Clay Holden
Project Team: JT Theeuwes, Bob Dolbinski, Adam Padua, Ken Kim,
    Tomohisa Miyauchi, Carissa Shrock, Sang Dae Lee, Laurie Groehler,
    Andrew Kao, Wing-Hon Ng, Stanley Anderson
Color and Materials: Tina Beebe
Landscape Architect: Olin Partnership
Executive Architect: Hughes Condon Marler, Karen Marler, Roger Hughes
Models: Model Concepts, Inc
Renderings: Al Forster, Charles Hellwig

GRANGEGORMAN MASTERPLAN

Client: Grangegorman Development Agency
Partners: John Ruble, Buzz Yudell
Principal-in-Charge: James Mary O'Connor
Associates: JT Theeuwes, Halil Dolan
Project Team: Kaoru Orime, Nozomu Sugawara, Toru Narita, Tony Tran,
    Carissa Shrock, Matthew Henry, Tristan Hall, Joyce Ip Leus,
    Alon Averbuch, Simone Barth, Pooja Bhagat.
Models: Mark Grand, Alon Averbuch, Evan Henderson, Jenny Lee,
    Michael Dammeyer
Local Architects: DMOD Architects, John Mitchell
Architectural Conservation Consultant: Shaffrey Associates
Landscape Architect: Lützow 7, Jan Wehberg, Tim Hagenhoff
Healthcare & Educational Environment Expertise: Prof. Bryan Lawson
Transport Planning/Civil & Infrastructure: Arup Consulting Engineers
Sustainability & Environmental Expertise: Battle McCarthy Ltd.
Renderings: Shimahara Illustration, Halil Dolan, Nozomu Sugawara,
    Matthew Henry, Tristan Hall, Tony Tran

TANGO, BO01 HOUSING EXHIBITION

Client: MKB Fastighets AB
Partners: John Ruble, Buzz Yudell
Principal-in-Charge: James Mary O'Connor
Project Team: Lisa Belian, Tony Tran
Color and Materials: Tina Beebe, Kaoru Orime
Interior Design, Exhibition Apartment: Tina Beebe, Kaoru Orime
Interior Design: Karin Bellander, Johanna Wittenmark
Landscape Architect: Moore Ruble Yudell with SWECO FFNS
Executive Architect: FFNS Arkitekter AB, Bertil Öhrström
Renderings: Ross Morishige
Models: Mark Grand, Chad T. Takenaka, Vely Zajec, Don Hornbeck, Joshua Lunn,
    Matthew Vincent, Lance Collins

SANTA MONICA VILLAGE

Client: The Related Companies of California
Partners: Buzz Yudell, John Ruble
Principal-in-Charge: James Mary O'Connor
Collaborating Principal: Krista Becker
Associate: Pooja Bhagat
Project Team: Halil Dolan, Joyce Ip Leus, Kaoru Orime,
    Toru Narita, Alon Averbuch, Tony Tran, Jason Pytko
Landscape Architect: Mia Lehrer + Associates
Associate Architect: Koning Eizenberg Architecture
Executive Architect: KTGY Group, Inc., Jack Price
Models: Toru Narita, Mark Grand, Katie Peterson

COMMUNITY CORPORATION HOUSING

Client: Community Corporation of Santa Monica, California
Partners: Buzz Yudell, John Ruble
Principal-in-Charge: James Mary O' Connor
Associate: Pooja Bhagat
Project Team: Martin Saavedra, Kaoru Orime, Jason Pytko,
    Toru Narita, Alberto Reano, Tony Tran
Color and Materials: Kaoru Orime, Pooja Bhagat
Models: Mark Grand

606 BROADWAY HOUSING

Client: JSM Construction, Inc.
Partners: Buzz Yudell, John Ruble
Principal-in-Charge: James Mary O'Connor
Project Team: Kyung-Sun Lee, Tony Tran, Halil Dolan
Colors and Materials: Tina Beebe, Kaoru Orime
Landscape Architect: Pamela Burton & Company
Executive Architect: DE Architects, Don Empakeris
Renderings: Nozomu Sugawara
Models: Model Concepts, Inc.

TIANJIN-XINHE MASTER PLAN

Developer/Client: Sunco Investment, Inc.
Partners: John Ruble, Buzz Yudell
Principal-in-Charge: James Mary O'Connor
Associate: Halil Dolan
Project Team: Tim Feigenbutz, Pooja Bhagat, Therese Kelly,
    Simone Barth, Tony Tran, Matthew Blake, Peter Sjöström, Rebecca Bubenas,
    Alexander Matthies, Michael König, Laura Flotho, Martin Sonnenberg
Color and Materials: Tina Beebe, Kaoru Orime, Yana Khudyakova
Landscape Architect: EDAW
Associate Architect: Yang Architects, Akai Ming-Kae Yang
Models: John Leimbach, Veronica Vela, Mark Grand, Tim Feigenbutz,
    Carissa Schrock, Model Concepts, Inc.

AMBER BAY RESORT MASTER PLAN

Client: Dalian Amber Bay Development Co., Ltd.
Partners: John Ruble, Buzz Yudell
Principal-in-Charge: James Mary O'Connor
Associates: Halil Dolan, Nozomu Sugawara
Project Team: Takuji Mukaiyama, Toru Narita, Pooja Bhagat,
    Tony Tran, Clay Holden, Michael Heise
Master Planner/Landscape Architect: SWA Group
Waterfront Commercial Center Architect: Graft Architects
Landscape Architect: SWA Houston
Associate Architect: China Northeast Architectural Design
    & Research Institute Co. Ltd.
Models: Toru Narita, Nozomu Sugawara, Kentaro Yamada

SERENDRA MASTER PLAN

Client: Ayala Land, Inc.
Partners: John Ruble, Buzz Yudell
Principal-in-Charge: James Mary O'Connor
Collaborating Principal: Krista Becker
Associate: Halil Dolan
Project Team: Peter Sjöström, Kyung-Sun Lee, David Cutler, Christian Robert,
    Tony Tran, Tim Feigenbutz
Color and Materials: Tina Beebe, Kaoru Orime, Yana Khudyakova
Landscape Architect: Mia Lehrer + Associates
Models: John Leimbach, Veronica Vela, Mark Grand, Carissa Schrock
Parking Consultant: International Parking Design

LUXE LAKES MASTER PLAN

Client: Chengdu Wide Horizon New Town Development Co. Ltd
Partners: Buzz Yudell, John Ruble
Principal-in-Charge: Michael S. Martin
Collaborating Principal: Mario Violich
Associate: Anthony Wang
Project Team: Alex Acemyan, Daniela Hammond, Takuji Mukaiyama, Katie Peterson, Annie Shu, Nozomu Sugawara
Color and Materials: Kaoru Orime
Landscape Architect: Famous Garden
Renderings: Shimahara Illustrations, Tony Tran
Models: Mark Grand, Jonathan Lynch, Jacob Pundyk

LUXE LAKES PARCEL 9 TOWERS

Client: Chengdu Wide Horizon New Town Development Co. Ltd
Partners: Buzz Yudell, John Ruble
Principal-in-Charge: James Mary O'Connor
Associate: Halil Dolan
Project Team: Michael S. Martin, Kaoru Orime, Takuji Mukaiyama, Philippe Arias, Anthony Wang, Annie Shu, Toru Narita, Matasaburo Murakami, Nozomu Sugawara, Tony Tran
Models: Takuji Mukaiyama, Toru Narita, Matasaburo Murakami, Nozomu Sugawara

CHUN SEN BI AN HOUSING MASTER PLAN

Client: Longhu Real Estate Development, Inc.
Partners: John Ruble, Buzz Yudell
Principal-in-Charge: James Mary O'Connor
Associate: Halil Dolan
Project Team: Kyung-Sun Lee, Pooja Bhagat, Therese Kelly, Chris Jonick, Tony Tran, Simone Barth
Color and Materials: Tina Beebe, Kaoru Orime
Landscape Architect: Pamela Burton & Company
Associate Architect: Yang Architects, Akai Ming-Kae Yang
Models: Mark Grand, Nicholas Worden, Joel Chappo

NEI-HU RESIDENTIAL TOWERS

Client: Win Sing Development Corporation Ltd.
Partners: John Ruble, Buzz Yudell
Principal-in-Charge: James Mary O'Connor
Associate: Pooja Bhagat
Project Team: Halil Dolan, Christopher Jonick, Kaoru Orime, Tony Tran, Takuji Mukaiyama
Executive Architect: LKP Design, Mr. Ko Hung-Tsung, Ya-Ting Chang
Models: Toru Narita, Benjamin Foster, Kentaro Yamada, Michael Heise

CONCORDIA MACAU RESORT DEVELOPMENT

Client: Empresa de Fomento Industrial E Comercial Concordia, Macau
Partners: John Ruble, Buzz Yudell
Principal-in-Charge: James Mary O'Connor
Collaborating Principal: Krista Becker
Associate: Halil Dolan
Project Team: Pooja Bhagat, Kaoru Orime, Tony Tran, Takuji Mukaiyama, Toru Narita, Kentaro Yamada, Nozomu Sugawara
Landscape Architect: ah'bé Landscape Architects
Models: Kentaro Yamada, Benjamin Foster, Model Concepts, Inc.
Renderings: Shimahara Illustration

LISI LAKE HOUSING

Client: Georgian Reconstruction & Development Company
Partners: John Ruble, Buzz Yudell
Principal-in-Charge: Mario Violich
Associate: Simone Barth
Project Team: Bob Dolbinski, Philippe Arias, Laurie Groehler, Chris Hamilton, Takuji Mukaiyama, Haekwan Park
Renderings: ArX Solutions
Executive Architect: Architects GE

WATERMARK TOWER CONDOMINIUMS

Client: Lend Lease Development
Partners: John Ruble, Buzz Yudell
Project Team: Michael de Villiers, Joan Young
Executive Architect: Kwan Henmi Architecture/Planning

CAMANA BAY MASTER PLAN AND MIXED-USE TOWN CENTER

Client: Cayman Shores Development Ltd.
Partners: Buzz Yudell, John Ruble
Principal-in-Charge: Michael S. Martin, Neal Matsuno
Associate: Anthony Wang
Project Team: Martin Saavedra, Dan Bajor, Krista Becker, Matt Blake, Mark Bittoni, David Cutler, Michael de Villiers, Richard Destin, Tim Eng, Bernardo Frias, Laurie Groehler, Anton Henning, Chris Hamilton, Clay Holden, Chris Jonick, Andrew Kao, Therese Kelly, Yana Khudyakova, Sang Dae Lee, Frank Maldonado, Tomohisa Miyauchi, Ross Morishige, Takuji Mukaiyama, Amy Newborn, Wing Hon Ng, Daniela Oberherr Hammond, Oscar Pineda, Alberto Reano, Haekwan Park, Kirk Soderstrom, Carissa Shrock, Nozomu Sugawara, John Theeuwes, Tony Tran, Matt Vincent, Vely Zajec
Color and Materials: Tina Beebe, Kaoru Orime
Interior Design: Stanley Anderson, Kinneret Atia, Amy Sklar, Jeanne Fitzgerald, Charlotte Thomas
Landscape Architect: Olin Partnership
Consulting Architect: Burns Conolly Group Limited, Burns Conolly
Executive Architect: AECOM, Lawrence Kline, Jorge Iglesias
Renderings: Al Forster
Models: Mark Grand, Philippe Arias, Jed Bunkowski, Chad Christopher, Joel Chappo, Benjamin Foster, Michael Heise, Matt MacDonald, Veronica Vela, Nate Wade, Nicholas Worden

在此，我们要特别感谢辽宁科学技术出版社对我们的鼎力帮助和支持，并将我们近期的大量设计作品传播到中国及世界各地。辽宁科学技术出版社凭借一流的图书出版质量，为当代平面设计、建筑以及其他领域设计作品的出版做出了杰出贡献。

同时，迈克尔·J·克罗斯比先生为我们的作品提出了宝贵评价，并将我们设计实践的背景和理念诠释得淋漓尽致，我们表示由衷的感谢。《未来空间》的设计概念由我们事务所的负责人和全体职员共同拟定，马修·克劳戴尔负责材料和概念的编辑整理。

维多利亚·林提供该书的封面、版式、字体设计，并对总体描述和信息专题进行全面布局。

凯蒂·卡利，丽贝卡·巴伯纳斯和托尼·特朗通过对图片和文字的调整为该书制作提供全面而细致的指导。他们对作品的价值和创作意图都具有深刻而独到的见解。

此外，摄影技术是将建筑作品呈现于纸上的前提，在此，我们要特别感谢安特·戈雷，提姆·格里菲斯，维尔纳·哈斯曼彻，奥兰·卡琪莫，约翰·爱德华·林登，大卫·马洛和科林斯·洛扎答为该书提供的图片摄制。

建筑事业，需要大家群策群力共同打造，每个项目凝聚了个体对设计的独特观点以及为之付出的不懈努力。我们在欣赏设计成果、展望未来的同时，还要特别感谢客户和同仁对我们在全世界进行人本主义建筑设计活动的支持和帮助。

We are indebted to Liaoning Science & Technology Publishing House for this opportunity to present a broad spectrum of recent work to China and the world. In their commitment to quality, and support of contemporary graphic design and presentation, Liaoning Science & Technology Publishing House continues to make a significant contribution to the publishing of architecture and design.

We especially wish to thank Michael Crosbie for his keen perspective on our work. His observations provide an understanding of the context and aspirations of our wide-ranging practice.

The concept for *The Future of Place* was developed collectively with our principals, with the able editorial assistance of Matthew Claudel, who provided much of the initial organization of material and ideas.

Victoria Lam provided both the very fine graphic design for the cover, layouts, and typography, as well as critical insight into the overall presentation and message of the monograph.

Katie Carley, Rebecca Bubenas, and Tony Tran provided thoughtful and attentive guidance from research through coordination of graphic and written material. They exhibited a deep understanding of the values and intentions of the work.

Any presentation of built work depends entirely on photography, and we are fortunate to have the diversity of talent that is represented here, including Art Gray, Tim Griffith, Werner Huthmacher, Alan Karchmer, John Edward Linden, David Marlow, and Colins Lozada.

Architecture is a collective enterprise, and each project is the result of the unique chemistry of individuals who bring their talents and commitment to the process. Both in reviewing the works presented here, and looking to the future, we are particularly grateful to the many clients and colleagues who continue to support our exploration of humanistic place-making around the world.

John Ruble, Buzz Yudell, James Mary O'Connor

鸣谢
ACKNOWLEDGMENTS

First published in 2010
by Liaoning Science & Technology Publishing House
Address: No.29, Shiyi Wei Road, Shenyang, Liaoning Province, China

ISBN: 978-7-5381-6561-6
©2010 by Liaoning Science & Technology Publishing House

Design: Victoria Lam with Matthew Claudel, Moore Ruble Yudell
Editorial Supervision, Copy Editing, Research:
Rebecca Bubenas, Katie Carley, and Tony Tran, Moore Ruble Yudell
Chinese Proofreading: Akai Mingkae Yang
Editorial advisor: James Mary O'Connor, Moore Ruble Yudell

This book is typeset in Verlag, designed by Hoefler & Frere-Jones.

Printed and bound in China
贺丽译

有关中国国内项目合作事宜征询，请直接传送电子邮件（中文或英文）
至本公司负责亚洲地区项目总裁
James Mary O'Connor 的邮箱 joconnor@mryarchitects.com